FIGHTING ON

General Sir Walter Walker KCB CBE
DSO** PMN PSNB

By the same author

The Bear at the Back Door (1978)
The Next Domino (1980)

FIGHTING ON

by

General Sir Walter Walker KCB CBE
DSO** PMN PSNB

NEW MILLENNIUM
292 Kennington Road, London SE11 4LD

British Library Cataloguing in Publication Data.
A catalogue record for this book is available
from the British Library.

Printed and bound by Morgan Technical Books Ltd,
Wotton-under-Edge, Glos
Issued by New Millennium*
ISBN 1 85845 131 0
*An imprint of The Professional Authors' & Publishers' Association

Acknowledgement

I would like to thank all those from whose books I have obtained a word picture of how they regard me as a soldier, leader and commander in battle, as well as in peace-time soldiering. I certainly have not quoted verbatim their opinions for my own self glorification, for there is no need for this. Rather do I regard most of the opinions as a riposte to those who sought, unsuccessfully, to unseat me by their nefarious designs.

I am grateful to my comrades in arms for having encouraged and persuaded me to write this Autobiography, mainly on the grounds that it would help to keep my mind off the agonising existence which I have been forced to lead for so long. Although they were well aware of the vicissitudes which I had encountered while I rose from the rank of Major General to full General, they were not privy to the bald facts, and the truth of each encounter with which I was faced, and which I successfully overcame. It is my hope that this book will satisfy their curiosity.

Without the wise advice of my friend, Brigadier 'Birdie' Smith – himself not only an author of no little repute, but also a gallant soldier – who acted as my editor, this book would never have seen the light of day.

I must thank Susan Hooper – my secretary for ten years who typed with such care the original manuscript and the many amendments, and displayed such patience and *sang-froid*.

Susan was succeeded by Tina Carter who carried on the good work with equal enthusiasm and efficiency.

Lastly, I must thank General Sir Peter de la Billiere for the most generous tribute he has paid me in his Foreword. Though I say it myself he has summed up my qualities, such as they are, and my personality in a remarkable manner. As such, his Foreword is in tune with the story I tell thereafter.

What more could one possibly ask from Great Britain's most distinguished post-war fighting commander and leader in battle - the nation's unsung Gulf hero and subsequently much maligned in quite a separate context.

Acknowledgement to publisher

I would like to pay a special tribute to my publishers, New Millennium. Their hard-working staff have given me much wise advice and extended to me the utmost courtesy and patience. I thank them one and all.

I dedicate this book to the memory of my late beloved wife, Beryl Catherine, after 52 years of such a happy, loving marriage, 9 November, 1938 - 24 June, 1990.

Contents

Chapter 1   My Biography, *Fighting General - The Public and Private Campaigns of General Sir Walter Walker* by Tom Pocock, published in 1973.   1

Chapter 2   My Grandfather and Parents.   7

Chapter 3   My Early Background.   13

Chapter 4   My Family   27

Chapter 5   1st Battalion 8th Gurkha Rifles and Waziristan, North West Frontier.   33

Chapter 6   The Quetta Earthquake, 31 May, 1935.   53

Chapter 7   First Burma Campaign 1942-1943.   59

Chapter 8   Commanding 4th Battalion 8th Gurkha Rifles - Burma 1944-45 and Malaya - 1946 - General Staff Officer First Grade (GS01) - Burma and Thailand 1945-46 - Japanese Surrender.   67

Chapter 9   As Some Others Saw Me While Commanding 4/8th Gurkha Rifles in Burma.   95

Chapter 10   Ferret Force - Far East Land Forces Training Centre (FTC).   111

Chapter 11   Officer Commanding 1st Battalion 6th Queen Elizabeth's Own Gurkha Rifles 1951-54 Malayan Emergency.   115

Chapter 12 General Staff Officer First Grade (GS01)
            Headquarters Eastern Command 1954-57.   125

Chapter 13 Commander 99 Gurkha Infantry Brigade - Malayan
            Emergency - Operation "Tiger" South Johore 1958
            and Internal Security.   131

Chapter 14 How Borneo was Won.   143

Chapter 15 The Ingredients of Success in Counter-Insurgency
            Jungle Warfare, whether against a Terrorist Type
            Enemy, or a more well-armed aggressive
            enemy.   147

Chapter 16 Some Personal Highlights of my Tenure of the
            Appointment Director of Borneo Operations, and
            Certain Subsequent Events.   157

Chapter 17 As Some Others Saw Me, while I was Director
            of Borneo Operations - Indonesian
            Confrontation.   187

Chapter 18 The Gurkha Saga.   219

Chapter 19 Headquarters Allied forces Central Europe
            (AFCENT) 1965-1967.   229

Chapter 20 General Officer Commanding-in-Chief, Northern
            Command, UK, 1967-1969.   239

Chapter 21 Commander-in-Chief Allied Forces Northern
            Europe (AFNORTH), 1969-1972.   247

Chapter 22 Retirement   289

Chapter 23 My Overseas Visits   319

Chapter 24 The Final Battle - My Legal Action against the
          Ministry of Defence for Negligent Medical
          Treatment.   367

Appendix I   Chronology of my life and career   373

Appendix II Promotions   377

Appendix III Medals Awards and Decorations   379

Photographs & Maps

Cover photograph: with General Westmoreland in
Washington, 1972

FAMILY

My grandfather, taken in 1883, when Commandant of
the Royal Military College, Bangkok, Thailand.   12

My father and uncle Walter taken during the Boer War in
1900, the day before my uncle Walter was killed.   26

RAZMAK - NORTH WEST FRONTIER

Picknicking at Hanna Lake, Quetta, 1936, aged 24, one
year after the earthquake.   49

Adjutant 1/8 Gurkha Rifles on road protection duty, 1939   50

Staff Captain Razmak Brigade on road protection duty,
1941   50

Staff Captain on Punitive Column against the Tribesmen,
1941.   51

My night accommodation while on punitive operations.   51

BURMA

Havildar Lachhiman Gurung, VC, Burma 1945. (Photo
1948).   66

Map of Burma   77

Havildar Lachhiman Gurung, VC (2nd from left) at the
Cenotaph Ceremony in London, 1997   94

MALAYSIA

Map of Malaysia   119
Farewell visit to Gurkha families 1/6GR, 1960.   124

BORNEO

Map of Brunei   145
With Commander Royal Marine Commando Battalion,   153
Borneo 1962.
Briefing officials on Hearts and Minds Campaign, Borneo 153
1963.
Flying over Borneo Jungle, 1963.   154
Visit of Peter Thornycroft as Minister of Defence to   155
Brunei and Borneo, 1963.
Investiture of the PSNB by his Highness The Sultan of   155
Brunei, January 1964.
Visit of Mr. Fred Mulley, Army Minister, Borneo 1964.   156
With Headman of a village deep in the Jungle, Borneo   156
1964.
Map of Borneo   165
Director of Operations. Climbing into my helicopter,   183
Borneo 1964.
In helicopter with Harry Tuzo, Brigade Commander,   183
Borneo 1964.
Working in my office, Borneo 1964.   184
Visit to 1/7GR Kuching. Dismounting from my helicopter, 184
Borneo November 1964. Lt. Col. Carroll, Major Kelly
and Mr. Henry, Commissioner Sarawak Constabulary.
With my wife and daughter, official residence, Brunei,   185
Feb. 1964.
Meeting with Prime Minister of Malaysia (Tunku Abdul   186
Rahman), Borneo 1965.
Farewell visit to 7GR, Borneo 1965.   186

AFCENT

Visit to Italy when Deputy Chief of Staff, AFCENT   228
1966.

NATO Senior Officers Advanced Weapons Orientation   228
Course 24-28 January, 1966.

NORTHERN COMMAND, YORK

The Queen and myself at the Ceremony of the opening   238
of the Tyne Tees Tunnel.

AFNORTH

Map of Scandinavia   256
Commander-in-Chief Allied Forces Northern Europe,   281
1969-72.
Ditto. In full dress.   281
Talking with Lt. Gen. Blixenkrone-Moller, C-in-C of the 282
Danish Army, Frederiksborg Castle 1971.
Sitting next to the Queen of Denmark at the ball in   282
Frederiksborg Castle 1971.
Visiting Units in Norway when C-in-C, AFNORTH   283
Saying farewell to C-in-C Allied Forces Southern Europe, 284
1971.
Queen of Denmark visits my HQ, Oslo 1971.   285
Sitting beside King of Norway at my annual study period 285
in my underground War Headquarters, 1971.
My farewell visit to General Westmoreland, Chief of   286
America's Defence Forces, Washington 1972.
Supreme Headquarters Allied Powers Europe with   287
Supreme C-in-C American General Goodpaster during
my farewell visit, February, 1972.
Citation presented to me by General Goodpaster at our   288
farewell meeting.

RETIREMENT

General Sir Walter Walker in front of house at East   316
Lambrook with his gun dog and Dachshund, 1972.
General Sir Walter Walker at home at Charlton All Saints, 317
1978.
Charlton House, Charlton All Saints   317
My medals and decorations, which I presented to my   318
Regiment after I had been crippled in 1985.

THE FINAL BATTLE

Christmas card from my son, Anthony, which my   372
solicitors had enlarged and hung in their office.

GENERAL SIR TAN SRI WALTER WALKER, KCB CBE DSO** PMN PSNB

"PLEASE ACCEPT MY HEARTIEST CONGRATULATIONS ON THE AUSPICIOUS AND HAPPY OCCASION OF YOUR 80TH BIRTHDAY. THROUGH YOUR GREAT ABILITY AND LEADERSHIP SARAWAK WAS SAVED FROM THE ENEMY. YOU DID MORE FOR MALAYSIA THAN ANYBODY ELSE WE CAN THINK OF.

MAY GOD BLESS YOU AND YOUR FAMILY ALWAYS."

DATO ANGLAI SOON.

xx

Foreword

There can be few people alive today with the breadth of experience in active military operations at all levels of command than that possessed by Walter Walker. In this self-analysis of his campaigns, most of them in the Far East, his powers of leadership stand out as an example which deserves study by all those interested in the management of military operations.

As I know from my own experience when, as an SAS officer, I served under his command in Borneo, Walter Walker has a magnetic personality, a clear sense of vision and an overwhelming sense of focus and dedication to attaining the objectives he has set himself. It is this single-mindedness that, as he grew in seniority and stature has increasingly brought him into conflict with his superiors and politicians: equally, it is this single-mindedness that led to the overwhelming success of the Borneo campaign of which he was the architect.

Perhaps the most outstanding example of his foresight is the clarity with which he identified the use of helicopters in support of modern operations and his unambiguous understanding of the need for operations to be tri-service in nature and in their command. Both these aspects were reinforced during the Gulf War and are now embedded in our military organisation at the very highest level.

Walter Walker has had a life of adventure and excitement which will be the envy of present day aspiring military leaders whatever their rank. However, his handling of the Borneo campaign gives a unique insight into the management of a successful military campaign and the political pressures and resource constraints under which a modern military leader has to fight and plan his battles.

From his early school-days Walter Walker has never flinched nor lacked in courage to face up to difficulties and problems whether they be military or personal in their construction. It is all the more credit that in recent years, despite being in considerable pain and virtually bound to a wheel-chair, he has, nevertheless, managed to produce these memoirs *Fighting On*. Never was there a more apt epithet of a man who will not give in to difficulties.

General Sir Peter de la Billiere

Chapter 1

MY BIOGRAPHY, *FIGHTING GENERAL – THE PUBLIC AND PRIVATE CAMPAIGNS OF GENERAL SIR WALTER WALKER*
by Tom Pocock, published in 1973.

Preface

It was while I was Commanding-in-Chief Northern Command, York, 1967-69, that the late Sir William Collins, head of the publishers, Collins of London, wrote to me and asked if I would be willing to have my biography written. He said that, "You were born into a family with a long tradition of service in India, and until your last and in some ways most spectacular appointments, saw all your Army service east of the Red Sea. The First and Second Burma campaigns, in which you played a prominent part, ranked with the bitterest defeats and hardest won victories of the British Army in the Second World War. You have also witnessed at close hand the beginning of the demise of the British Empire, in the form of the Partition of India into the self-governing States of India and Pakistan."

Sir William continued: "After 1945, Britain had achieved two total victories, both of them almost unsung and both of them in the Far East. The first was the Malayan Emergency, in which a communist guerilla revolution was annihilated: and the second was the Indonesian Confrontation, when a far more serious attack, both internal and external, met a complete military defeat. In both of these you played a crucial part. In the first as the pioneer of training in jungle warfare and a brilliantly successful battalion and brigade commander; in the second as the operational director of a unified force that included all land, air, sea, police and local auxiliaries as well as regular troops from Australia, New Zealand and Malaya."

1

Sir William said that if I agreed to his proposal, he would strongly recommend that the author should be Tom Pocock, who had covered the Borneo campaign as a war correspondent, and that there seemed to be mutual respect on the part of the latter and me. I immediately agreed for I held Tom Pocock in high esteem, not only as a war correspondent but also as an author. At that time his earlier biographies were about Nelson and the Chelsea artist, Walter Greaves. Since then he has written many more books.

When the book was completed, there was a certain amount of head scratching about the choice of title. When Sir William Collins read the book he said that what it showed loud and clear was that the title should be "Fighting General" Why? Because for almost the whole of my time in the Army, ever since I joined the Gurkhas as a subaltern in the thirties, I had been in command of troops actively engaged in operations. The blurb on the jacket of the book said: "Few officers, and no Generals, came near the variety and extent of his frontline experience. When not employed in exchanging fire with the enemy there had been more than a whiff of grapeshot left over for colleagues and superiors in Whitehall."

The full title of the book was: *Fighting General – The Public and Private Campaigns of General Sir Walter Walker.*

The blurb went on to say: "His successes certainly aroused jealousy. And his passionate loyalty to the Gurkhas who played so large a part in all these victories came near to wrecking his career. In his final appointment NATO Commander-in-Chief Allied Forces Northern Europe, he showed the same fearless contempt for political consequences, the same ruthlessly professional determination in the discharge of his military obligation that he had learned fighting the tribesmen on the North West Frontier thirty years earlier."

The blurb continues: "Tom Pocock first met General

2

Walker when he was covering the Borneo campaign as a war correspondent. The years that have followed only confirmed his first impression that here was an outstanding soldier and a most unusual man."

After I retired I chose brick making and brick laying as my Resettlement Course at Aldershot. One afternoon the Military Assistant to the Chief of the General Staff – General (now Field Marshal) Sir Michael Carver – telephoned me to ask if on my way home, I would call in at the Ministry of Defence to see the Chief of the General Staff. I told him that I would be returning home in exactly the opposite direction, namely Somerset! He asked me if I would kindly let him know when it would be convenient for me to go to London. Later I gave him a date when I would be going to London to see my bank manager.

I duly saw Michael Carver who said he understood that a book would shortly be published about me in which reference to the Top Secret 'CLARET' cross border operations would be included. He said that he understood that neither my successor, Major General Sir George Lea, nor I, had revealed any mention of CLARET cross-border operations. I assured him that this was the case as far as I was concerned. He then said I was to read the proof copy of the book and that if any reference was made to CLARET, I was to insist that it was to be expunged. I replied with my tongue in my cheek that I would comply with his order.

Accordingly, I immediately went to Sir William Collins' office and told him what I had been instructed to do. He was furious and said he would not reveal Tom Pocock's sources and hastened to assure me that they were neither Major General Sir George Lea nor I. He then said he would be grateful if I would take no action whatsoever and leave the matter entirely for him to handle in his own way. I readily agreed and was absolutely delighted to see, when I received my complimentary copies of the book, that an accurate and complete account of CLARET was included in the book. I do not know to this day who Tom Pocock's sources were. All I do know is that every Regiment was highly delighted to read that CLARET was included in the book, for this would now enable them to write about these highly successful operations in their news letters and regimental histories, which were waiting to be published.

So another "battle" had been won. Carver was known throughout the British Army as 'Creepy Carver'. I do not know who coined this name, but he was certainly very unpopular, unlike one of his successors, Field Marshal Lord Bramall, who was universally liked and highly respected.

When I was Commander-in-Chief Allied Forces Northern Europe, my opposite number on NATO's Southern Flank was an American admiral. He and his wife invited Beryl (my wife) and myself to Naples for a few days. I was his official guest and attended a number of briefings and the usual inspections. While we were there the Admiral received a message from Carver to say he would like to pay him an official visit on a certain date. The Admiral was furious, not only because Carver had given him such short notice when I was his official guest, but also because he and his wife had arranged a relaxed dinner party for us at which among the other guests would be the famous singer, Gracie Fields and her husband, who lived on the island of Capri. After a very nice dinner, Gracie Fields' husband said to me: "Please do not press Gracie to sing, for she will do so on her own accord if she feels like it." We were all delighted when she decided to entertain us.

In my absence, Carver had informed my headquarters at Oslo that he wished to pay a visit to Oslo after leaving Naples. This meant that I had to send a message to say that a dinner party was to be organised with as many British Officers and

4

their wives as possible to be invited, and my house staff alerted.

Carver asked me to travel back to Norway in his aircraft which was faster than mine. My wife was not amused and showed it by resting on a bed throughout the flight. I put up a newspaper as I did not intend to talk shop.

Normally I gave the full briefings to VIPs visiting my headquarters. But I had sent a message ahead to say I would not be doing so on this occasion and that individual briefings were to be given by the heads of the various branches of my headquarters.

The next morning following the dinner party, Carver was about to leave our house after breakfast, having said goodbye to my wife, when she stopped him and said: "I expect you would like to say goodbye and thank the two army cooks who gave us such a good meal last night and at such short notice." He said: "Oh yes." My wife was so particular about proper man management and rightly so. She looked after the house staff as if they were her own sons. This incident must have been related by my wife to our village rector when she was dying, for he mentioned it – without giving names – in his address at my wife's funeral service, to emphasise what a caring and lovable person she was.

6

Chapter 2

My Grandfather – Thomas Nicholls Walker 1837-1902

My grandfather, Thomas Nicholls Walker entered the 60th Regiment Bengal Infantry (B.I.) and sailed for India, arriving in Calcutta just before the Indian Mutiny broke out. He served the Hon. East India Company as a Cadet. He subsequently served with the 2nd European Fusiliers in the Indian Mutiny Campaign 1857-58, including the whole of the siege operations before Delhi and the capture of the city.

During the Indian Mutiny, he was selected as one of the Subalterns of 'The Forlorn Hope' Ladder Party at the storming of the Water Bastion at the siege of Delhi, composed of 3 officers and 75 men of his Regiment. He commanded it from the Custom House and was reported to the Commander-in-Chief for outstanding bravery.

Next he took part in the capture of the heights of Sonah, and the surrender of Forts Rewarrie, Jugghur, Kanouda, Furruknugger and Bullumbghur. When the 60th Regiment B.I. mutinied at Umballa, the sepoys rushed to seize their arms and ammunition, Walker ran to the bell of arms of his company and defended it singly, at the imminent risk of his life, which was constantly being threatened, and prevented the men from breaking into the armoury.

He also saw active service with the 17th Punjab Regiment during the Rohilkund Campaign in 1858, when he took part in the actions of Amsoth, Bagawalla, Nugeena and the Relief of Moradabad.

He was then invalided home and was wrecked in the ship Alma off the coast of Socotra.

He joined the 2nd Gurkhas for one year and was then promoted to Lieutenant Colonel and served in the Naga Hills Expedition, 1879-80, where he commanded the 44th Gurkha Rifles (the present 8th Gurkhas). He was one of the first to enter Fort Khonoma, the Nagas' great stronghold.

He commanded the 44th Gurkhas Rifles for three years when he retired with the rank of full Colonel. He was twice wounded and frequently mentioned in dispatches. He possessed the Mutiny Medal with clasp, and the Naga Hills Expedition Medal. He was presented by the Royal Humane Society with a Bronze Medal for courage and humanity for jumping into the River Alipore, Bhutan, at night and saving four lives from drowning after the capsizing of their boat. One was a sentry fully armed with accoutrements and wearing his great coat.

He was a keen sportsman and devoted to the Volunteer Movement. He compiled a *Guide for Mounted Infantry* which he dedicated to the Commandant of the Assam Valley Light Horse, in which corps three of his sons were serving.

Two of his sons served in South Africa with 'Lumsden's Horse', where one Sergeant Walter Larkins Walker was killed at Boxburgh, near Johannesburg, whilst successfully and gallantly defending this post, of which he was in charge with only 20 men, against an attack made by about 300 Boers. The other, Corporal Arthur Colyear Walker, (my father), was wounded. Walter was buried with full military honours, having been decorated with an honour for bravery.

My grandfather wrote a book entitled *Through the Mutiny* (now in the Gurkha Museum) of his reminiscences of thirty years active service and sport in India from 1854 to 1883.

In 1883 he raised and organised the Royal Military College, Bangkok, Thailand, and subsequently was appointed Commandant.

My Father – Arthur Colyear WALKER 1873-1947 and Mother – Dorothea Catherine WALKER 1886-1964

My parents had four sons and two daughters.

My father was a tea planter who opened out and became Manager of the Tara Tea Company in Upper Assam, India.

He served for 25 years in the Volunteer and Territorial Services and was awarded The Volunteer Officers' Decoration – V.D. – for meritorious Service with the Assam Valley Light Horse. During this period he was a first class marksman, winner of the All Comers Challenge Cup and Best Man at Arms. He also won the Sirocco Cup for two years running with a score of 110 out of a possible 112. The competition was open to five separate Volunteer Mounted Corps.

Not only was he Master at Arms with army weapons but also an exceptionally fine big game shot, equally good with the rifle with big game as the target, and with the shot gun at feathered and ground game. The hall of our house was carpeted with mounted tiger, panther and snake skins and the walls hung with rare and valuable horns.

He was an exceptionally fine horseman and the best polo player in Assam and probably in all of India, captaining the Assam polo team for several years. He was invited to return to England to captain the English Polo Team during the celebrations to mark Queen Victoria's Jubilee. He could not afford the return journey by boat and leaving the managership of his Tea Estate. Furthermore his polo ponies were in Assam. He was also a fine tennis player. In all he won over 300 prizes at athletics, polo, tennis, shooting, gymkhanas and military events.

At the outbreak of the South African War, he and his older brother, Walter, served with Lumsden's Horse (8th Mounted Infantry). He served through the South African War, where he was wounded and was awarded the Medal with three Clasps.

At the outbreak of the 1914-18 War, he offered his services immediately war was declared. First he served with the 5th Battalion Gloucestershire Regiment and was later transferred to the 9th Battalion Oxfordshire and Buckinghamshire Light Infantry, and saw fighting in Ypres Salient (Hell Fire Corner) with them.

In 1916 he was appointed a captain in the 2nd Battalion The Devonshire Regiment, but because of ill health after a serious stomach operation, he was posted to a labour company, 1500 strong, distributed over a wide area, and was the commanding officer for two years. He formed a War Savings Association and in nine months raised so much money that he received a letter of gratitude from the Chancellor of the Exchequer (Mr. Bonar Law). The Air Ministry authorised an aeroplane to be named after the unit.

In 1919 he was demobilised and the family moved to a house named *Tara* after the name of his tea garden in Assam. This was in Tiverton, Devon, where he took up chicken farming to supplement his war and disability pensions. One of the reasons for moving to Tiverton was for the education of his four sons at Blundell's School. The founder of the school, Peter Blundell, had laid down a clause which stated that all public school boys whose parents lived in Tiverton, could be educated at Blundells School at an exceptionally low fee. With four sons, this was quite a consideration.

The following year he was commissioned to the Imperial War Graves Commission at St. Omer, and was appointed director of the very large Bethune Area. He had been working at high pressure and struggling against ill health for a long time and was forced to resign shortly before completing a year in the appointment.

10

He then took up chicken farming on a large scale, also vegetable growing in four acres of ground with a large fruit orchard. He made a steady income from these activities.

On the outbreak of the World War II, he and my mother, Dorothea, moved to a fairly large house at Weybridge, with enough accommodation to be able to have their grown up family to stay.

My mother was the dominant figure in the family. She must have been very pretty as a girl for she was strikingly handsome and one felt proud of her when she attended various functions whether at school, Sandhurst and later at Investitures at Buckingham Palace.

She was a forceful character, a strict disciplinarian, a much sought after organiser and ultra efficient. She was chairlady of the Mothers' Union and was closely involved in all manner of charitable work. She was a keen and knowledgeable gardener. As if all this was not enough, plus the bringing up of six children, she bought a Royal Enfield ladies model motor cycle and played first class tennis and hockey all over Devon. She did this in addition to running a large house and cooking for a large family with only one young maid.

She kept a tight grip on the purse strings, unlike my father, who was happy go lucky, hale fellow well met, and who had a daily flutter on the horses. There is no doubt that the strong character of my mother and the military feats of my grandfather and father, and the latter's diverse sporting prowess, combined to have a significant influence on me.

After their death, three of us clubbed together to raise money to build a wing for visitors in memory of our parents, at the Wadebridge General Hospital, which was named the *Walker Ward*.

My grandfather, taken in 1883, when he was Commandant of the Royal Military College, Bangkok, Thailand

Chapter 3

My early background

I and my three brothers were educated at a preparatory boarding school, St. Petroc's, Bude, Cornwall, which I believe is still going strong. I was not only getting myself into constant trouble by always larking, but I also objected strongly to being taught by women. My school reports were so appalling that I was wasting my parents' money, and after my first year the school took the initiative by stipulating that I should be sent elsewhere. After exhaustive enquiries my parents selected Norwood School at Exeter, where the headmaster, a parson, had the reputation of being an absolute martinet and a fine teacher. I had to catch an early morning train from Tiverton to Exeter every day and return home in the late evening, having played football and cricket after afternoon class and before catching the slow return train from Exeter to Tiverton, when I started my prep during the journey. On arrival home I had to finish my prep for the next day after supper, so I was pretty tired by the time I got to bed.

The Headmaster, The Reverend Bird, had played football and cricket for the county, so he expected one to excel at both these games. He was also a fitness fanatic, so the gymnasium featured prominently in the weekly programme. He drove me hard in the classroom and when one made a stupid mistake or could not answer a question, I received a sharp clout on the back of my head.

I was taught Latin by a witch of a woman with pebble glasses and her hair wound in a circle against her ears. She was as ugly as sin, but a good teacher. Forgetfulness or making too many mistakes were rewarded with several strokes on the knuckles with the sharp edge of a ruler.

I learned to work hard and play hard. The eagle eye of the Reverend Bird was riveted on me in the classroom and on the playing field. The reward for doing well on the playing field and at gymnastics was to be selected to help in the cricket score box on the county ground during the cricket season. I owe a lot to him for he taught me the meaning of hard work, discipline and physical fitness. Work hard and play hard was his motto. At the age of thirteen I passed the common entrance examination quite well into Blundell's School, and joined my elder brother.

The reason why my parents settled in Tiverton, Devon, was because the sons of local families could be educated as day boys at greatly reduced fees. There were several army families who took advantage of this concession and at one period there was a special army class. One of these families was called Harper, and it was Alec Harper, who was my best man when I married Beryl Johnston at St. John's Church, Calcutta, on 9th November 1938. Alec was in an Indian Army Cavalry Regiment and at the time of our wedding was commanding the Governor of Bengal's Bodyguard. After World War II he made his name as a polo player of world class in England. His younger brother, Jim, lost his life when the submarine, HMS *Thistle* was sunk.

I had the highest regard for the new headmaster, Alexander Wallace, who came during my last year. He was ex-Indian Civil Service and Indian Cavalry. Later he was ordained, became headmaster of Sherborne School, Dorset, and finally Dean of Exeter. He ran the school like a regiment – stern, strict, demanding the highest standards, yet approachable, a good sportsman who knew the name and character of every boy in the school.

When I became head of the school's day boys, I found them to be a motley bunch of idle, unpatriotic, unkempt, and 'couldn't care less' type of youths. I decided to straighten them out and I encouraged them not to allow themselves to be contemptuously referred to as 'daybugs' by the boarders. If we couldn't shine on the playing field because of the low strength of our numbers, at least we could show the school what smartness on the parade ground meant, and also the precision of our foot drill and musketry. We were all members of the Officers Training Corps (OTC), as it was then called.

I decided to become an amateur boxer and was coached during the term and during the school holidays by an ex-warrant officer, by name, Company Quarter Master Sergeant Sturrock. He taught me my craft and turned me out as a tiger of a boxer whose aim was to attack from the sound of the bell and knock out my opponent in the first round. In this I succeeded. I also decided to sort out the school bullies who received a straight left to the nose or an uppercut to the jaw if they insulted me, tripped me up or ruffled my hair etc. I drove the day boys hard and they gradually began to have pride in their house, pride in their appearance and self-respect. But I overstepped the mark. The headmaster summoned me to his study and explained the difference between driving and leading. While being grateful to me for what I was achieving, he wrote in my terms report: "He must not allow his zeal to outrun discretion." He referred to me as 'a tiger' on the rugger field as well as in the boxing ring, and emphasised my powers of leadership. He prophesied that I would go far in the army.

As school monitors, we were authorised to cane erring boys, but for more serious offences the boy's housemaster, or even on occasions the headmaster, administered corporal punishment, 'six of the best' and trousers down. Corporal punishment certainly achieved its aim and to my certain knowledge no boy ever transgressed again.

At the day boys end of the school year house supper,

when I was leaving at the age of eighteen, Ross Wallace was a guest. At the end of the supper, he rose to his feet and having made a rather complimentary speech about me, ended by saying: "On behalf of all parents I have been asked to present you with this inscribed silver cigarette case, which you richly deserve." Also presented to me was a scrubbing brush inscribed: "I have earned you more friends than enemies." This referred to my insistence on having the long table, on which the boys 'blancoed' their equipment and cleaned the brasses, always scrubbed clean and kept spotless. Likewise, the locker and changing room.

The school report that Ross Wallace wrote for me was as follows: "I am most grateful to him for his most valuable work as School Monitor and Head of Day Boys House.

"He is in my opinion one of the most efficient and capable Heads of the House that the Day Boys have ever had and I personally am extremely grateful to him for the way in which he pulled them together during his last year.

"I regard him as in every way one of the most promising boys I have met, and I foresee myself a very distinguished career in front of him.

"We are all sorry to lose him."

Alexander Ross Wallace must also have given me a very good report to the selection board for entry into the Royal Military College (RMC), Sandhurst, for at the interview I was awarded four hundred out of four hundred. Also I seemed to 'click' with the board.

From then until he died at the age of ninety, we kept up a yearly correspondence. He was so interested in the progress of my career. Both my wife and I attended his funeral and also his memorial service.

I entered the Royal Military College (RMC) Sandhurst, now Academy (RMA), in the autumn of 1931. On arrival I was shown my room in the old building and told to go to the centre of the building called Piccadilly Circus, and read and absorb all the notices. I hadn't been there more than a minute or two when an officious looking Junior Under Officer bawled at me, "Why the hell aren't you wearing your mufti cap? Caps are b...y well worn by all junior cadets in Piccadilly Circus, and don't you forget it, or you will be for the high jump and b...y high jump at that." This turned out to be my platoon commander a Junior Under Officer (JUO) for my first term, and his last term. 'Sandhurst', as this institute was more commonly known, was organised into seniors, intermediates and juniors, and the course lasted two years.

The whole day seemed to be devoted to square bashing, then changing into a red and white striped blazer with brass buttons, silk striped scarf, long white trousers and a 'pillbox'. Thereafter proceeding to the gymnasium for rigorous physical training. Before leaving for the gym we were fallen-in with our army bicycles and paraded just as for a drill parade, with every bicycle correctly 'dressed' by the right, given the order, 'Prepare to mount', and then to ride with ram-rod backs to the gym, and the same procedure after the PT parade was over. We would then bicycle in formation, wheel to wheel, dressed by the right, back to our quarters, and change into drill uniform for more square bashing under the Company Sergeant Major, with several drill sergeants watching one's every movement and rewarding one with a yell of anger for any mistake. Later on in the first term, equitation featured prominently in the daily programme. For this one had to change into breeches and leggings, and again bicycle in strict formation to and from the equitation school.

I remember my first weekend so well. We juniors all spent the whole time indoors polishing our boots and rifles. Brown Kiwi polish with spit and methylated spirit was worked round and round the toe cap until a shiny smooth surface with a smooth shiny thickness of polish was achieved. I could see my eyes reflected in their shiny mirror-like surface. A certain amount of heal-ball was also applied. One's rifle received the same loving care with polish, oil and so on, and the bayonet was burnished until it gleamed. Then there was the webbing equipment to be scrubbed, blancoed and the brasses polished like mirrors.

On the first Sunday evening my platoon commander, JUO Young, entered my room where my boots, leather belt, rifle, bayonet and webbing equipment were laid out neatly for his inspection. He picked up my boots, examined them closely, snarled "bloody shit", and chucked them out of the window on to the gravel surface below. When I retrieved them the surface of the toe caps was pitted with holes, and so much so that I had to clean off all the polish and start all over again. The JUO had snapped at me that he would inspect my boots again before lights out. I went without supper and just about met the JUO's time restriction with his grudging approval.

For church parade every Sunday, new cadets wore blue suits and 'gore-blimeys' (mufti caps) while our uniforms were being cut. The inspection before being marched to church was meticulous for any sign of a single speck of dust or dandruff. One Sunday, the Duke of Connaught inspected the whole parade and took the salute at the march past. I had taken the precaution of having the hair at the side and back of my head cut down to the white skin by the college barber using electric clippers. When the Duke had inspected the front rank, he then inspected the rear rank. All of a sudden I sensed he had halted behind my back. In a loud voice he said: "Why has this gentleman cadet got long hair?" Immediately the adjutant barked: "Take his name." Down the crocodile line I heard a succession of yells: "Junior Gentleman Cadet Walker, sir. Take his name. Got it."

For this misdemeanour I was given 'restrictions', which meant I had to stay in my brown canvas-like uniform all Saturday and Sunday, answer innumerable bugle calls throughout the whole day by reporting to the orderly room in the main entrance hall with rifle and webbing equipment, and closely inspected. In addition, at intervals throughout the whole day, I was subjected to arms drill and foot drill by the CSM, Cobb was his name, of the Coldstream Guards, and then doubled around the lake performing arms drill while at the double. The sweat poured off one, which made one's highly polished rifle slippery and difficult to handle.

On the Saturday afternoon my father appeared unexpectedly at the steps of my Number 4 Company block. CSM Cobb was standing there watching me in the distance. My father said to him: "I am Captain Walker and have come to see my son, Gentleman Cadet Walker, who is not expecting me, but I happened to be passing through Camberley." CSM Cobb saluted him smartly and said: "Sir, you see that figure in the distance being chased round the lake by a sergeant and performing arms drill at the double, that is your son, sir." My father replied: "What on earth has he done to deserve this? Nothing too serious, I hope?" CSM Cobb told him what had happened, and added: "I shouldn't be saying this, but it was pure bad luck. He had one single tiny piece of dark hair protruding below the bottom rim at the back of his cap on church parade last week, when unfortunately the Duke of Connaught spotted it. I am as much to blame because I should have seen it when I did the preliminary inspection. But there is nothing for you to worry about, sir, your son is doing very well and I have marked him out as one of the best junior gentlemen cadets of his intake."

My father said to me: "I have been longing to be able to do this to you, and now its been done for me!"

The CSM told me to have a shower and said there would be no bugle calls for me to answer for at least one hour, so as to enable me to have a good chat with my father in my room.

It amazed me that the highly polished rifles whose brass butt plates we crashed on to the ground during arms drill, were the same rifles which we would have to fire on the rifle range. I was astonished that so little attention was paid to weapon training. The rifle was treated as if it took pride of place on the parade ground, not on the rifle range. Also, not nearly enough time was paid to minor tactics on a sand-model and in the field. The same applied to military history and practical map reading.

During my very first term I was promoted to lance corporal – referred to as 'a stripe off the square'. This was regarded as a feather in one's cap and was awarded only to a handful of cadets in each of the four Gentleman Cadet Companies. I don't quite know when the title Gentleman Cadet was abolished but I imagine it was during the time of a Labour Government, who are always so class conscious and brimming over with envy.

I continued with my boxing and every evening trained in the gymnasium under the ex-army champion, 'Dusty' Miller. In the inter-company boxing I won all my fights by a knock-out in the first round and became the feather-weight champion of the RMC. I was about to represent Sandhurst against the Royal Military Academy, Woolwich – where gentleman cadets were trained for the Royal Artillery and Royal Engineers – when I dislocated my left elbow. One of the instructors, called Captain MacIntosh Walker, drove me in his car several times to a renowned physiotherapist in Windsor who did his best to treat the damage and get me fit in time, but a proper cure fit enough for me to box and train for the contest was not achieved in time.

The most heinous punishment that could be meted out by the senior under officer of one's company was what was erroneously called a 'puttee parade'. The wretched victim had to be in full uniform – plus fours, puttees, boots, jacket, collar and tie – carry a pack on his back, be hounded along the corridors at double time and lashed with a leather belt as he passed the door of each cadet's room. Fortunately this barbaric punishment was abruptly stopped when a certain cadet burst his appendix wound as he was being doubled up the stone staircase to the top floor of the building.

During my last term I was promoted to senior sergeant of my company which gave me certain privileges and special duties. Also, I was right hand man of the line when marching past the saluting base. Our company commander was a bachelor major in a cavalry regiment and one did not see much of him unless you were the senior under officer, or one of the four junior under officers or, like myself, the senior sergeant. He committed suicide at Dunkirk, rather than be captured.

Two out of the three senior under officers in my cadet company during my time committed suicide as officers well before the beginning of World War II. The reason for this I do not know, but it was not difficult to discern that they were both living on their nerves as senior under officers while at Sandhurst. I would say that a very small percentage of those who achieved under officer rank at Sandhurst went on to achieve dizzy heights in the army. In too many cases I have a sneaking feeling that the cadet's public school had some influence on the decision.

I had already been accepted for commissioning into my grandfather's regiment, the 1st Battalion, the 8th Gurkha Rifles. But prospective officers for the Indian Army had to spend their first year attached to a British regiment. In the case of officers accepted for Gurkha regiments they served their one year's attachment in the Rifle Brigade or the King's Royal Rifle Corps, to which they were affiliated. But my elder brother's Punjab Regiment was stationed at the garrison town of Multan in the

21

Punjab, where the 2nd Battalion, the Sherwood Foresters was also stationed. In the hot weather Multan was the hottest military station in India, with the temperature rising to 120 degrees. In the hot weather half of the battalion took it in turns to move up to the delightful hill station, Dalhousie.

The battalion's primary task was 'Internal Security', for Congress leaders were stirring up trouble and mass demonstrations soon turned into riots. My training and practical experience of internal security were to stand me in good stead many years later when I was commanding a brigade in Singapore.

The Sherwood Foresters were a very fine regiment, exceptionally well trained, smart, highly disciplined and very efficient. I was fortunate to be posted to a company commanded by a Captain MacDonald Walker, who, although a pugnacious officer with a very quick temper, was a brilliant instructor of tactics, map reading, internal security, weapon training and musketry. Only the highest standard of every aspect of one's military profession would satisfy him. He drove one very hard indeed and demanded perfection in the field, on parade, in the office, on the playing field and in the officers' mess. Once I had got to know him and proved my worth, we established an amicable relationship, but woe betide me if I transgressed and stepped out of line.

One of the 2nd Lieutenants, by name John Baxter, attached to the Foresters with me had his father in Multan commanding my brother's Punjab Regiment. After a month or two he asked his son and me to go and live in his large bungalow with him and his wife. I gladly accepted for this would be real comfort, although we would continue to lead a normal officers' mess life. But I learned a great deal from his father for he was a brilliant tactician and engaged one in absorbing conversation.

One night I was working late in my room, as was my wont, studying for the lower standard Urdu exam, when John

Baxter entered the room and froze rigid in the doorway. He whispered to me: "There is a large cobra behind your chair with its head and body raised ready to strike." At that very moment Colonel Baxter returned from a guest night in his regimental officers' mess. He was dressed in hot weather mess uniform and wearing spurs which jangled. John whispered to his father who could see the cobra rearing its head. Colonel Baxter withdrew silently and a few minutes later entered my room by the open door behind me. As I learned later, he was armed with a long thick curtain pole which his orderly had taken down from the drawing room. His orderly had removed the colonel's spurs which enabled him to enter my room silently. Although I could not see the action he took, he quickly swung the curtain pole in an almighty swipe and struck the cobra between the head and the neck, felling it immediately. By now another orderly had joined the colonel, armed with the colonel's army revolver. The cobra was wriggling wildly on the floor so the Colonel gave it a *coup de grace* with two bullets in the head. Both his orderlies were terrified and shaking with fear. I had sat motionless throughout this drama, not daring to move a muscle. The colonel said to me, "You remained steadfast under fire!"

Cobras were not the only danger in Multan, for they were matched by the small but highly poisonous snake, the Krite, which could climb up a curtain and hide in its folds. I always felt more secure when I had climbed into bed under my mosquito net and tucked it in firmly for the night, especially when one was sleeping outside in the hot weather. It took the colonel's two Punjabi soldier orderlies some time to mop up the blood and dispose of the dead cobra for the night. The next day it was skinned by a taxidermist and later mounted for the colonel.

In due course the Battalion moved to Bombay for Internal Security duties. There I met the Governor of Bombay's daughter when playing tennis. Later, and much to all the senior subalterns' chagrin, she invited me to join her parents' party for the Governor's Annual Ball and stay the night. We danced together most of the evening and after the national anthem had been played, she suggested that we should go for a drive along the sea front. The car was driven by one of the governor's chauffeurs and he had been told to drive us so far and then return, for her parents would be sitting up waiting for us!

I only had three months in Bombay after which I would be due to join my Gurkha battalion in Quetta, Baluchistan. Captain MacDonald Walker and all the subalterns gave me a most happy and enjoyable farewell dinner. The commanding officer was kind enough to give me an excellent Confidential Report, which was to stand me in good stead. He wrote:

"Plenty of character, and an attractive personality.

"Tactful and reliable – plenty of initiative and sound judgement.

"Strictly temperate.

"He has shown exceptional zeal and energy during his year in this unit, and has acquired quite a good amount of professional knowledge.

"He is steady and has the courage of his convictions.

"If this young man goes on as he has begun, he has a good future and may go far."

Bombay, 1 April 1934.

After World War II and the Partition of India, Britain absorbed four of the Gurkha regiments, each of two battalions, and India absorbed the remaining six regiments, including my own, the 8th Gurkha Rifles. The Sherwood Foresters said they would be pleased if I was to transfer to them. They had a vacancy for an officer of my age and length of service. Because the Major General, The Brigade of Gurkhas, could not give me a firm assurance that a British officer already qualified as a staff officer would be eligible to serve world-wide just as any officer of a British regiment, I decided to accept the vacancy offered by the Sherwood Foresters.

I was immediately posted to a plum staff job, GS01, Military Operations Directorate, General Headquarters, New Delhi, and was 'cap badged' as a Sherwood Forester in 1946. It was not until I received a written assurance in 1947 that, as a qualified and experienced staff officer in peace and war, I would be eligible to serve on the staff wherever the British Army was stationed, that I transferred back to the Gurkha Brigade. I was cap badged to the 2nd King Edward VII's own Gurkha Rifles, on paper, but never served with them for I was appointed to raise and command the Jungle Warfare School and also the Far East Land Forces Training Centre. I was then promoted to command the 1st Battalion 6th Queen Elizabeth's Own Gurkha Rifles in Malaya at the height of the Malayan Emergency.

My father and uncle Walter taken during the Boer War in 1900, the day before my uncle Walter was killed

Chapter 4

My Family

I was born in India in 1912, educated at Blundells School and the Royal Military Academy, Sandhurst, and commissioned into the Indian Army, 1/8th Gurkha Rifles – my grandfather's Regiment – in 1933.

I was married with twin sons and a daughter, both sons followed me into the army, but much to my wife's and my own disappointment, they both resigned and, later, they both suffered the consequences, i.e. finding long lasting employment in 'civvy street'.

The elder of our twin sons was commissioned in the Rifle Brigade – now the Royal Green Jackets – and the younger one – by half an hour – entered my regiment, the First Battalion of the 6th Queen Elizabeth's Own Gurkha Rifles. The latter, Nigel, served under me when I was Major General The Brigade of Gurkhas, and again when I was Director of Borneo Operations, and he was serving with the Gurkha Parachute Company. The elder, Anthony, served in Borneo with The Rifle Brigade, so also came under my command.

Our daughter, Venetia, married a young officer in the Royal Irish Rifles, called Richard Venning, whose father served in the Fifth Royal Gurkha Rifles. It was on Armistice Day in 1967, when I was General Officer Commanding-in Chief, Northern Command, York, and happened to be convalescing from a particularly bad attack of 'flu that Venetia, who was living with us, came into my dressing room where I was resting to wish me a happy birthday. When she left the room and opened the door I saw the figure of Richard standing outside. He entered the room and stood to attention opposite me and said: "I have come, sir, to ask your permission to marry your daughter, Venetia." I asked him if he had obtained the permission of his commanding officer to get married. He replied: "Not yet, sir, I thought I should first ask you, not only as her father, but also as my army commander." I replied: "You should go far in the army, Richard, for resorting to such tactics! Of course, it gives me and I'm sure my wife, great pleasure to grant our permission. But you are to telephone your commanding officer immediately and if he grants his permission, I shall know by the sound of champagne corks popping in the drawing room, that you have obtained the permission of your CO, as well as the permission of my wife and myself." Apparently his CO said to Richard: "It is about time too; why have you taken so long to pop the question?"

They were married in York Minster. Richard transferred to the 2nd King Edward VII's Own Gurkha Rifles, a battalion he later commanded.

As I write this in 1995, Venetia has been a wonderful daughter to me ever since my beloved wife died so tragically in June 1990. Never a day goes by without her either visiting or telephoning me. She has done so much to comfort me and give me the physical and moral courage to fight my severe disablement and to bear the excruciating pain which struck me more than ten years ago. I am, indeed, fortunate that she and Richard live in their own house only twenty minutes away by car.

My wife and I were very happily married for fifty-two years. She had been suffering from polycythemia for several years which she fought with amazing courage, but finally had to have her spleen removed. She asked the surgeon how much longer she had to live and insisted on him telling her. He replied three months. She returned to our house to die. On arrival home she handed me her obituary which she had written in her own handwriting. During those three months I watched her wither from a human being to a living skeleton. It is difficult to describe how terribly she had to suffer, but she displayed amazing courage and determination and won the admiration and respect of all her doctors and nurses. She died quietly at 8.30 a.m on the 24th June 1990. She had asked in her obituary that any donations, if desired, should be sent to the Gurkha Welfare Trust. A record £700 was donated which is some indication of how much she was loved by individual members of the Gurkha Brigade Association and by many other relations and friends.

Tom Pocock, the author of my biography – *Fighting General* – wrote this appreciation of my wife:

"Beauty of looks and beauty of spirit combined in Beryl Walker, the one reflecting the other. All who met her remembered the radiance, which came from within and for which her physical grace was the natural setting. It was not a self-conscious beauty for hers was a generous spirit, living for others and, most particularly, for her family.

"The lot of a soldier's wife can be hard, especially when it includes as much active service as her husband's service. Yet such was her serenity that the observer would never know how much she must have worried and how many difficulties she had to overcome. Only her husband can know how much her support meant to him in those momentous times. Indeed it must be that some of his great achievements were also hers.

"Beryl Johnston met Walter Walker and their partnership began, appropriately, in India. In those pre-war years they can have had no hint of the trials that lay ahead. It must have seemed a secure and conventional future within the boundaries of the British Empire to the young couple. It was enough that they had recognised in each other the partner of a lifetime. She must have been an exceptionally pretty girl – maturity and experience were yet to give her the look of kindly wisdom and humour that gave her looks such distinction – and all were agreed that Walter was a dashing and promising young officer.

"Surprisingly, in retrospect, the path to partnership was not smooth for there was initial family opposition to the principle of their marriage, if only because Walter was aged only twenty-four, young for a married officer.

"They were married on 9th November 1938, at St. John's Church, Calcutta, and at once the trials, faced by all young couples dedicated to the Indian Army, began. For Walter, there would be service on the North West Frontier and, now that Italy was showing such aggression in Africa, perhaps farther afield. So both following the 8th Gurkhas, Walter as one of their officers; Beryl at his side whenever that was possible. Inevitably there were long separations but this only served to intensify the happiness of their times together.

"When war broke out in 1939 and Japan struck in the East two years later, their testing time began. Walter's war was to be in Burma, but it was in Quetta, where he was briefly an instructor at the Staff College, that he was with Beryl when their twin sons were born. Then, for him, it was back to the war in the jungle.

"The end of the Second World War did not bring peace for, within a few years, it was to be followed by The Emergency in Malaya and, when that guerrilla war had been won, Confrontation with Indonesia in Borneo.

"For the Walker family, to which a daughter had now been added, active service was now a way of life. To some extent, the demands of soldiering were offset by the security of army life and the increasing scale of their domestic arrangements as Walter was promoted.

"Beryl, too, had her duties. She was confidante to other army wives and almost a mother-figure to the Gurkhas her husband commanded and they both loved, as well as a loving mother to their own children. Far from the daunting *memsahib* of fiction, she was loved and admired in return. It is only possible to make a shrewd guess at the enhancement of happy relations between the British and the Asians that was due to Beryl's tact, charm and intelligence.

"History has recognised that victory over Indonesian aggression in Borneo with minimum loss of life was a great military achievement, particularly when seen in contrast to the long horror of Vietnam. For this, prime credit is rightly accorded to Walter Walker but Beryl shared in the triumph. For much of the time, she was there too, living at their official residence in Brunei and so, to some extent, sharing the dangers of warfare that could include assassination. Indeed there were occasions when this seemed possible; once when an attack on the house seemed imminent, Walter told Beryl that, if shooting started, she should take Venetia and lie down in the empty bath.

"Yet visitors to Muara Lodge found a tranquil household, a warm welcome and a calm that inspired confidence in the leadership and conduct of the Allied cause. In retrospect, it is extraordinary that at this very time Walter should have been subjected to political difficulties within the British Army itself. That, of course, was triumphantly overcome but it took time and added another burden to those of command in time of war. Again, the support and advice he received from Beryl is something that he alone can appreciate but others can make an assessment that is probably close to the truth.

"After victory over the Indonesians and over problems in Whitehall, Walter's career reached new heights in Northern Command and then in Northern Europe. No Commander-in-Chief could have hoped for a more charming, yet dignified, consort than Lady Walker, as she had now become. As in Brunei, so in Oslo, her unaffected friendliness and quiet wisdom inspired both calm and confidence.

"Retirement from an active career in the army, early in 1972, meant little reduction in Walter's activity because, freed from official restraint, he preached the need for defence against military threats from without and political threats from within. Writing, lecturing and organising, he was constantly on the move and, once again, Beryl provided the secure base for his work and for their family life. Once again, their characters – apparently so different yet so clearly in tune – complemented each other.

"When past seventy, Walter remained fit and active in mind and body, keeping abreast of world affairs as eagerly as he enjoyed field sports. Both he and Beryl seemed set for the long and happy years of peace which were surely their due. Yet, as so often in war, the unexpected was to be expected and this proved to be the most formidable that the couple had ever had to face together. Beryl's decline in health coincided with the catastrophic effects of the surgical disaster and the years of crippling pain that followed for Walter. For both of the partners it was to be another battle against adversity that would have defeated most other human beings. Beryl, despite serious illness from which she knew there was little chance of recovery, shared Walter's satisfaction in his final victory against odds, for which credit was due to her, too.

"Beryl's spirit lives on in the lives of those who knew and loved her. The two conditions go together, exactly like the qualities that shone through her beauty and had created it."

Chapter 5

1ST BATTALION 8TH GURKHA RIFLES AND WAZIRISTAN, NORTH-WEST FRONTIER

Having completed the statutory one years attachment to a British Regiment, I joined the First Battalion the 8th Gurkha Rifles in 1934, at Quetta, Baluchistan, then in India, now Pakistan. I was greeted most warmly by the Gurkha rank and file, led by their viceroy commissioned officers (VCOs). In the VCOs mess hung a large portrait of my grandfather, of which they were very proud and even more so now that his grandson had been commissioned into the Battalion. I was made to feel that I was someone special and I, therefore, was determined to excel on and off the parade ground, 'in the field', and on the playing field. The first things that struck me were the amazingly high standard of the turn-out of every officer and man, the marksmanship throughout the battalion and the fantastic *esprit de corps* – 'Second to None'. Above all, perhaps was the strong sense of comradeship between all the officers, British and Gurkha.

The Commanding Officer (CO) was a charming man but too kind to the World War I Majors who were heavy drinkers and bachelors to boot. It took the next CO only a few months to sort them out and to find convenient extra-regimental employment for them. The previous CO was a great horseman and because I was slim and light and a keen horseman, he decided to turn me into something like a show jumper. I was put through my paces for an hour after lunch every day, much to the annoyance of the adjutant because sometimes I missed a football training session. I coached the battalion boxing team in the late afternoon and would then return to my bachelor's bungalow for one hour's study of oral and written Urdu under my munshi (teacher) in preparation for the higher standard Urdu exam, including reading and writing Nagri script. I had to pass this exam before I was eligible for my nine months UK leave, after completing three years regimental duty.

Another exam to be passed was the retention exam to prove that one had reached the exacting standards demanded by the battalion. The subjects included regimental history, weapon training with all weapons, marksmanship, semaphore, minor tactics, night compass march, fire orders, map-reading, physical training, athletics, first aid, horsemanship, keeping regimental and company accounts, drilling a rifle company followed by executing all formations of battalion drill, and current affairs. This stiff exam was also a convenient way of getting rid of an officer who had not fulfilled expectations.

Not long after the Quetta earthquake, 1935, the battalion moved to our depot at Shillong, a journey by train from one side of India to the other – five days and nights by troop train. Then, from rail head at Gauhati in the plains to Shillong itself involved a tedious road journey up a steep one way mountain-like road. Shillong, the administrative capital of Assam and the hill station for Calcutta, was about five thousand feet above sea level with an ideal temperature of about eighty degrees Fahrenheit. The one disadvantage was that the average rainfall was as high as almost anywhere in the world.

Shillong was well known to me by repute for my father's tea garden 'Tara' was in Assam and his elder brother was Commissioner of Police, Assam, with his headquarters at Shillong.

We soldiered hard and played hard – football and basketball with our Gurkhas, and polo and tennis several days a week, with a dance at the club once a week. During the hot weather in the plains, Shillong was the refuge for the British living in the plains, and with them came their daughters – whom we unkindly called 'the fishing fleet'. It was now 1936 when, having completed the three years service since leaving England, I was due for long leave in England. For experience, I decided to fly home by Imperial Airways flying-boat from Calcutta, a journey which in those days took five days. In the middle of the flight home I developed malaria, diagnosed as such by a fellow passenger who happened to be a doctor.

My parents were horrified to see how thin and pale I was on arrival home. After two more attacks of the shivers – one while watching the open air annual Aldershot Tattoo when I felt frozen with cold – I had blood tests at the army Millbank hospital in London. It took about three visits to Millbank before I was proved positive and by this time I had wasted more than six weeks of my leave. However, I soon made up for it and spent most of my time playing in tennis tournaments around Devon and Cornwall. I also hunted regularly with the Tiverton Foxhounds and sometimes hired a mount for my sister, on condition that she kept clean my small Morris car! There were a number of hunt balls for which the only permissible dress for gentlemen was white tie and tails. The Master of Foxhounds was a General Butler, whose son was in an Indian cavalry regiment, and later he and his wife became firm friends of ours. Sadly, they both met a tragic end.

I returned to Shillong well before the 1937 season started. It was shortly afterwards that I met my future wife, Beryl Johnston, who had recently arrived from England to stay with her parents at her father's tea estate in Assam. She had studied ballet dancing in England after leaving school and planned to teach it in Shillong and Calcutta. She knocked me over with her beauty and charm from the very first moment we met at a big dance. We danced together the whole evening and from then on were inseparable whenever my military duties and playing games with my Gurkhas, gave me the free time to meet her at the club. She soon met all the officers, middle-aged and young, when she came to watch us playing polo and, of course, she was with me at all the parties and picnics. Within three months we were engaged to be married. I astounded everyone for I was regarded as likely to be the bachelor of the family, like my uncle in the Indian police.

The commanding officer (Roy Harrington) retired to England and was succeeded by Lieutenant Colonel Bruce Scott of the 6th Gurkhas, who had recently vacated command of the famous Tochi Scouts in Waziristan on the North West Frontier of India (now Pakistan). He arrived with the reputation of being a strict disciplinarian and a stickler for one hundred percent efficiency in every sphere of soldiering. This proved to be so, but 'off parade' he was relaxed, quite charming and extremely friendly. He thought very highly of our small band of junior officers – all subalterns.

He appointed me as his adjutant and made it quite clear that he did not approve of married Adjutants. However, he and his wife returned to England on three months leave and the second-in-command (Major Eric Langlands) officiated as CO. The battalion then moved from Shillong back to Quetta in preparation for three years active service on the North West Frontier where we would be located at Razmak. Before we moved to Quetta, I had been adjutant to Eric Langlands, who saw my work at close hand and the long hours I worked each day. One day he said to me that I could not be expected to wait three years before Beryl and I got married and furthermore he knew me well enough to realise that my regimental duty would come first and foremost. On his return from home leave Bruce Scott was not best pleased that his temporary replacement had given permission for me to get married. However, he seemed well pleased with my performance as his adjutant and after about two months we became close friends. He taught me to shoot partridge on the dusty plains and in the barren hills, and snipe in the lakes. He was also keen on swimming in Hanna lake, a few miles from our barracks, and always took me with him, plus two or three other subalterns. He would generally organise a picnic and make a day of it. He was also keen on tennis and we had many needle matches. Little did I dream then that we would remain firm friends until his dying day.

Beryl and I were married at St. John's Church, Calcutta. It had to be a small wedding because the great distance from Quetta across India to Calcutta prevented my brother officers from being present. My best man was an Old Blundellian who was then commanding the Governor of Bengal's Bodyguard, Alec Harper, later of polo fame. So we were driven in style in a horse-drawn carriage after the wedding.

We spent our idyllic honeymoon at a seaside private resort, Puri, on the east coast of India, in the State of Orissa. An uncle of mine had been Commissioner of Police, Orissa, with his headquarters at Puri. We were given the honeymoon suite in an excellent hotel within walking distance of the beautiful sandy beach and warm sea as calm as a mill-pond. Our two weeks there went all too quickly. We had a long train journey in front of us and knew we would probably arrive in Quetta to find snow on the ground. Such was the case. We were allotted a bungalow badly damaged by the earthquake and no one was allowed to sleep indoors. Everyone slept in wanahuts – a fairly large tent but with mud walls and a fireplace to help to keep out the snow and the cold.

As adjutant I was out of the office most of the morning accompanying the CO on his inspection of the barracks, mule lines and Gurkha married quarters, and then inspecting the numerous training cadres – weapon training, signalling, mountain warfare and so on. I got down to all my office work

37

after recreation had finished and was in the office until 8.30 p.m., when I would return to Beryl for supper. The CO used to walk his dog through the lines after his evening meal with his wife and invariably passed by my office where the lights were on, with me engrossed in my office work and drafting letters for the CO's approval the following day. One evening he came into my office and said: "I have been watching you for the past few weeks and never have you left your office before 8.30 p.m. You really must be more considerate to Beryl and arrive home not later than 6.30 p.m. This is an order. You have got everything in 'apple-pie order' and can now afford to relax. After all we shall be on the frontier shortly where no wives are allowed. This will mean long periods of separation so soon after you have been married. I take back everything I said about not wanting a married Adjutant. A married adjutant has far more responsibilities than a bachelor, and you have shown great dedication and a high sense of duty."

Beryl and the CO's wife, Nancy, had already established a close relationship and met every morning to visit the Gurkha family quarters, weigh babies and, with the amah (nurse), deal with the sick.

This close relationship between Bruce and Nancy Scott and ourselves was to last for more than thirty years, in fact until they both died. Furthermore, their younger son, Colin, joined me as a second lieutenant when I was commanding the lst Battalion 6th Queen Elizabeth's Own Gurkha Rifles, during the Malayan Emergency, fighting the Chinese Communist Terrorists (CTs). I took good care that he was closely watched by a Gurkha officer when on operations for it would have been tragic if he had been killed or badly wounded. Unfortunately, after he retired when in his fifties, he had a heart attack on a London underground station and died immediately. He broke his widowed mother's heart. I had chided him about his girth, his chain-smoking and his lack of exercise, but to no avail.

Beryl and I had about three months of married life in Quetta when, in about March 1939, the battalion moved to Razmak for a tour of three years. This meant a very long separation with a few weeks leave each year, providing punitive operations against the Pathan tribesmen permitted it. But we had discussed the inevitability of long and frequent partings and if Beryl had felt that this would be too much to bear we would not have become engaged, let alone married. We wrote to each other every day and continued to do so throughout our married life.

Razmak was a large fortified base deep inside hostile tribesmen territory and garrisoned by a brigade HQ and six battalions, supported by artillery, engineers and a full complement of administrative units including a 'train' of mules. The whole Brigade was completely self-contained, ready to move out as a punitive 'column'. In support of 'Razbrigade' was a brigade at the garrison town of Bannu in the plains, linked to Razmak by a motorised mountainous road, winding its way through hostile territory and overlooked by bare brown hills. There was another brigade in support at Wana. We were briefed on the current situation along the frontier, which was that the tribesmen had been extremely hostile for the past three years and were completely united under their magnetic and elusive leader, the Fakir of Ipi. The brigade had two principal roles; first, to keep the road open to Bannu twice a week, and second, to launch punitive operations against the tribesmen. On road open days, columns of civilian lorries – called Bagai lorries – supplied Razmak with everything for the existence and replenishment of the brigade. The task of the battalion was to establish piquets, generally of platoon strength, on the crest of the commanding heights. On their steep upward climb the soldiers were supported by their own medium machine guns (MMGs) and by artillery mountain guns, all sighted on the crest of the hill, and ready to switch immediately to a target on a flank. As soon as the piquet was firmly and tactically in position, the platoon signaller would communicate by semaphore and helio to battalion HQ below that the crest, as far as the eye could see, was clear of hostile tribesmen. There were no wireless sets in those days.

I was adjutant, and with Colonel Bruce Scott by my side, watched through binoculars the steady climb of each piquet and would note any mistakes that may have been made, or if everything had gone like clock-work and a *shabash* (congratulations) was therefore their due.

As adjutant it was my responsibility to keep the CO constantly in the picture throughout the morning and afternoon, so that he would never be caught off guard. He was an expert and very experienced mountain warfare warrior. The bars to his North West Frontier medal were so numerous that the ribbon had to be lengthened. He was also a Pushtu linguist and so was able to converse with the local Khassadors (loyal auxiliary tribesmen) and exact information from them. He had also held down several key intelligence posts on the frontier, so all in all he was an absolute expert on the problems of the frontier and the characteristics and tactics of the Pathan tribesmen. These were the same hostile tribesmen who the Russians failed to defeat fifty years later in spite of all their sophisticated armour and air-power. At that time they were called the *mugahideen*.

During road opening days we were invariably sniped, sometimes quite heavily. One grew used to the crack of rifle fire and the 'tock-dong' of bullets over one's head. But it was my job to try to locate the source of the rifle fire and inform the CO so that he could bring artillery fire to bear. As adjutant it was also my job to supervise the opening of the gates of the 'fortress' and see the leading rifle company safely through. One day I was standing by one of the pillars of the gates, together with a Gurkha officer, when a sniper targeted us and mortally wounded the Gurkha officer. Obviously the bullet was meant for me for the colour of my face must have stood out in the early morning gloom. A fighting patrol was immediately deployed and they found the fresh empty bullet case which showed clearly from where the sniper had fired. The range was 800 yards which is some indication of the high standard of marksmanship of the Pathan tribesmen.

The first time my behaviour in action was to be noted was on a punitive expedition against a Pathan village called Mir Khan Khel Kalai in August 1939. Typed on a buff army form W-3121 was the brief commendation: "It was greatly due to the energetic staff work of Lieut. W. C. Walker that the 1/8 GR were successful in reaching very difficult objectives during the night. At light next morning under heavy sniping fire, he helped to supervise the changes in the dispositions of forward troops." And, in the same area, a few weeks later: "Lieut. Walker's energetic work as adjutant greatly facilitated the task of the rear guard commander. On several occasions when the rear party was difficult to withdraw, he went forward under heavy fire and personally conducted the withdrawal of platoons in difficulty."

In the autumn of 1939, Colonel Scott left Razmak to take command of a new brigade being formed in Upper Burma – a quiet part of the Empire with little or no prospect of active service – it seemed – and had been succeeded by Lieutenant Colonel Eric Langlands. Before he left he wrote this confidential report on me: "A thoroughly efficient and hard working officer, who by his zeal and smartness makes a first class adjutant and is a fine example to all ranks. Conscientious and indefatigable, he is thorough to the smallest detail and possesses every attribute necessary to his appointment. Extremely popular with both British and Gurkha ranks. Reliable and tactful, with a pleasant manner to both superiors and subordinates. I consider Lieut. Walker shows promise of going far in his profession. Of active habits – a good horseman and all round sportsman – strictly temperate. I recommend him for the staff college."

The brigade commander was Christison, who was to be a corps commander in Burma during World War II. He wrote in his report on me: "I agree. A particularly good adjutant, and would do well at Sandhurst. His industry, military knowledge, popularity and application to details make him a suitable candidate for the staff college."

For a few months I became a company commander with direct tactical responsibilities in the field. I was also adjutant. A testing time was soon to come.

During 1939, the battalion had fought several brisk skirmishes with the Pathans, two of them in covering the withdrawal of the Leicestershire Regiment from untenable positions. In March 1940, another somewhat similar action was fought over the same ground as the last of the previous year's actions, but this time in support of the Suffolk Regiment. It was typical of many small battles fought to cover the withdrawal of a high piquet. This was coming down from a hilltop to the left of a ridge, known to be held by Pathans, and two of my platoons, which were covering the move, were also being withdrawn. Then four shots were fired from near the position the piquet had evacuated and a Gurkha was wounded. I at once threw the deployment into reverse to recapture the high ground. This was done, but another rifleman was wounded. I now called for artillery and machine-gun fire, not so much to cover any further advance or a new withdrawal, but to rescue a badly wounded Gurkha, who was lying in the open between my and the Pathans' position. I called for three volunteers to crawl forward to rescue him. I, directing operations from a sangar – a low breastwork of loose stones – came under accurate fire, one shot hitting the light machine-gun beside me, splinters cutting my hand deeply. As firing became general, the rescue party reached the wounded man. But in retrieving him, a Gurkha machine-gunner was killed and two more wounded. The battalion's withdrawal on Razmak could now be continued. All the dead bodies and wounded were evacuated so I signalled to the CO that I was ready to act as rearguard to the withdrawal. The Pathan tribesmen had been routed with severe casualties.

Many such actions were being fought on the North West Frontier at this time, but what was to be important for my future prospects was that my successful conduct of the battle had been watched by both my colonel and my brigadier. That night Colonel Langlands wrote to Beryl: "Just a wee note to tell you that Walter has really distinguished himself today. He was in command of our rear party during a withdrawal on Razmak when one of our piquets was heavily fired on ... He really was excellent – organised things fast just as if he was on peace training in Shillong. The Brig. was with me – watching him and says he has never seen a show – under heavy fire – so well directed. Tomorrow I shall do my very best to get something for Walter with the strong support of the Brig. He really is a first-class soldier – you must be so terribly proud of him."

About three weeks later, she received another letter, reading: "By now you will have heard from Walter about his show for which he was put in for an immediate MC. I thought I should like to let you know how sorry I and everyone else in the battalion was that the recommendation was stopped by district. If anyone ever deserved the medal Walter did and it's most shockingly bad luck that the district commander should have seen fit to do as he did." Instead of the Military Cross, my name appeared in a long list of those 'brought to notice by His Excellency the Commander-in-Chief'.

The brigade commander ordered the CO to have a

portable mud model made of the action and that I was to visit each battalion in turn in order to demonstrate how a rearguard should be conducted in close contact with the enemy, and how wounded and dead should be evacuated under heavy and accurate small arms fire.

Shortly after this my CO called me into his office and handed me a note in his handwriting, which read: "The brigade commander has personally selected you to be appointed his next staff captain of Razmak Brigade. In doing so he has commended your zeal as adjutant and your courage and leadership in the face of the finest mountain warfare warriors in the world."

Eric Langlands, a Scotsman, said: "I thought you might like to send this wee note to Beryl." He then handed over to me my Annual Confidential Report, which read: "I have a very high opinion of this officer and consider him much above the average of his rank and age in professional ability. His outstanding characteristics are – zeal, energy, initiative and self reliance. He is very smart in appearance. A strict disciplinarian, and in every way sets an excellent example to junior officers. Cool and collected under fire. Has a phenomenal capacity for work – in office – during training, and in the field. Is always cheerful and never loses his sense of humour. Has good power of command. Very popular with all with whom he comes in contact. He will, in my opinion, make an ideal staff officer. At all times he considers his work before anything else. It would be in the interest of the service for him to go through the staff college as early as possible. Strictly temperate."

I received a mention in dispatches in 1940, when I was adjutant of the 1/8th Gurkhas, and a second mention in Dispatches in 1942, when I was Staff Captain Razmak Brigade.

Because of its strategic position on the North-West Frontier, Razmak Brigade was always on a war footing. It followed, therefore, that a posting on the staff of Razmak Brigade was regarded as a key appointment. The North-West Frontier was where Afghanistan presses against India – now Pakistan – and through Afghanistan ran the invasion routes into India-Pakistan. The great gateways of India were the Khyber, the Kurram, the Tochi, the Gomal and the Khojak and Bolan passes.

Astride the frontier and the passes, living in the mountains, were the formidable Pathans, the fierce war-like tribes beyond whose homeland and beyond Afghanistan itself lay Russia. Russia, like Britain, desired India. It was on the North-West Frontier that was played what came to be known as The Great Game. Were the Frontier tribesmen in the pay of the would-be invaders, preparing his way? It was the primary task of the British sophisticated military and civilian frontier intelligence service to ensure that every hostile movement on and beyond the frontier could be traced, and that surprise invasion could not be achieved. Thus the Frontier Scouts, commanded by British officers, and consisting of loyal tribesmen, were raised to command all the invasion gateways. Meanwhile the regular British and Indian regiments on the frontier were constantly conducting punitive operations against the recalcitrant Pathan tribesmen.

These were the same fiercely hostile tribesmen – the mujahideen – that a modern Russian army and air force failed to defeat after their post World War II invasion and occupation of Afghanistan.

The job of Staff Captain Razmak Brigade, was no desk job, for one of my tasks was the organisation of the temporary camps occupied and evacuated when the brigade was on operations. But to my despair my first duty as staff captain was to decipher a signal ordering the 8th Gurkhas to prepare to leave Razmak instantly for an unspecified destination.

For me this was a bitter moment. For years I had trained to go to war with the 8th Gurkhas. I had been blooded on active service with them but now – so it seemed – they were probably going to war and I could not go with them. As the column of lorries disappeared down the road, I stood at the gates of Razmak, with tears in my eyes.

Razmak Brigade had now been built up into what was virtually a division and I found myself responsible for an immense variety of duties. With only the help of one Indian clerk, I had to handle the supply of rations and ammunition, all legal problems, building projects and the relief of units. When 'on column', it was I who drew up the order of march, laid out the temporary camps including the mule lines, and supervised their efficient and tidy evacuation.

The siting and laying-out of these camps had to be carried out with punctilious attention to detail. Whether the site had been used regularly by columns, or whether it was new, the procedure was the same. The column would stop at two o'clock in the afternoon to begin the long routine. First, the chosen ground was occupied and searched for mines and booby-traps. Piquets were sent out to any commanding heights. Then, to the plan sketched by me, slit trenches would be dug and sangars built. When all was ready, there would be a practice stand-to and, finally, all but the piquets would be withdrawn within the perimeter before dusk.

The slit trenches provided shelter from sniping and this would begin as darkness came on, the bullets often snapping over the sleepless soldiers until dawn. Dry stone walls had been built to protect the mules but the beasts were often hit, bullets sometimes passing clean through the body without touching the vitals, so that all that would be visible in the morning would be a small pool of blood on the ground and a tiny puncture on each side of the mule.

While striking camp next morning, I had to make certain that all rubbish had been buried and the latrine trenches filled in, because the site might soon be used again. The column could then move on, and the process repeated the same afternoon.

If I needed a lesson in the dangers of the slightest disregard of instructions I was to be given a fearsome reminder. A column from Razmak was moving through the mountains and the Pathans were known to be hovering beyond the crests in force. Particularly strong piquets were being sent up to cover the progress, but one of them did not withdraw down the mountainside with the speed and efficiency this inherently dangerous manoeuvre demanded.

Twenty or more Indian sepoys had made up the piquet and, seeing and hearing nothing of the enemy, they walked rather than ran down the mountain and, instead of taking the more difficult route along the sharp edge of a spur, chose the easier way down a dry ravine. It was there that they were ambushed by the Pathans.

Forty-five minutes later, I saw an exhausted sepoy stagger towards the column. He was, he said, the only survivor of a massacre. At once a counter-attack was mounted and I went forward to retrieve the dead. The enemy had, of course, disappeared but what they left behind made that day in the mountains unforgettable. The sepoys all lay dead in a welter of blood. The Pathans had gone to work with their knives and the bodies lay, strewn on the rocks, beheaded, castrated, their eyes gouged out. It was, of course, known that this was a Pathan custom, but it was rare to see one mutilated corpse – so important was the recovery of the wounded – but to see some twenty was an appallingly effective lesson in the dangers of relaxing discipline and tactical technique for one instant.

At a time when twenty soldiers might be killed in Europe by a single shell, such a loss might have seemed trivial. But the

47

fact that the Indian Army could suffer such a defeat at the hands of mountain guerillas threw a shock wave from Razmak through Quetta to New Delhi itself. Later, when I heard myself described as a strict disciplinarian and a martinet, my mind's eye would see again that terrible blood-stained mountainside.

Now Beryl was able to come within a hundred miles of Razmak and, for several months, she stayed at the Abandoned Wives' Hostel at Bannu. But I was only able to visit her there twice, once when I was recovering from a bad attack of jaundice and malaria, both at the same time. I was rather ill and the brigadier ordered and supervised all my meals. The brigadier was posted to China but sadly he was killed in an air crash before he could assume his appointment.

After I had completed three and a half years on active service on the North West Frontier, the time arrived for me to attend a course at the Staff College, Quetta. I had acquired much valuable practical experience both as a regimental officer and as a staff officer. Little did I realise it at the time that this experience was to stand me in such good stead, not only in World War II, but in the Malayan Emergency and also in Borneo against Indonesian Confrontation.

"When you're wounded and left on the Waziristan plains,
And the women come out to cut up the remains,
Jest roll to your rifle and blow out your brains,
An' go to your Gawd like a soldier ..."

(With apologies to Kipling)

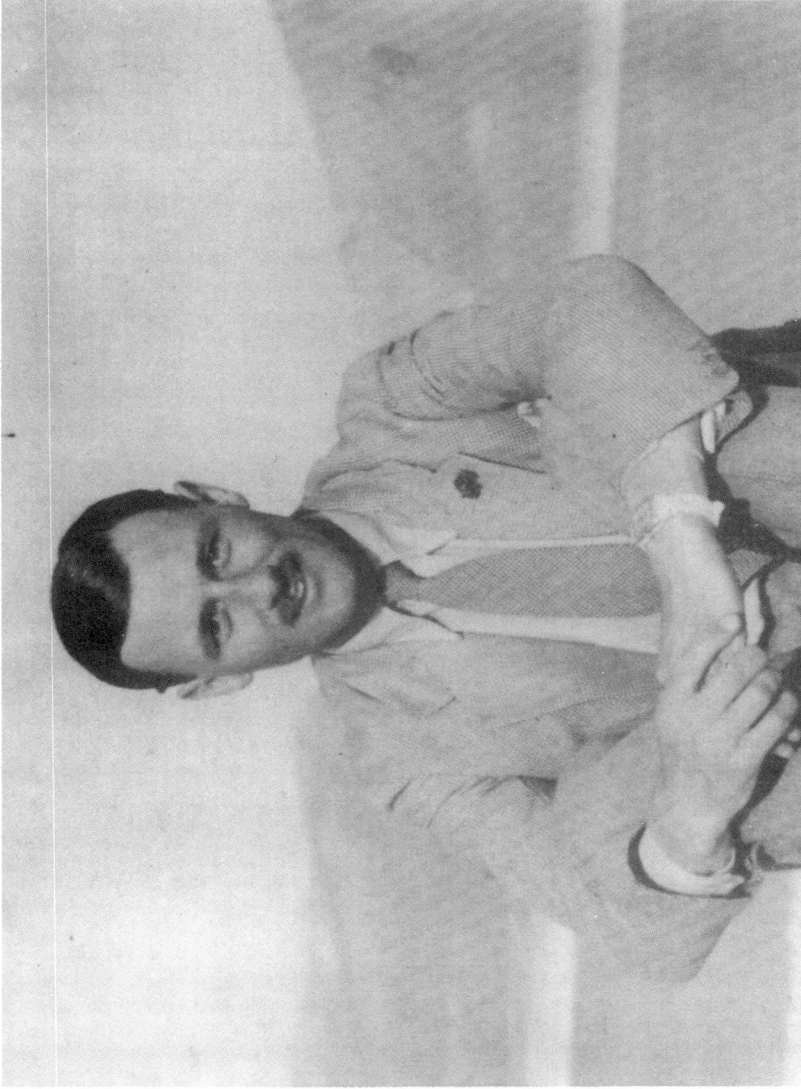

Picknicking at Hanna Lake, Quetta, 1936, aged 24, one year after the earthquake

Adjutant 1/8 Gurkha Rifles on road protection duty, 1939

Staff Captain Razmak Brigade on road protection duty, 1941

Staff Captain on Punitive Column against the Tribesmen, 1941

My night accommodation while on punitive operations

Chapter 6

The Quetta Earthquake, 31 May 1935

On 30 May 1935, we had all enjoyed a good weekly guest night in the officer's mess and went back to our quarters, well-wined, at about midnight. It was the very first day of the beginning of the hot weather, so I had told my bearer to put my bed outside on the bungalow lawn. I climbed into bed under my raised mosquito net and was soon asleep. I shared the bungalow with a brother officer, Dick McGill, who had also decided to sleep outside.

At three minutes past three in the morning I was woken with a tremendous jolt and a nightmare of an express train roaring and screaming down on me. My bed was heaving up and down and my mosquito net had collapsed on me. It was pitch dark and it took me a little time to untangle myself from the collapsed mosquito net. The lawn was heaving up and down and so was the corrugated-iron roof of the bungalow, making such a noise that I had to shout at Dick to make myself heard. My immediate instinct was that the ground was going to open, so I ran across the lawn and jumped and climbed up a cherry tree! I shouted to Dick that I was in a cherry tree and he shouted back, 'So am I.'

The roaring and rumbling rolled down our hill leading to Quetta City, and as I looked towards the city from my perch in the tree, there suddenly appeared in the sky the light of fires covering the whole city. Almost immediately I heard the alarm being sounded by several buglers in our barracks about a mile away. Dick and I rushed to our respective rooms in the bungalow and pulled on our hot weather uniform, which had been laid out by our bearers after we had changed from mess kit three hours before.

In the dark we mounted our bicycles and pedalled to our battalion lines where we found our respective rifle companies, already fallen in under the three Gurkha platoon commanders – all three Gurkha officers. We marched towards the city and before reaching the outskirts I had been allotted the area for which I was to be responsible.

I will now quote from the official account published by the Government of India three months later.

"In Quetta the scene is indescribable," the narrative ran. "A whole sleeping city; men, women and children crowded in small rooms, large rooms and corridors, on roofs and on pavements; animals tethered in tiny enclosures; a mass of humanity sleeping in a house of cards, each card of which weighed a ton ...

"The street lamps are alight; police constables patrol their beats ... then, a sudden dynamic convulsion; a surging implacable wave roared over the surface of the earth and made Quetta – in less than half a minute – a shambles, a catacomb ... The wave passed through Quetta leaving few fissures, no boiling mud or other outwards marks – except a heap of debris and ruins, the city which was once Quetta.

"For the next ten minutes no one knew what had happened. Then humanity began to re-assert itself and our imagination will help us to visualise the heart-breaking scenes ..."

There was no moon and the electricity supply had failed, so I and my company had made our way downhill towards the light of the fires where broken oil lamps had ignited splintered timbers. As the first light of day came up over the ridge of mountains, we saw a vast cloud of dust hanging over the ground where Quetta had stood.

My company made straight for the residency where I had mounted the agent-general's guard the day before. Sir Norman Cater himself had escaped but almost his entire staff and guard had been killed beneath the collapsing house. Some of my Gurkhas had been trapped under the masonry by their rifles to which they were chained as an added precaution against stealthy rifle thieves.

The 8th Gurkhas were allotted to the south-east of the town and there we began to dig. But only one in ten of those found in the rubble was alive.

Two of the bodies I dug from the ruins of a bungalow were those of a young English man and his wife who had just returned from their honeymoon. Very sad. He was on the staff of the British Agent-General.

The town itself had been destroyed, its houses shaken down into heaps of rubble. It would never be known how many people were killed in the twenty-five seconds of earthquake, or how many died later, buried under their homes, but the government finally put the total at between fifteen and twenty thousand.

The RAF station had also lain in the path of the worst shock wave and had been destroyed, the barracks reminding one officer of "a village in the front line in France after three years of war". Of a total strength of six hundred and fifty-six British and Indian on the air station one hundred and forty-eight were killed and about two hundred injured.

After two days the corpses began to smell and we were issued with face masks to enable us to work without continually vomiting. The Indian dead were carried to vast funeral pyres, and the living were moved away from the ruins which were surrounded by barbed wire and sentries to contain potential disease and exclude looters. Refugee camps were set up on the racecourse and polo ground. I and my Gurkhas were sent to hold back huge crowds besieging the railway station in the hope of escaping by train. Baluchi tribesmen were circling closer to the town in the hope of loot and looters who were caught were sentenced under martial law to flogging.

Unfortunately, in the rubble of a collapsed building, I trod on a sharp spike which pierced the sole of my boot and entered my foot. I carried on until I could feel the blood in my boot and the pain creeping up my leg. My foot was so swollen that the Gurkha medical orderly had difficulty in removing my boot. I was evacuated to the now tented home of one of our married officers, and his wife – Yeo Gardner, who took one look at it and rushed me to hospital, where I was diagnosed as having developed septicaemia. By this time my leg was completely paralysed. Our regimental doctor dressed my foot and warned me that if I was to live, Yeo Gardner would have to apply hot poultices every hour to extract the poison and bring the swelling down. Yeo Gardner nursed me for twenty-four hours with my leg raised. I then put on gym shoes and against her better judgement reported for duty much against the colonel's wishes. But I insisted on doing my share. That day we spent in excavating and evacuating all dead bodies not more than three feet under the debris. Everyone wore antiseptic masks for the stench was appalling – the bodies having been there for over fifty hours and for half of this time with the Indian sun doing its worst. The bodies were dreadfully swollen and covered in flies and worms. However, we all had to do our share and handled them without really caring. We unburied three men who were still breathing. Besides excavating corpses, we had lorries evacuating the remaining inhabitants' luggage and families, as from that night the city and bazaar had to be clear.

At 1500 hours we had a very bad shock. I was standing in the middle of the road and was knocked off my feet, and lamp posts rocked and swayed to about sixty degrees. At 1600, the Queen's Royal Regiment, the West Yorkshires and ourselves formed one long line and did a complete drive from one end of the city to the other. We allowed no one to remain and on several occasions I had to enforce obedience with the point of my revolver. One man had lost his mother and father, two out of three brothers and five out of six children and all his belongings. I came upon some frightful sights during this so-called drive. Men, women and children lying with their insides hanging out and babies crushed to pulp.

The Viceroy of India came to Quetta some weeks later to thank the whole garrison. The general put on a big ceremonial parade for which we had several rehearsals because of the number of regiments and bands involved. The Viceroy made a very good speech, paying us a handsome tribute, after which the whole garrison marched past him at the saluting base.

Gradually our tentage accommodation was converted into 'Wanahuts', which were tents but with the sides replaced by walls of mud bricks, just as was the accommodation at Wana on the North West Frontier of India; hence the name Wanahut. Sleeping inside any bungalows was strictly prohibited for all of those that were still standing were thoroughly unsafe with crevices in the corner of every room.

To relieve the accommodation problem, the Quetta garrison was reduced and my battalion was to be sent to Shillong in Assam on the far side of India, where our regimental depot was located. While we were under orders to move I had to spend one hour each day with a munchi-Hindustani or Urdu teacher – and also learn the Nagri script. This entailed at least two hours home work each night. I was due for six months home leave in 1936, but before being eligible, I had to pass both the lower and higher standard language exams – oral and written. I was not allowed to learn Gurkhali until I had qualified in Urdu. This was a great disadvantage because on return from home leave I would have to learn Gurkhali with a clerk as my teacher. There was no Gurkhali language course as there was in later years. The result was that my standard of Gurkhali was always mediocre and nowhere near my proficiency in Hindustani.

It was not long before the weekly drag hunt started early every Wednesday. I gradually found myself being the 'fox', which entailed riding my charger at a brisk gallop and dragging behind me a jackal's tail soaked in jackal urine. I was given about ten minutes start, and always did my best to choose the most difficult and hazardous route. This entailed jumping across the wide and deep fissures which had been opened up in the ground by the earthquake. Being young and adventurous I took risks which my elders and betters thought twice about emulating. The senior officers of the hunt drag generally chided me for setting such a difficult scent. I soon was able to recognise those who were likely to show dash and fearlessness in battle and lead from the front; my commanding officer was always at the front of the 'field' for he was a good and fearless horseman. He certainly approved my tactics and always gave me a 'shabash (Well done) Walter' at the end of the hunt.

We would then return to the officer's mess for a hearty breakfast followed by a hot bath. The remainder of the morning would be spent doing office work, keeping the company financial accounts, and general administration. Always the afternoon was spent playing football with the Gurkhas, followed in my case by coaching one's company boxing team. We were the best boxing battalion in the Indian Army.

Chapter 7

First Burma Campaign 1942-1943

In 1942, when the Japanese were cutting their way down the Malay peninsula towards Singapore, the posting came for me to attend the staff college at Quetta. I had served on the frontier for three and a half years, far longer than I had expected. It might have seemed at the time that I had had to waste my military talents in a backwater of the currents that were scouring the world. It is unlikely that any officer in that year could have foreseen that the years in Waziristan would prove to be the best possible preparation for the ordeals to come.

The staff course at Quetta had been cut from a year to six months in order to mass-produce staff officers for the war against Japan. But, for this time, I could be with Beryl in a married quarter and enjoy a little reminder of the social jollities of Quetta I remembered from the time before the earthquake.

For about three years, I had suffered from occasional stomach pains. Being something of a Spartan, I had put this down to indigestion, or perhaps physical strain, and taken no action. The pain had become increasingly severe but, so long as it continued to be temporary, it was ignored. Then, at one of the Saturday night dances at the Quetta Club, which would last until dawn, I collapsed in agony. I was rushed to hospital and an immediate exploratory operation was arranged. My appendix, it was found, was bent double.

My appointment after the staff college was to be as a a general staff officer (Grade 3) on the staff of Lieutenant-General William Slim, who had commanded the 1 Burma Corps since 19th March 1942. 'Burcorps', as it was known, comprised the 1 Burma Division of Burmese and Indian troops (now commanded by Major General Bruce Scott (my former Commanding Officer), 17th Indian Division and 7 Armoured Brigade. Since the Japanese had attacked across the Siamese border in January, and Rangoon had been evacuated, all that was generally known of Burcorps was that it was conducting a fighting retreat somewhere in Central Burma.

Slim's headquarters had been retreating every few days with its light covering screen of infantry and, when I found it on 16th April, it was encamped to the north of the oilfields. As was the custom, the headquarters was spread out under trees – trestle tables, maps and notice boards, wireless trucks and hastily-dug slit trenches. There was intense activity because, as I was at once told, the Yenangyaung oilfields had been blown the day before, and the Japanese were now making one of their encircling sweeps behind the troops retreating from the huge canopy of black oil smoke above the ruins.

This was no time for any exchange of gossip with new colleagues but there was one brief moment of gratified recognition. I recognised Major Brian Montgomery, the GSO (1), as an old and reliable friend. Montgomery, the brother of the future Field-Marshal Viscount Montgomery of Alamein, had been GSO (2) of Waziristan District Headquarters and we had often met during operations against the Fakir of Ipi.

A brilliant staff officer, Montgomery was something of a disciplinarian and punctilious to a degree: I never knew him draw a line on a message pad without using a ruler. He was brisk, sometimes finicky but, I knew, highly professional and unlikely to become flustered in a crisis. For his part, Montgomery seemed pleased to see me and said he well remembered my achievements on the North-West Frontier. Montgomery told me that that same night I would start work as duty staff officer under instruction. So, knowing nothing of the tactical situation, I found myself helping to mount a counter-attack against the Japanese who had set up a road block between corps headquarters and the troops retreating from the oilfields. Somehow in the confusion and darkness this was successfully achieved.

Corps headquarters was necessarily small – no larger than the customary brigade headquarters – and there was little equipment that could not be packed into a column of jeeps. It was to be my task to reconnoitre the next site for the headquarters and lay it out. Thus, every two days or so, I would drive north up the road or track to look for a suitable place that offered concealment from the air, a natural defensive position and the best possible overland communications. Occasionally I chose a village but these were obvious targets and the Japanese Zero fighters, which dominated the air, regularly struck at the corps' line of retreat. More often the site would be in a patch of jungle or under coconut palms. It would be dangerous to choose an isolated clump of trees to which Jeep-tracks could be seen to lead, so I tried to put myself in the position of a Zero pilot looking for the headquarters and then choose the least likely site.

Usually I chose well – each new site being some twenty miles to the north of the last – but once there was an alarm when the Japanese, using river craft on the Chindwin, outflanked corps headquarters itself and a counter-attack had to scramble into action to force them back. In following this hectic routine, I found that my long experience in the very different terrain of the North-West Frontier proved its value. Then too, I had belonged to a light-scale, highly-mobile headquarters, always under threat of attack by a skilled and courageous enemy. Both Montgomery and I had had this grounding but so too, had the corps commander. Slim had also been on the frontier and, more recently, had commanded a Gurkha battalion in the Middle East and, later, a division during the last year's operations in Iraq.

Tough and imperturbable, Slim quietly dominated his corps, radiating a confidence that he cannot have felt himself, although, even at this stage, he had not given up all hope of catching the Japanese off balance and delivering a counter-blow that would drive them south. Working day and night shifts of eight hours, I saw much of Slim and later only remembered one occasion when he showed strong emotion.

General Scott's division had been encircled and was hoping to break out in a night move. The complex orders for this, and for various covering and diversionary moves by other formations, had been passing through my hands and copies were being circulated in the usual manner. A major action seemed likely and Slim was prowling the headquarters site, sunk in thought. Then I saw him look up at the board on which were pinned copies of the orders I had circulated. Suddenly Slim frowned in anger and, striding over to my table, stormed at me. I had, said Slim, omitted to include the director of medical services among those due to receive copies and that, with a battle imminent, was unforgivable. I never forgot it again.

In fact I used it to good effect when I was later an instructor at the staff college, Quetta, and the students thought I was being too strict and finicky in my correcting of their message writing, written operation orders and written appreciations of the situation.

Slim's own superior, General Alexander, was directing the strategy of the campaign from his headquarters near Mandalay, but I occasionally passed him on the road and I would be stopped and asked for the latest news. In contrast to Slim's relaxed appearance, Alexander always wore his high-crowned Guards' cap and a polished Sam Browne belt. But like Slim, he never appeared ruffled, however disastrous the outlook.

The last practicable line of defence within Burma was the river Irrawaddy. Mandalay, on the east bank, had to be evacuated by the end of April and what was left of Burma Corps withdrew across the road and rail bridge over the river and, on 30th April at one minute before midnight, this was blown. The explosion announced the loss of Burma to Japan.

During this long retreat – some one thousand miles in about three and a half months – the Burma Army had never disintegrated. It had had to fall back constantly not only in the face of fierce Japanese attacks and encirclements, but in the hope of reaching India or some stable defensive positions before the monsoons broke in May. The final act was the crossing of the Chindwin and there the last of the heavy weapons and vehicles were destroyed or abandoned. I myself lost most of my kit when my Burmese batman deserted to the Japanese, taking with him Beryl's wedding present: a pigskin case fitted with ebony-backed brushes.

The first monsoon rains fell on 12th May but, by then, Burma Corps was straggling in India. I, watching them, was glad to see a Gurkha battalion still marching in military formation and each man still carrying his rifle slung. Corps headquarters had suffered badly. We had long lacked protection against malarial mosquitoes: no nets, no mepacrine, no protective oil. When Slim's staff crossed into India only half a dozen of us were still on our feet. On 20th May it was all over, officially, when General Alexander's now non-existent command was formally disbanded and the surviving troops came under command of an Indian Army corps.

The Burma Army had suffered a total of 13,463 British, Indian, Gurkha and Burmese casualties, against 4,597 Japanese killed and wounded. It had lost virtually all its weapons – except personal arms – ammunition, transport and supplies. In the air, losses had been almost exactly equal, with just over one hundred aircraft lost by each side.

So the first Burma campaign ended in total victory for

Japan. Not only was the country itself occupied, but the Japanese had succeeded in cutting the vital Burma Road to China, so that now the only supplies from the outside world reaching that country had to be lifted in aircraft flying 'over the hump' of dangerously high mountains. With success throughout the Pacific and South-East Asia complete, the enemy could now prepare for the invasion of India itself.

Once safely inside India, the survivors of Burcorps faced a humiliating shock. We thought we would be housed in clean, dry transit-camps to await leave. This was not to be the case. Arriving at the frontier garrison town of Ranchi we were appalled to find the hospitals filled to overflowing and the comfortable transit-camps non-existent. Those able to march or rather, to walk, were directed away from the town and told to make our own bivouacs just as we had in Burma. And, as for the mighty, avenging Indian Army, that was nowhere to be seen.

At Ranchi, I was asked by Montgomery to write the corps' war diary. Meanwhile I was one of those granted leave and, soon after, began the week-long rail journey back across India to Quetta for a month with Beryl. There, just as the veterans of the Libyan desert had once been the talk of the staff college, now it was this thin, sallow-skinned staff officer from Burma. I was asked to lecture on my experiences and did so. But that evening an instructor from the staff college came up to me as I dined with Beryl at the Quetta Club. Both staff and students wanted to hear more, he said. Particularly important to them was my account of conducting the campaign from a small, highly-mobile corps headquarters. When the time came for a return to Burma these would be needed again, these streamlined headquarters able to move quickly by jeep, or even aircraft. Would I therefore lecture again? Protests that I was still tired and was meant to be resting had to be dropped and I found myself indoctrinating the future officers of the avenging 14th Army with the ways of jungle war.

The respite could not be long and soon I received orders to return to Ranchi as Deputy Quartermaster-General of a division preparing for the return to Burma. Shortly before I was due to leave, there was a change of plan and I was asked to remain at Quetta as an instructor at the staff college to lecture on staff duties. Again I found myself directly junior to Montgomery, who was in charge of his division at the college, and was delighted to find that the new commandant was Brigadier Geoffrey Evans, who had won the Distinguished Service Order in Eritrea.

Beryl and I could now enjoy some domesticity and we were grateful that chance had brought us together for the birth of our first child. One morning while I was lecturing to my class, I saw the adjutant peer through the window, grin and give what I took to be a rude gesture with two fingers of his right hand. I returned the signal but the adjutant shook his head and called out, 'No, no! It's twins!'

The students cheered, the commandant, who had heard the uproar, asked what it was all about and I leapt on my bicycle to ride to the hospital where I saw Beryl and our twin sons. The peaceful interlude had become idyllic.

Havildar Lachhiman Gurung, VC, Burma 1945

Chapter 8

Having been adjutant of a crack Gurkha regiment, staff captain of the famous Razmak Brigade and on the staff of probably the most distinguished field commander in World War II, Field Marshal Lord Slim, I was not going to lower my standards.

On joining the 4/8th Gurkhas – a war-raised battalion – I was fully conscious of the fact that they had been severely blooded, been through a prolonged ordeal of battle and were war weary and physically drained. However, making full allowance for this, it was perfectly obvious to me that the battalion had to be retrained and transformed in five months, if I was to command and lead it to victory against an enemy as ruthless, efficient and adept at jungle warfare as were the Japanese.

Therefore I set about retraining them to the standards to which I myself had been trained. In the chapter *As Some Others Saw Me* (Chapter 10), Patrick Davis and Scott Gilmore give as accurate a description as any of my characteristics and reputation. Certainly there had been blood, sweat and tears, but by the 20th December 1944, the battalion was ready for battle, and with confidence, I issued an 'Order of the Day' which is reproduced in the chapter already mentioned.

The major battles which the battalion fought under me are described in the same chapter under the sections devoted to Patrick Davis, Denis Sheil-Small and Scott Gilmore.

Unbeknown to me the ferocious battle of Taungdaw, fought in May 1945, (Chapter 10) when one of my Gurkha riflemen earned the Victoria Cross and Major Peter Myers a bar to his MC, was planned to be my last in command of the 4/8th Gurkha Rifles.

We could never have won these battles had it not been for the magnificent artillery support that we always received from the battery of the 136th (lst West Lancashire) Field Regiment, Royal Artillery.

I was asked to write a foreword to this regiment's life story entitled *The Rose and The Arrow*. I wrote this on the 6th October 1986, and this is what I said:

"136 Field Regiment owe G. W. 'Robbie' Robertson a great debit of gratitude for the way he tells this story and the stirring story he tells. Much of the value of this history lies in the style in which it is written, a style that must surely satisfy even the most fastidious.

"Many of the actions described will not be found in the divisional history and certainly not in the official history of the Second World War. All the more important, therefore, is it that this war history of such a fine regiment, a regiment which was certainly second to none, should be recorded for posterity.

"It will give immense pleasure not only to those who had the honour to serve in its ranks, but also to those of us who served alongside the regiment and received such magnificent artillery support. Certainly I, myself, regard it as a great honour to be asked to write this foreword.

"Speaking as a former battalion commander in the famous Golden Arrow Division, I know what a great morale booster it was for one's company and platoon commanders to know that their accompanying forward observation officer (FOO) had on call the artillery support of twenty-four 25-pounder field-guns and that when that close support came it would be so deadly accurate.

"One of my officers, Patrick Davis, wrote a book called *Child at Arms* which was first published, to very considerable praise, in 1970 and won the *Yorkshire Post* Best First Work Award. A new edition was published in 1985 and contains a specially written afterword by the author.

"In this Afterword, Patrick Davis writes that not only were the reviews of the original edition of his book mostly kind, which was pleasing, but that what was heart-warming and fascinating were the letters that arrived sometimes years later. Gunners serving with the 7th Indian Division were particularly active in writing to him. In his words, "Artillerymen providing close support to infantry are blind without observation posts, and those O.P's were usually manned by a gunner officer and two or more men with wireless. They sat with the infantry in the most forward positions, often accompanying them on patrols, and so came to know some of us, and we some of them, very well."

"He then proceeds to quote extracts from letters he has received from Gunners of various ranks. The friendship and comradeship expressed in these letters bring a lump to one's throat. One of the writers was Lance Bombardier Eric Williams of 136, now running a boarding kennels at Great Yarmouth in Norfolk. Such was the admiration and affection he held for my own soldiers, that he not only became closely involved with the Gurkha Welfare Appeal, but personally paid for the education of both sons of one of my riflemen, who was awarded the Victoria Cross at the Battle of Taungdaw on the nights of 12/13 May 1945.

"Both Eric Williams and Patrick Davis have recently travelled to Burma and visited the actual sites of where many of the actions fought by 89 Brigade took place.

"Putting on my former NATO hat as the Commander-in-Chief of the Northern Flank, I know very well how the field artillery has become integrated with nuclear weapons and guided missiles into the nuclear battlefield. Our field artillery will always be there on the battlefield, always ready with fast and accurate support for the infantry, thanks to an organisation and fire control system well in advance of our allies. Our modern artillery is still 'Queen of the Battlefield' and once again ready to act as the backbone of the defence and the spearhead of the attack.

"To revert to the substance of this book. Well do I remember studying the situation one day with Geoffrey Armstrong on his map. I noticed that the contours on his map had been coloured in various colours so that the commanding ground and dominating features stood out in stark relief. From that day onwards I did the same to my map, often by the light of an oil lamp or torch at night. It helped me to plan my patrols, to plan my operations and more often than not to put my finger on the enemy's most likely dispositions. I have Geoffrey Armstrong to thank for a tip that paid my battalion and me some handsome dividends. I continued to use this device throughout the remainder of my forty years service in the British Army."

The commanding officer was Lieutenant Colonel Geoffrey Armstrong, DSO, MC, TD, who was the finest type of 'gunner' CO, highly professional and greatly admired. He wrote to me the following letter of gratitude:-

"You have been kind enough to write a foreword to this book and no general officer could have known 136 so well or been more involved in its period of action in Burma. We are too modest to claim that the successful outcome of these battles, or of your own considerable and gallant part in them, was due entirely to our support – but where would we have got without each other?

"On behalf of all who served in 136 – perhaps the happiest family in the Royal Regiment of Artillery – I am charged to offer you this signed copy as a small token of our appreciation of a fine soldier and a good friend."

Shortly after the Battle of Taungdaw, I was working on my map in my dug-in command post choosing the objectives which might be occupied by the Japs and to which I would send reconnaissance patrols. So engrossed was I that unbeknown to me, the divisional commander, Major General Evans, had tip-toed into the command post and had been standing behind watching me colouring the contours of my map so that the highest features stood out in stark relief. He coughed and I turned round to find him standing there. He shook me warmly by the hand, congratulated the battalion and me on the tremendous victory of the battle of Taungdaw, and then asked me to put him in the picture about my immediate plans. This I did with the aid of my map which I had just coloured. He then said quite casually: "How is your second-in-command shaping and would he be fit to succeed you when the time comes?" I replied that he was fairly raw when he first joined me but being an intelligent man had 'picked up the ropes' quite quickly and could take over command of the battalion if anything were to happen to me. I added that I had known him well for a number of years.

He gave me his future plans and we then talked about old times, for he had been commandant of the staff college, Quetta, when I was an instructor, so we knew each other well. A few weeks later my brigadier came to see me and told me that Geoff Evans had informed him that he had decided to appoint me his general staff officer (Grade 1), and that I was to hand over command of my battalion to my second-in-command. I protested strongly to my brigadier on the grounds that this was not the moment to change command, just as the battalion had emerged from a period of hard fighting, with more shortly to come.

General Evans was adamant. As a sop he said I was looking rather drawn and under-weight, and a spell of leave would do me good before I took over the somewhat arduous appointment of his principal staff officer. So I set out for the long journey to Quetta in Baluchistan to have a week with my wife and our twin sons, now nearly three years old. When I arrived at the nearest airfield, the Dakota aircraft which had been arranged to fly me to Calcutta was unserviceable for passengers. I was armed with a special priority pass signed by the general, and showed it to the pilot. He said that he and his co-pilot would have to fly the aircraft to Calcutta for urgent repairs because one engine was not functioning properly. He was prepared to take me as his sole passenger if I was prepared to take the risk. He explained that he and his co-pilot both had parachutes but that there was not one for me. I said I would give him a Jap officer's sword if he would get me to Calcutta. He jumped at this and so we took off and after a rather anxious and slow flight we arrived safely at Calcutta. I duly presented the pilot with the Jap sword.

I flew from Calcutta to Karachi as a priority passenger and then boarded the train from Karachi to Quetta. At the junction station of Mach, less than halfway up the final climb to Quetta, I telephoned the 8th Gurkhas depot at Quetta to request them to inform my wife that I would be arriving at Quetta railway station at such and such an hour. I had already sent a signal from Calcutta that I would be arriving in about three days time, but as I suspected, the signal never got through to my regimental depot. In the event my wife received only half an hour's notice of my return on one week's leave from the war in Burma!

When I first arrived home at our earthquake-proof 'hutted' accommodation allotted to 'abandoned wives' I was somewhat taken aback to find our Gurkha amah (nurse) holding a baby and a large dog – Great Dane – barking at me. After a rapturous reunion with Beryl and the twins I said – "When on earth did we get these?" My wife roared with laughter and replied – "They belong to my next door neighbour, whose husband (also commanding a Gurkha battalion) has also come back on a short leave. I offered to look after their baby and Great Dane while they went off to the hills for a two days break."

After a gloriously happy week which passed all too quickly, I flew from Quetta to Karachi where I changed aircraft and then flew all the way across India to Calcutta and thence to Burma. I arrived at Divisional Headquarters and reported to the general in his caravan. He gave me a very warm and friendly welcome and then briefed me on the current battle situation and his future intentions and plan. Next I took over my appointment of GSO 1 from an old friend of Quetta staff college days, Hugh Ley, and was introduced to all the members of the headquarters. My caravan was adjacent to the general's. I thought to myself, a caravan would be a luxury after sleeping in a bunker or slit trench for so long and being shelled and mortared during the night.

Geoff Evans was a hard task master, seldom smiled and throughout the day was very much 'on parade'. It was not until the evening that he relaxed when he and I played badminton for half an hour or so close to our caravans so that I could break off to answer any urgent wireless or telephone calls. After an improvised shower I would go to his caravan for a pink gin and this is when his demeanour changed to one of relaxation. It was then that I brought up any tricky problems from the three brigades about which he had proved to be so stubborn and inflexible during the day time. He would hear me out and provided I presented the facts clearly and tactfully and gave him the pros and cons and then my own reasoned opinion and recommendation, he would usually agree. Of course it was a great advantage having served under him as an instructor when he was commandant of the Quetta staff college and, more important, as a battalion commander, having fought several successful battles against the Japs soon after he had arrived as the new commander of the 7th Indian Division. In fact he visited me without warning one evening just as I had arrived back at my headquarters after conducting a very successful attack against the Japs at a village called Milaungbya. He was delighted at my battalion's success when my Gurkhas showed their true mettle and fought like tigers. I would not like to have been at the receiving end of their ferocious onslaught. I shall never forget their grinning faces and their singing with pride as they passed me at my tactical headquarters after a day's long slogging match during which they carried all before them, and not only slaughtered the Japs, but routed them. They gave me a great cheer as they passed me, so I knew they had a lot of fight left in them and that their morale could hardly be higher.

About a month after I had become GSOl to Geoff Evans, I received a private signal from the commanding officer of the 4/8th Gurkhas, who had succeeded me. The battalion had fought a heavy but losing battle for the vital bridge over the Sittang river, which had been the scene of such an agonizing defeat three years before during the retreat from Burma. The battalion was deployed in flooded ground unable to dig in and were easy targets for accurate shell and machine-gun fire. The withdrawal through deep water was a nightmare. The casualties were heavy and there is no doubt that the battalion and its leadership were badly shaken. Most of the old hands among the British officers who served under me had been sent on leave and therefore were not in the battle.

The battle and its leadership were severely criticised by the new brigade commander. The commanding officer who had succeeded me decided to send me a private and personal signal asserting that the brigade commander had failed to provide him with the necessary support. I decided to ask Geoff Evans if I could immediately visit the brigade commander, followed by the battalion commander. Before I did so, I left my caravan to brief the senior GSO2 on the action he was to take on certain problems during my absence for the morning. While I was doing this Geoff Evans entered my caravan and saw the signal lying on my desk. He spoke to the brigade commander on the wireless and was given his account of the battle. When I returned to my caravan Geoff Evans said he had read the signal which was highly improper of the commanding officer to have sent to me, thus going behind his brigade commander's back. He told me to visit the brigade commander and then my old battalion and conduct a thorough investigation. He gave me the authority to relieve the CO of command of the 4/8th if this was necessary, and resume command myself while still remaining as the senior staff officer of divisional headquarters. This was a tall order.

I knew the brigade commander well for he had been my instructor during my first term at the staff college, Quetta. This made it so much easier to be frank with each other. He told me that the CO had deployed the battalion in a tactically unsound position in the flooded paddy-fields, and on the rail embankment and in the village of Sittang and that he had lost confidence in his conduct of the admittedly difficult battle. He was adamant that the CO was no longer fit to command the battalion in war. Furthermore his manner left much to be desired, he was abrupt, argumentative, belly-ached over trivialities and was not popular with his British officers. In short he was no longer battle-worthy and was unfit to remain in his brigade. He already knew that I had been authorised by the general to relieve him of command. This was a most unpleasant task but it had to be done and in doing so I did not mince my words. I told the CO that he was

75

to depart unobtrusively that very day. It was sad to see my battalion, formerly second to none, so glum and shaken. I realised only too well that I would have my work cut out to restore it to its former high morale if it was to be fit in time to be thrown into another battle. Fortunately the end of the war in Burma came to my aid.

On 6th August 1945, the atomic bomb was dropped on Hiroshima. A second atomic bomb was dropped over Nagasaki on 9th August and, next day, Japan acknowledged defeat.

We in the 14th Army had inflicted upon the Japanese the most decisive defeat they were to suffer during World War II.

I was awarded the Distinguished Service Order. The citation written on 16th May 1945, by my brigade commander said:

"15 Feb. – 15 May 1945 IRRAWADY OPS.

"Lt. Col. Walker has been in command of 4/8 GR since 26 November 1944. During the period under review he has led his men with conspicuous gallantry on several occasions. In March an enemy force was organised from CHAUK with orders to destroy NYAUNGU Bridge head. The destruction of this force in the three battles of MILAUNGBYA on 7, 18 and 20 March 1945 was entirely due to his meticulous planning and leadership. During these battles his Tac H.Q. was invariably sited right forward where he could exercise personal contact and control regardless of his own personal safety. During recent operations WEST of the IRRAWADY he has again shown entire disregard for his own well being in order to lead his men in the destruction of the enemy."

There were now four main tasks for the 14th Army to tackle with the utmost speed. First, was to re-occupy the immense areas of territory captured by the Japanese earlier in the war. Second, was to take the surrender of the Japanese.

TIBET

BHUTAN

INDIA

Ledo

ASSAM

Silghat

Dimapur

Shillong

Kohima

CHINA

Sylhet

Ukhrul

Myitkyina

EAST
BENGAL

Imphal

Bhamo

Tamu

Chindwin River

Irrawaddy River

Dacca

Lashio

Chittagong

Kan

Shwebo

Salween River

Gangaw

Tilin

Mandalay

Cox's
Bazar

Sinthe

Pakokku

Pagan

Nyaungu

Seikpyu

Milaungbyas

Meiktila

ARAKAN

Maungdaw

Chauk

BURMA

INDO-
CHINA

Akyab

Yenanyaung

Minbu

Bay
of
Bengal

Taungdaw

Pyinmana

Theyetmyo

Kama

Prome

Sittang River

Pegu
Yomas

IRRAWADDY

SITTANG
BRIDGE

Nyaungkashe

Pegu

Rangoon

Hlegu

BURMA

Moulmein

0   50   100   200
miles

THAILAND

Andaman
Sea

N

Third, was to rescue the many thousands of Allied prisoners held in prisoner of war camps throughout the Far East theatre of war. Fourth, was to evacuate these thousands of prisoners to their respective countries.

The task given to the 7th Indian Division was the re-occupation of Siam (now Thailand).

General Evans with a small headquarters flew ahead to Bangkok leaving me to follow with divisional headquarters. I had a separate Dakota aircraft for the essential members of my staff, and the essential equipment and files, plus a Gurkha escort. We took off very early in the morning to avoid the hazardous turbulent cumulus cloud which built up at about midday when the sun was at its hottest. Half-way between Rangoon and Bangkok the pilot informed me that we would have to return to Rangoon because one engine was racing. He alerted me to the possibility of having to make a crash belly-landing in the rice paddy-fields. Only the crew had parachutes, so the pilot asked me to organise the Gurkhas plus the other passengers to move all the personal kit, baggage and office equipment opposite the door ready to be jettisoned immediately should the aircraft have to prepare for a crash belly-landing.

The suspense on the flight back to Rangoon was somewhat nerve racking so I decided to unbuckle my seat belt and walk down the aircraft to talk to each passenger. There was no need to raise the spirits of the Gurkhas for they were singing their favourite songs and bursting with laughter!

The Dakota flying at fairly low level landed safely at Rangoon, and with all speed its load was transferred to another Dakota aircraft. Speed was essential for it was now late in the day and valuable flying time had been lost, thus allowing the dangerous cloud base to begin to form over the mountains between Burma and Siam.

We took off again from Rangoon and before the pilot attempted to begin the dangerous crossing of the mountain range, now shrouded in dense cumulus black stormy clouds, he climbed to the Dakota's maximum height of twenty thousand feet, but to no avail. He called me to the cockpit and told me there was nothing for it but to fly through the cumulus cloud and hope for the best. He asked me to check that each passenger was securely strapped in and suggested that I should then join him in the cockpit, so that I could transmit any orders to the passengers in the event of an emergency.

We flew straight through the teeth of an electric storm. The aircraft was tossed violently up and down and from side to side. It had a ferocious cork-screw effect made worse by the blinding flashes of lightning, and the straining noise of the bodywork which made one feel that the aircraft would break up. The pilot appeared cool and steadfast although he must have felt, as I did, that violent death was on the cards. Water was dripping through the canopy on to the three of us – pilot, co-pilot and myself and visibility was nil. Several times I said a silent prayer to God for safe deliverance, and for some uncanny reason I remained perfectly calm and resigned to almost certain death. I decided to open the cockpit door and show myself to the passengers. The British soldiers were pale and tense and most were vomiting, while all the Gurkhas were fast asleep!

It seemed impossible that the aircraft could survive in one piece, but eventually it emerged from the mountainous barrier and flew into relatively calm weather. Sadly two other Dakotas met with disaster. One, with a full complement of British soldiers completely vanished in the storm. The other, flying in the opposite direction, also vanished, tragically, carrying one of the first parties of Allied prisoners of war to be released in Siam.

Eventually the Dakota made a safe landing at Bangkok. At first General Evans, oblivious of our near disaster, appeared annoyed, and certainly impatient, that I and the essential communication equipment and staff had taken so long to join him. I had foreseen this and suggested to the pilot that I should introduce him to the general so that he could explain in professional terms the reason for the delay. This he did with great clarity to an astonished but complimentary general. Geoff Evans thanked and congratulated him on his skill and courage and added that he would bring his feat to the notice of his air vice-marshal.

Geoff Evans said to me with a broad grin: "Now, Walter, you can make up for lost time for there is much work for both of us to do without delay." The first priority was to take the Japanese surrender in a formal parade and instil in them that they were part and parcel of a totally defeated Japanese Army. As these particular Japanese formations had not actually been defeated in battle on Siamese soil, they were behaving in a proud and arrogant manner. Their convoys would attempt to force British and Gurkha convoys off the road. I was determined to bring the Japanese to heel with an abrupt shock which they would not quickly forget. I was in charge of negotiations for the formal surrender at which the Japanese officers would lay down their swords at the feet of General Evans and myself.

Geoff Evans and I were accommodated in style in one of the King's palaces, complete with servants, one behind each dining room chair in smart white uniforms. The senior members of the headquarters staff joined us for meals with the delicious food which was provided by the main palace. At the rear of the palace was a small office building in which I housed a senior Japanese officer and small staff to whom I would daily transmit orders for strict obedience by the Japs, and mete out harsh punishment to those who transgressed in the slightest degree.

Not only was I responsible for deciding on the programme for the daily fly-in of essential supplies and medical aid for our occupying forces, but also for the many Allied ex-prisoners of war. I called for volunteers from the fit and more healthy officers of the ex-prisoners of war to remain in Bangkok for a short period to form a team to be called "Returned Allied Prisoners of War", to accompany me on flights to every prisoner of war camp. There was no shortage of volunteers. These war criminals were transported under escort and incarcerated in the large Bangkok jail. Once the correct procedures had been completed those guilty of atrocities such as torturing, beating, starving and killing Allied prisoners of war were eventually executed. A number were executed in the Pudu jail at Kuala Lumpur, Malaya, where I subsequently found myself once again commanding the 4/8th Gurkhas, and having to witness the hangings.

Every evening I summoned the Japanese liaison officer to my office and issued him with stringent orders for the work to be carried out the following day by the surrendered Japanese soldiers. Each British and Gurkha battalion and unit was allotted a Japanese working party to restore the accommodation to the standards to which the British Army was accustomed, and to employ them as working parties for the numerous other day to day tasks. I read out to the Japanese liaison officer the name of every war criminal and ordered him to produce a typed list of names the following day. I passed to him all complaints transmitted to me by our occupying forces and issued him with strict orders for immediate compliance. I was absolutely ruthless and would not accept any excuse and demanded immediate action on my orders. Within a comparatively short time every surrendered Japanese officer and soldier had been brought to heel.

It was I who had to scrutinise the priority order for the flying in of personnel, medical and army equipment, supplies and all those urgent items essential for the day to day existence of an occupying force. I well remember the occasion when Lady Mountbatten arrived and transformed the whole medical scene from one which was just about ticking over to one which was put into top gear. General Evans brought her into my office late one evening and having introduced her to me, said: "Walter, I have agreed to the request by Lady Mountbatten that the whole of tomorrow's fly-in should be allotted to her for the arrival of urgent medical supplies and equipment. If you have already completed tomorrow's 'plot' and sent it out, please unscramble it." "Certainly sir, no problem", I replied. Lady Mountbatten gave me a friendly smile and thanked me.

In addition to my responsibilities of GSO1, 7th Indian Division, I was also now once again the commanding officer of the 4/8th Gurkhas. This meant that somehow I had to fit in at least one hour each day with the battalion, one of whose responsibilities was the guarding of prisoners, mostly surrendered traitors of the Indian Army who, after the surrender of Singapore in 1942, had deserted to the Japanese and formed themselves into the Indian National Army (INA).

The scourge of Bangkok was rampant venereal disease. A certain Gurkha battalion had suffered such a high rate that I was determined that the 4/8th Gurkhas would not follow suit. Having consulted my senior Gurkha officer (the 'subedar major'), I promulgated an order that any Gurkha soldier who contracted VD would have the letters VD painted in red on the front and back of his white physical training (PT) vest, which he would wear at all times. In addition his name would be reported to the headman of his village in Nepal. This would mean that he would be ostracised or banished by his village. My remedy had the desired effect, although I incurred the displeasure of one of my superior officers, but the approval of another, and more senior one, at that. These Siamese diseased females went to any lengths to reach the soldiers, including crawling through the double apron barbed wire fence surrounding our camp. One of them was found by a night patrol in a cookhouse – the cook being the oldest and somewhat wrinkled Gurkha in the battalion!

In the Bangkok harbour were about six ships in which were embarked British and Allied ex-prisoners of war. My younger brother, who had been a tea planter in Assam, India, had enlisted in my elder brother's Punjab regiment and was taken prisoner in the surrender of Singapore. My parents had heard nothing from him during the whole of the war, except that he had been put to work with thousands of other POWs, on the infamous Burma railway, so they did not know if he was dead or alive. Therefore, I asked my adjutant, Peter Wickham, to visit each ship and find out if my brother was aboard one of them. As far as I can remember he was traced to the very last ship visited. Therefore, I was able to send a message to my parents that he was alive and returning on such and such a ship, and due to arrive in England on a certain date.

I learned later how my brother had been mercilessly tortured and beaten and his health ruined. He spent many months in a London hospital but he never recovered his health.

I had been able to cross question members of my team of Returned Allied Prisoners of War on the precise atrocities committed by the Japanese in the various POW camps. I was so horrified at what I was told that I compiled a dossier which I submitted to General Evans for onward transmission to the highest authority. I reproduce this in the succeeding three paragraphs. I also had it translated into Japanese and made my Japanese liaison officer read and inwardly digest it. I then went through it with him line by line during several sessions. Having done so I rubbed more salt into the wound by making him learn it off by heart and repeat it to me.

Most of the ex-prisoners of war were emaciated, diseased and exhausted. Most of them had toiled on the Burma-Siam Death Railway, a 260 mile stretch of track laid through jungle to complete the Japanese supply route from Bangkok to Rangoon, which claimed the lives of 16,000 of the 61,000 Allied prisoners and 100,000 of the 300,000 Asian labourers. One man died for every sleeper laid, killed by sickness, dysentery, malaria, beri-beri, cholera, starvation, liver complaints, neglect, beatings on their injuries and sores, torture and beheadings. Dust and sun had severely damaged their eyes. Rats, fleas, lice and mosquitos contributed to the diseases. There was the intense humiliation they had to endure, such as going on parade with dysentery and diarrhoea running down their legs. Atrocities such as holding rocks above their heads, for not bowing low enough to their guards, kneeling for hours in front of the guardhouse covered from head to foot in flies. Prisoners were killed for sport, for bayonet and sword practice, in the course of martial arts demonstrations. They even went into camp hospitals and forced seriously ill prisoners to work for up to 13 hours a day.

The lives of their labour force were of little consequence to the Jap guards. In one place the railway was cut into the sheer rock face. Prisoners were dangled over the edge on ropes and made to drill holes for explosives. Some of the men cracked and started screaming, so the Japs would cut the ropes, letting them plunge to their deaths in the river Kwai below.

The sense of impotence the POWs experienced was appalling. For example, they had to stand by and watch men – often their close friends – being brutalised, and could do nothing about it. They had to listen to a man screaming as he was being beaten. All they could do was to put their hands over their ears. If they intervened it made things fifty times worse. My own brother, Peter, intervened once. He was beaten mercilessly and then tied to a stake with his head tilted upwards and made to stare into the sun. As the sun moved in the sky, so was he rotated on the stake. Their friends died in terrible conditions while those who survived endured the cruelest slavery. They were deprived of medical care where disease had always been rampant and kept on starvation rations.

All these thousands of POWs should have been compensated fully. Besides the POWs, there were millions of other victims – the inhabitants of the countries over-run by the Japanese.

In addition to the atrocities inflicted on the POWs there was the terrible treatment suffered by those innumerable women who were taken from their camps and forced into becoming what the Japanese called 'comfort women' for the carnal pleasure of the Jap soldiers, sailors and airmen. They were raped throughout each day, week in and week out, for months on end. After the war they suffered mental torment and the majority required surgical treatment while many found themselves infertile. None of these victims have received compensation, let alone an apology by the Japanese government.

Then there were the ten million Chinese subjects killed by the Japanese, and the 150,00 Korean girls forced into prostitution.

In the land fighting the Japanese often killed newly-taken prisoners by bayoneting or beheading and there were even instances of cannibalism.

Had the atomic bomb not been dropped on Hiroshima and Nagasaki and the invasion of Japan taken place, the Japanese had plans to exterminate all their prisoners of war.

In fact Japan, with the help of Germany, particularly the supply of uranium, had their own plans for the atomic bomb, both for the Army and the Navy, and would not have hesitated to use it had the war been prolonged long enough.

Many POWs applied for a pension. They were hauled before medical boards. It was like a court martial. Some received their first pension of twelve shillings and six pence a week, years after the war. Others were awarded a forty percent disability pension worth between forty-seven and thirty pounds a week. They would have got more than this if they had fallen off the pavement. My own brother had contracted a serious liver complaint that took years to clear, with prolonged admissions to the hospital at Roehampton. He was given the same pittance of a disability pension until some years later when the panel included a doctor who had been a POW with him in the same camp. His disability pension was increased immediately to ninety percent.

It was not until I returned to England on short war leave that I met my brother who confirmed the unspeakable atrocities committed by the Japanese guards and of their sub-human treatment of the Allied POWs. As far as some are concerned the dropping of the atom bomb on Hiroshima and Nagasaki was Japan's just reward for the atrocities and indescribable war crimes committed by their inhuman countrymen. The imposition of reparations on Japan should have included the payment of full compensation to every ex-prisoner of war for the barbaric treatment that they had received at the hands of these evil monsters. But as usual our servicemen were let down by our political 'servants'. Our politicians were and still are so puffed up with their own importance that they fail to realise that they are the servants of their countrymen, not their masters.

Fifty years after the surrender of Japan, the VJ Commemoration took place on 19 and 20 August, 1995. The Commemoration was not the time to forget what happened, to forget past injustices, or forget past crimes. Those who suffered unbearable suffering can never forgive their former impenitent Japanese enemy.

Two months before, Japan had produced yet another of its weasel-worded expressions of nebulous regret. Their Prime Minister had sought a more frank and honest statement to clear the air before the anniversary, but parliament in Tokyo would have none of it. Japanese politicians still sought to excuse Japan's offensive war and to deny the barbarity. Japan had funked its chance to make a sincere and full written apology on behalf of the government and the whole Japanese nation. There had been no act of genuine atonement or payment of meaningful compensation. Veterans refer to the reparations made by Germany which has given, or promised, 120 billion DM (£55 billion) in one-off payments and pensions to those deemed 'Victims of Nazism'.

Generations of Japanese children have been kept in total ignorance by the deliberate teaching of distorted history. Officialdom denied atrocities against prisoners of war and the subjugated peoples of South East Asia.

Therefore, on August 19th and 20th, 1995, the nation did its duty in memory of those of their gallant countrymen who never came back. They died that the present generation were able to breathe the air of freedom.

Functions were held throughout the United Kingdom. In London during the march past the Queen down the Mall, the loudest and most spontaneous applause by the crowds was reserved for the Gurkhas.

The official commemorations ended with a ceremonial retreat in front of the Royal Family on Horse Guards Parade. When the lights were extinguished, out of the darkness came the pipes and drums of the Brigade of Gurkhas, who performed by themselves with the crowd in complete silence. As they marched off the Parade ground, a tumultuous applause broke out, such was the demonstration of affection and admiration of the British people. Then from the roof of Buckingham Palace, a lone Gurkha Piper was silhouetted and played a lament. The crowd, not only on Horseguards Parade, but down the Mall once again broke out into thunderous applause.

The Army Board held a large dinner to which I was invited. I had to decline the invitation because of the severity of my disablement. The next day I received the following telemessage from the Chief of the General Staff:

"You were much missed at last night's Army Board Dinner which was held to commemorate victory over Japan.

"You are one of the few senior officers we have who played a part in the defeat of Japan and of course we owe you so much for what you did subsequently in the Far East and for the Gurkhas.

"Several of our guests spoke of you and the Army Board would like you to know that you were remembered and send their best wishes."

In the little hill town of Kohima in the Naga Hills, close to the Indian border with Burma, stands one of the most poignant of all war memorials. The inscription reads:

When you go home
Tell them of us and say
For your tomorrow
We gave our today.

Hiroshima and Nagasaki were in no way retribution for the Japanese aggression, sub-human criminal acts, atrocities and barbarity in the most devastating war in history. The truth is that at the beginning of 1945, the Japanese commanders were committed to fighting to the last man and last round in defence of their homeland. The fanaticism of Japanese resistance on Iwo Jima in February 1945, demonstrated most vividly to the Allies what the cost in human lives would be of defeating a suicidal enemy.

The Japanese government refused to contemplate unconditional surrender. They even remained adamant after the dropping of the Nagasaki bomb.

The Japanese sense of superiority was such that it was on that very day that General Anam, the Minister of War, told the Supreme War Council: "That we will inflict severe losses on the enemy when he invades Japan is certain. It is far too early to say that we have lost the war." Only later that night, when the Emperor overruled their objections at a second meeting, did the generals agree 'to fall on their swords'.

It is Japan, by its own evil, that must bear historic responsibility for the obliteration of the two cities of Hiroshima and Nagasaki in August 1945. It was the demonstration of the atomic bomb that took place in 1945 which has preserved the world from its horrors ever since. The stability of the bomb has warned dictators that they cannot, as in the past, get their way through violence.

Japan's war criminals slipped back into their communities so quietly that few if any of the men, women and children they had so grievously oppressed ever found out how long they had spent behind bars.

Unlike Germany, many Japanese war criminals reassumed prominent roles in society. An official society of former war criminals exists and still exerts an influence on conservative opinion. Even the most prominent of Japanese war criminals benefited from the eagerness of post-war Allied governments to cement relations with Tokyo. The Allied attitude reflected the general lack of interest in the Far East war, combined with a concern to keep the new Japan firmly within the Western sphere of influence. It was the old, old story of currying favour with the Japanese. We have been doing this ever since the war finished, even though Japan reached the depths of depravity.

To return to the 4/8th Gurkhas. When the time came for the battalion to leave for Malaya I, once again, became the full time CO. We occupied a bashi (semi-hutted) camp on the outskirts of the capital, Kuala Lumpur. I was fortunate to have the 'battle blooded' Peter Myers as my second in command. My aim was two-fold. First, to revert to a high standard of peace time soldiering. Second, to prepare for war in the former British, Dutch and French eastern empires where it stood out a mile that the repression of nationalist guerrillas was an obvious commitment ahead of the battalion. Few, if any, of my superiors and contemporaries had the foresight to look very far beyond their noses, so engrossed were they in settling back into the piping days of peace.

None of my officers had the experience of having served in a peace time regiment, so I had my work cut out in moulding the battalion to a peace time role, but up to the high standard of my pre-war 1/8th Gurkhas. The battalion was located in a tented camp on the outskirts of Kuala Lumpur, the capital of Malaya. There was only one main small wooden building and that became the officers' mess. The rest of us, British and Gurkha officers and the rank and file, lived in tented accommodation. I had a working party of Japanese prisoners of war whose task it was to perform all the menial tasks, to keep the camp spotlessly clean and to carry out the many alterations that I required in order to improve the living conditions and the appearance of the camp.

The garrison, commanded by a brigadier for whom I had scant regard, had already settled down to the 'piping days of peace' and the daily round of social and sporting activities. No one seemed capable or willing to look beyond the immediate or distant horizon and yet there were warning signals staring them in the face. With the collapse of the British, Dutch and French eastern empires imminent, it was obvious that there were bound to be conflicts ahead.

I worked all day and far into the night, not only to raise the battalion to the pre-war standards to which I was accustomed, but also to sharpen its cutting edge for what I was certain would be the fighting that lay ahead.

My subedar major reported to me one day that there was a threesome of newly joined Gurkha officers who were out to give trouble and were not amenable to my strict regime. Forthwith I had my eagle eye daily on these three potential trouble makers at close quarters and on and off parade. They were not true Gurkha hill-men of fighting stock, but rather the clerical plainsman type of Gurkha. I was always accompanied by the Gurkha major on my daily rounds of the whole battalion, and it soon became apparent that this trio were a surly lot and well below the high standard of their contemporaries. One day the subedar major reported to me that this bunch of malcontents was undermining his authority, setting a bad example to the rank and file and were neither loyal to him nor to me. He recommended their immediate removal. Thereupon I decided to rid myself of them. By then a new brigadier had taken over as garrison commander who was, furthermore, a former pre-war officer serving in a Gurkha regiment. I reported the whole matter to him. He realised at once that because the subedar major himself had requested their discharge elsewhere, he would visit my battalion immediately and hear at first hand the circumstances of the case and the opinion of the subedar major. The outcome was that the brigadier gave his full support to the subedar major and me. The three 'bad hats' were interviewed by me, given their 'marching orders' to take effect from that very day via the transit camp and thence to the depot at Quetta.

There are 'bad hats' in every sector of society and this does not exclude Gurkhas. That is why the background of every recruit is scrupulously scrutinised. It is the responsibility of the Gurkha Major (previously called the subedar major) to keep his ear very close to the ground. It has to be remembered that The Communist Party is strong in Kathmandu and in the plains, as opposed to the hill tribes of Nepal.

In August 1946, I handed over command of the battalion on being appointed to a key posting in GHQ, New Delhi, India, that of general staff officer Grade 1, Military Operations Directorate.

In 1946 I was due my first home leave for ten years, so after handing over command of the 4/8th Gurkhas, I proceeded to India to be reunited with Beryl and the twins at Karachi ready to embark by troopship to England. The twins were bounding with energy and were fluent in Gurkhali but could only speak a few words of English. Fortunately Beryl found a children's nurse on board who was returning to England having been with a family in India for several years. She took the twins off Beryl's hands so we were able to have the day time together. Little did we realise it at the time that she was to remain with us for a number of years and long after our daughter, Venetia, was born.

All the officers were accommodated separately in four-berth cabins and the ladies likewise. Beryl, the twins and the nurse had their own four-berth cabin. Fortunately for me I fell ill with an undiagnosed fever and spent the latter half of the voyage home in the sick bay on a special diet with several nurses to look after me. I enjoyed the peaceful atmosphere and complete rest and Beryl was able to sit by my bed.

On arrival in England we stayed with out respective parents, and all too soon my short leave came to an end and I flew to India to assume the appointment of general staff officer, Grade 1, (GSO1) of the Military Operations Directorate of General Headquarters, New Delhi.

Beryl, the twins and our children's nurse (Nanny) were to follow by sea once I had obtained separate family accommodation in the army quarters on the outskirts of New Delhi. On no account would we countenance being housed in a family camp.

Meanwhile, as I had predicted, there had been fighting going on in Java between the 23rd Indian Division and the Indonesians since September 1945. The casualties were such that the 5th Indian Division had to reinforce this theatre of war. But what is remarkable is that the surrendered Japanese had to be rearmed and they fought on the side of their former enemies against the Indonesians. Towards the final stages of this campaign the 4/8th were sent to Java as reinforcements and fortunately suffered only a small number of casualties in killed and wounded. The battalion returned to Malaya in November 1946, and on the partition of India between India and Pakistan was absorbed into the Indian Army, together with five other Gurkha regiments. Four Gurkha regiments joined the British Army. There are, in fact, now eleven battalions of the 8th Gurkhas in the Indian Army. I believe the latter have at least forty Gurkha battalions, some of which are armoured. Compare this with Britain which cuts its armed forces to the bone.

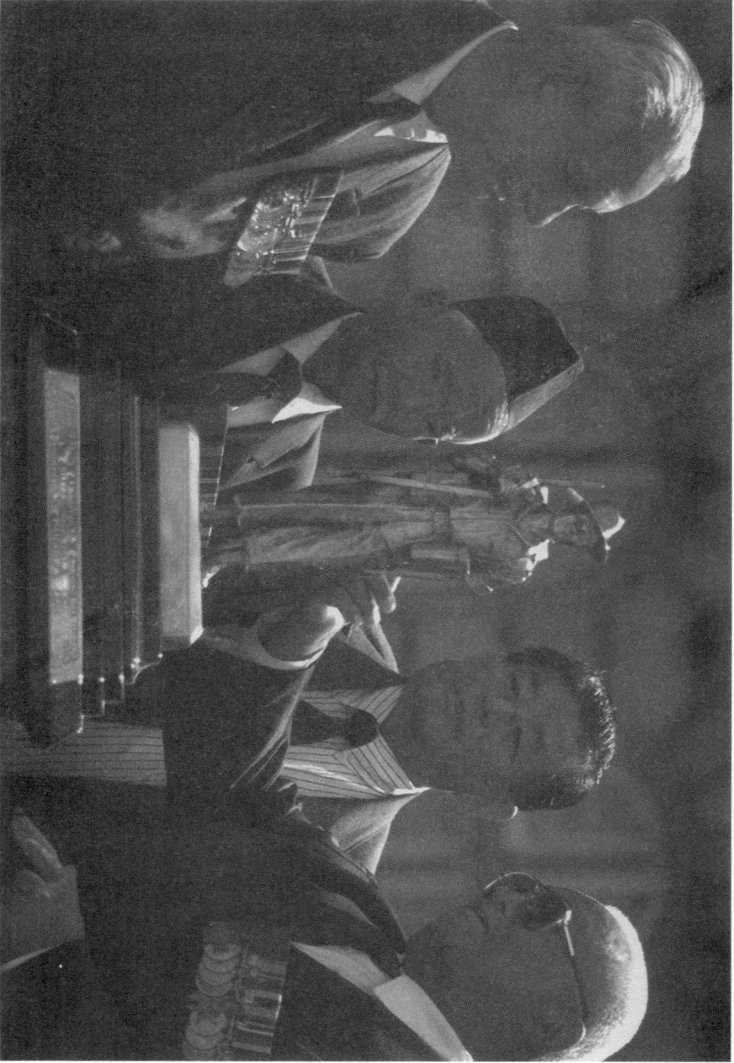

Havildar Lachhiman Gurung, VC (2nd from left) at the Cenotaph Ceremony in London, 1997
Photograph courtesy of *The Sunday Telegraph*

Chapter 9

AS SOME OTHERS SAW ME WHILE COMMANDING 4/8TH GURKHA RIFLES IN BURMA

Patrick Davis
Author of: *A Child at Arms*. Published in 1970

The Motto that I gave to the 4/8th Gurkha Rifles in 1944 when I became the commanding officer was: "Live Hard, Fight Hard and when necessary Die Hard."

One of my young officers, Patrick Davis by name, wrote a book after World War II against the Japanese called *A Child at Arms*, first published in 1970 by Hutchinson and Co. It proved to be a tremendous success and won a well deserved award.

I now quote what he thought of me as his commanding officer in the fierce fighting against the Japanese:

"Walter Walker drove us hard. During this long period of recuperation and re-training he caused much heart-ache, much grumbling, sometimes feelings for which grumbling is a polite euphemism. He was strict. He insisted on high standards. He was not afraid to punish. He was not afraid to winnow: a few left, other ranks and officers, but not many. Occasionally we thought him unjust, but only occasionally. For myself, I was in awe of him, but committed to his way of running things. I thought it right that he was tough and hard on us. We were not playing a game. There would be no umpire to rule the enemy offside. No one would bring back to life our dead.

In his early thirties, medium height, lithe, dapper, dark hair and trim dark moustache, at Kohima I seem to remember the colonel always with an officer's swagger stick under one arm, upright, alert eyes watching, ready to praise as well as to criticise, often smiling, by no means unapproachable. At Kohima he was the only pre-war 'regular' officer among us heterogeneous war-collected emergency-commissioned civilians. He knew what he wanted and how to get it. If he had his doubts, they were hidden. He dominated events and was never, in my experience, caught by surprise. What more could a soldier ask of a commander? Probably those who were nearer to him in age and service would give a different picture. For me, very junior, rather diffident, inexperienced, but reasonably intelligent and potentially most willing, he was a beneficial dragon. I gained confidence. I was given five months in which to learn more about this lethal trade under a man who was an expert.

"The colonel was the head and heart of the battalion, could make or break it, but every officer was important.

"Order of the Day by Commandant 4/8th Gurkha Rifles, Lt. Col. W. C. Walker, 20 December 1944:

1. The Battalion is once again about to proceed on active operations against the Japanese.

2. Most of us have had leave and most of us have undergone intensive training to fit ourselves for active service.

3. The results of our training have been excellent, and if we all not only remember what we have learned but put it into practice against the Japanese, we shall annihilate him on every occasion we fight him in battle.

4. We have had to face difficulties but all ranks have never given up trying, never lost faith and never forgotten the cause which has brought us together in this battalion. And the result – the joint result – of it all is a real live regiment, with a morale and soul of its own.

5. Those of you who have not fought against the Japanese before have no knowledge as to what your real strength or

96

weaknesses may be. Some of you, hitherto undistinguished, will come into your own and cover yourselves with glory. Only war itself can discover the qualities which count in war. But I am absolutely confident that the supreme Gurkha virtue – the virtue of holding on, and holding on, and holding on, until our task is accomplished – will not be found wanting in a single one of you.

6. The fighting in front of us will be tough and we shall have to exert every ounce of our strength. But we shall defeat the enemy just as we have defeated him before, and just as other Gurkha battalions have defeated not only the Japanese but the Germans also.

7. The reputation of Gurkhas as fighting men is unsurpassed. You are known throughout the world as the best fighters of any army, and the enemy respects you and fears you. The Gurkha Brigade has already received 7 V.C.s, the highest award that can be won for gallantry. We ourselves have received 2 I.O.M.s, 3 M.C.s, 3 I.D.S.M.s and 1 Gallantry Certificate. All these have been Immediate Awards. There are more awards to come as a result of our fighting in the Arakan and Imphal area. As yet no battalion of the 8th Gurkhas has received a V.C. in this War – let us be the first battalion to achieve this signal honour. (Three British officers of the regiment had won the V.C. in earlier wars: one during the Indian Mutiny, one in the Naga Rebellion of 1879, and one in Tibet in 1904.)

8. I know we shall kill and utterly destroy the Japanese whenever and wherever we meet him. As commandant of this battalion I pin my faith in you. You have character; you have grit and guts; you have supreme courage; you have high morale; you have discipline; you have pride in your race; and now that you have confidence as a result of our recent training you are all going to be an everlasting credit to the cause which roused the manhood of Nepal and the land which gave you birth."

"Wherever Walter Walker went he generally took me: visits to forward companies, visits to brigade headquarters, to conferences here and there. He sent me on missions to impart and collect information. Walter Walker was an admirable commanding officer. We would not have changed him. But he was a demanding one."

"The counting of enemy dead: the colonel was adamant that totals should include only those dead bodies that could be seen to be counted. No possibles or probables were allowed, no guesswork about bodies removed (the Japanese always tried to remove their dead, often at great risk to the living). Counting was done by an officer or senior N.C.O. Thus, our totals were, I hope, reliable."

When the Japanese were in full retreat I was given the task of blocking and destroying the desperate attempts of elements of the Japanese 54th Division breaking south in the Irrawaddy Valley. I decided that the time had come to move Pat Davis from his post of my intelligence officer – a task which he had performed with great distinction – and transfer him as second-in-command of one of the rifle companies. He had already proved himself leading patrols in close contact with the enemy and had come under fire from bullets, mortar bombs and artillery shell fire. I wanted him to gain experience and show his metal with a rifle company in close combat with the enemy. On his very first mission with two platoons of his company he won his spurs. He had a narrow escape. As he stepped under the stone porch of a building which he had made into a first-aid post, and where a couple of lightly wounded Gurkha riflemen were being dressed, an enemy mortar bomb exploded on the roof of the porch and showered the space he had just left.

On his safe return to his company battle location, he had this to say in his book:

"About midday Walter Walker came on the phone. "You all right, Pat?"

"We-re fine, sir."

"Good. Hold on as you are and we should have Denis to you during the afternoon."

"O.K., sir."

"Oh, and Pat, I'm making you a captain with immediate effect."

"Even in our vaster wars there cannot have been many who were promoted over the telephone while cut off and under shot and shell. It was certainly a morale raiser."

It was at about this time at a place called Yenanme when the war in Europe ended. Meanwhile Pat was in night ambush on a track down which some of the retreating enemy could come. How many in England realised what a bloody war we were still fighting against such a barbaric and ruthless enemy?

THE BATTLE OF TAUNGDAW

My battalions next task was to cut off the formidable 54 Japanese Divisions retreat, and the point chosen was the village of Taungdaw. Here the only Japanese road of retreat ran through a valley some fifteen hundred yards wide, dominated by steep hills rising to more than nine hundred feet. I knew my hastily dug-in companies – the cork in the bottle – would be subjected to ferocious Japanese suicide attacks by day and night, supported by intensive and accurate artillery, mortar and machine-gun fire. My citation recommending rifleman Lachhiman Gurung for the immediate award of the VC, gives some idea of the ferocity and intensity of the battle lasting three days and nights.

I deployed two companies to block a valley down which

I appreciated the Japanese would be retreating in strength. The Japanese attacked both companies in strength supported by artillery fire and suffered casualties. It was now the 13th May. Between me and them was a col and a ridge now held in strength by the Japanese. I decided to attack this col and ridge the following day. Meanwhile that night my HQ and my reserve company were attacked by a suicide squad of ten Japs led by an officer armed with a sword. The officer killed one of my Gurkhas. We were also shelled and mortared. All the Japs were killed. At dawn stand-to the next day I went round our perimeter to speak to my Gurkhas to satisfy myself that they were in good spirits, when my eye caught site of a pile of small pieces of gold. My Gurkhas had extracted the gold teeth from the dead Japs who had attacked us during the night!

Meanwhile the attack on the col and ridge had been held up and the company commander, Mike Tidswell, mortally wounded by a Jap sniper in a tree. When he was evacuated on a stretcher to me I could see that he was fatally wounded. He was a charming young man, every inch a gallant English gentleman. He died in the jeep taking him back to the advanced dressing station.

I called the brigadier on my wireless set and asked him for an immediate air strike by Hurricanes, not only to support the company attacking the Japs on the ridge, but also to clear any enemy who might be forming up to attack again the two companies which were the other side of the ridge – the 'cork in the bottle' – both of which had already fought such a gallant battle.

I spoke on the wireless to poor Mike Tidswell's company second-in-command – an American called Scott Gilmore – known with affection as Scotty. I told him that he would be getting close air support and that if he could capture the col, I would promote him to captain on the field of battle.

I also spoke to the senior pilot of the Hurricanes as they flew over me and said: "If you succeed in helping to kill or dislodge all the Japs on the ridge overlooking the village of Taungdaw (I gave him the map reference) I will give you a Japanese officer's sword. He replied, "WILCO – we will not fail you." I then told him that one of my companies was now attacking the ridge and that they would identify themselves.

Scotty and his company, together with my reserve company climbing the ridge behind the Japanese, captured the col and ridge the following day. The track to my two companies the other side of the ridge next to the village of Taungdaw was now open. We had won the battle with heavy casualties to the Japs who had been forced to abandon seventy five trucks, their guns and their stores.

It was now 14th May, which I heard on the wireless had been declared 'Victory Day', but not for us, for there was still much fierce fighting ahead. I was anxious about the plight of my two companies the other side of the ridge next to Taungdaw, who had repulsed every Japanese attack for three days and three nights. They had wounded requiring urgent medical treatment and were short of food and ammunition.

I set off with an escort well ahead of me and my doctor behind me. I now quote from Pat's book:

"The colonel was holding out for me a wrapped-up tin of fifty cigarettes which had just come with an air-drop. My parents' supply line had worked even to this remote corner. The colonel seemed pleased with us. He was an extraordinary man, and I use the word extraordinary with care. He was extra ordinary. I knew how I longed for sleep, how my own nerves were worn thin, like an over-used truck tyre, how almost everybody was to a greater or lesser extent suffering in the same way. I also knew that Walter Walker took less sleep than any of us, could never relax, was for all of every day and much of most nights thinking, planning, encouraging, prodding, looking ahead both in time and space, whether on the move or chained to his command post, never inactive. Yet now, as he came briskly across from his jeep with the package for me in his hand, smiling, he seemed much the same as ever. The shadows about his eyes were perhaps deeper, the bones on his face a little more prominent. He was certainly living on his nerves, he must have been, but it hardly showed."

"The Taungdaw battles had proved to be another success, and once again our casualties were light compared with those of the enemy. We lost ten killed and thirty-three wounded (none of them in Pat's company) and in return counted 218 dead Japanese; there would have been more from artillery-fire and air strikes, torn bodies hidden by torn jungle. Despite our anxieties and whatever the apparent risks – and I was not the only one to fear disaster – the colonel had put us into a major battle and brought us out again with remarkably little damage. This time the whole battalion had got sucked into the fighting, leaving nothing in reserve, which must have given him acute anxiety. But his nerve held (as did the brigadier's); it was the Japanese who broke. That was why we trusted him, and I was glad to see him, and despite my waning courage, I would have tried to do anything he asked."

"So we marched back to Shandatgyi, a few fewer, a lot wearier. There was no lingering at the scene of our trials. There was nothing to hold once the enemy had gone. We trudged over the col which Mike had died to reach, and had no time, nor any real desire, to digress to see the ground. But for Ken Bark, the artillery lieutenant with the sniper's bullet in his stomach, relief came too late. He had clung to life so long it seemed doubly sad that he could not have lasted a little longer."

I sat down on a bank and wrote a citation recommending Peter Myers for an immediate MC, for it was his company which had borne the full brunt of the ferocious Japanese shell and mortar fire and not flinched nor given one inch of ground.

Peter gave me a written account of Rifleman Lachhiman Gurung's outstanding bravery, who was so severely wounded, losing an eye and an arm. I spent about an hour writing the citation for the immediate award of the Victoria Cross. I had been a staff officer on active service on the North West Frontier, and also with Bill Slim – later Field Marshal Lord Slim – in the retreat from Burma, not to know how meticulous one had to be if the citation was to be approved by the various higher authorities.

Citation in respect of no 87726 rfn Lachhiman Gurung 4/8th Gurkha Rifles for the award of the Victoria Cross

At Taungdaw in Burma, on the west bank of the Irrawaddy, on the night of 12/13th May 1945, Rfn Lachhiman Gurung was manning the most forward position of his platoon. At 0120 hours at least 200 enemy assaulted his company psn. The brunt of the attack was borne by Rfn Lachhiman Gurung's section and by his own post in particular. This post dominated a jungle path leading up into his platoon locality.

Before assaulting, the enemy hurled innumerable grenades at the position from close range. One grenade fell on the lip of Rfn Lachhiman Gurung's trench; he at once grasped it and hurled it back at the enemy. Almost immediately another grenade fell directly inside the trench. Again this Rfn snatched it up and threw it back. A third grenade then fell just in front of the trench. He attempted to throw it back, but it exploded in his hand, blowing off his fingers, shattering his right arm and severely wounding him in the face, body and right leg. His two comrades were also badly wounded and lay helpless in the bottom of the trench.

The enemy, screaming and shouting, now formed up shoulder to shoulder and attempted to rush the position by sheer weight of numbers. Rfn Lachhiman Gurung, regardless of his wounds, fired and loaded his rifle with his left hand, maintaining a continuous and steady rate of fire. Wave after wave of fanatical attacks were thrown in by the enemy and all were repulsed with heavy casualties.

For four hours after being severely wounded Rfn Lachhiman Gurung remained alone at his post, waiting with perfect calm for each attack, which he met with fire at point-blank range from his rifle, determined not to give one inch of ground.

Of the 87 enemy dead, counted in the immediate vicinity of the company locality, 31 lay in front of this rifleman's section, the key to the whole position. Had the enemy succeeded in over-running and occupying Rfn Lachhiman Gurung's trench, the whole of the reverse slope position would have been completely dominated and turned.

This rifleman, by his magnificent example, so inspired his comrades to resist the enemy to the last that, although surrounded and cut off for three days and two nights, they held and smashed every attack.

His outstanding gallantry and extreme devotion to duty in the face of almost overwhelming odds were the main factors in the defeat of the enemy.

Peter also gave me an account of the outstanding gallantry of the Gurkha officer whose forward platoon had borne the full ferocity of every attack launched by the Japs. I wrote his citation for the Immediate Award of the MC.

I let it be known that I had submitted a recommendation for the award of the VC for I knew it would be a tremendous morale booster to the whole of my battalion.

All three Immediate Awards were approved. Some

months later the Viceroy of India, Field Marshal Lord Wavell, held a ceremonial VC Parade in New Delhi, India, to which my wife and I were invited. I could not attend because I was so involved with performing the dual role of GS01 of 7 Indian Division in Bangkok and at the same time resuming command of my battalion again.

Because I was so overloaded with the burden of fulfilling a dual role, I was denied the pleasure of meeting and escorting my wife to the VC Parade and to the Viceroy's dinner that night. So instead I sent my best and gallant company commander, Major Peter Myers, who had already been awarded a MC and Bar. Furthermore he was the company commander of the Gurkha rifleman who had won the VC at the Battle of Taungdaw. He, of course, was too badly wounded to attend, having lost an arm and an eye in the ferocious battle.

SCOTT GILMORE with Patrick Davis
Author of *A Connecticut Yankee in the 8th Gurkha Rifles – A Burma Memoir.* Published in 1995.

Scott Gilmore's fascinating and brilliant account of his active service with, and command of, the Gurkha warriors of the 4/8th Gurkha Rifles in World War II, against the savage and brutal Japanese soldiers, is in a class of its own.

Scott Gilmore, or Scotty as he was called by his brother officers, was the only American to have fought with one of the forty Gurkha battalions in World War II. Before joining the 4/8th Gurkha Rifles, he had already taken part in the Battles of Tobruk and Alamein in North Africa as an American field service ambulance driver.

Scotty was several years older than his brother officers, but junior in rank until he climbed the ladder to company commander with the rank of major. It would be no exaggeration to say that he was the most popular officer among his British comrades and with the Gurkha officers and riflemen in the battalion. He was unflappable, always cheerful and always cool, calm and collected under fire.

I regarded it as an honour to have this 'Connecticut Yankee' under my command while I was the commanding officer of the 4/8th Gurkha Rifles.

How did he regard me? I quote from his truly magnificent book, an autographed copy of which he kindly sent me by airmail, with this inscription:

"Walter Walker

Your outstanding leadership has turned out a surprising number of scribblers, hope you like this one!

Scott Gilmore."

"For the first weeks in Kohima the pace of training was easy, to allow the men to rebuild from their run-down condition.

"As strength returned, discipline and the work schedule tightened.

"This toughening of life was accelerated by a change of commander. Major Walter Walker, the career officer who had joined us in the Arakan in April, moved up from second in command to take over as colonel.

"From this moment the pride, confidence, and spirit of the battalion soared. While Walker could be a cold, aloof, and unreasonable person, he was also an outstanding commander. The pace and calibre of the training immediately stepped up; all day and often by night we practised weapons training, battle drills, digging, patrols, and section, platoon and company exercises. Discipline became strict, fitness was compulsory. It was a time for absorbing the lessons learned from the battalion's first ten months in action, for practising those lessons and teaching them to the new arrivals.

"The firm hand of Walker's discipline did not spare the

officers. To acquire the colonel's displeasure would often result in instant demotion. On the other hand, new responsibilities immediately brought the rank for the job. We learned to keep a supply of pips and crowns so that we could switch rank as fast as our orderlies could sew.

"When we got command of a company, which carried the rank of major, the trick was to avoid the C0's wrath for six months. Under wartime regulations, holding the rank of major for six months insured that an officer could not under any circumstances (other than court-martial) again sink below the rank of captain.

"To return to Colonel Walker, he often worked late in his office tent. We could see the kerosene lamp glowing through the canvas. Sometimes he went through until dawn and reveille. This was a deliberate part of his own self-training. He told Peter Wickham, now adjutant, that in case the time might come when he would not be able to get any sleep, he needed to know that he could remain alert even when totally exhausted. We were permitted to sleep, but by day he demanded hard work from all of us, and got it. Very soon we knew that we had a most able leader and a well-organised and confident battalion.

"Walter Walker was later to be recognised as an outstanding soldier. He became general commanding the entire Southeast Asia forces during the 1964 confrontation with Indonesia over Borneo. Then in Europe he was to become the general commanding NATO's northern forces at a critical time in the Cold War confrontation with the USSR. He was knighted in 1968.

"To maintain discipline and respect, Walker held himself aloof. His only chance to relax came with the occasional visit from one equal in rank – for example, his friend Derek Horsford who had become CO of the 4/1st Gurkhas.

"The CO insisted on efficiency and cleanliness throughout

the battalion. Occasionally he would order punishment for the mess staff for some infraction. More than once he would demand to know where his breakfast was, only to be reminded that the entire mess staff was at the moment performing pack drill.

"By this time I was no longer the new boy on the block. Those months of training at Kohima, of comradeship on the march, in the mess, and in our company lines, had put me in good health and confident of our commander, Walter Walker."

I, myself, snatched a week's leave towards the end of our retraining at Kohima. Beryl travelled right across India, from Quetta to Calcutta, and thence to Shillong, where we spent a wonderful week's leave together. Half way to Calcutta, her train – the express from Lahore to Calcutta – was derailed at night by Congress militants. The loss of life was tremendous. The compartment next to Beryl's coupe was smashed to pieces, but the Almighty spared her. I, of course, was unaware that there had been such a terrible rail derailment and such a loss of life. About two days later, I received a telegram from friends in Calcutta which read: "Beryl escaped injury in the disastrous rail derailment of Calcutta night express train and is safe with us. Lost most of her clothing when suitcase was smashed. Her delay to Shillong will be two days only."

When we met at Shillong, Beryl told me that she had thought of bringing our twin sons with her, but had decided they were too small – two years old – and it would be too tiring for them. Had they been with her they would all three have been killed, for the compartment in which they would have been travelling in was smashed and all the occupants killed.

Beryl had spent all the night down the railway embankment attending to the injured. She used all her own blankets and clothing to keep the injured warm. It was a terrible experience for her, but when we met in Shillong one week later, she was as cool as a cucumber and quite unshaken.

I will now revert to Scott Gilmore's account of the war.

"In mid-December 1944, the routine and mood of the camp suddenly changed. Firm orders came for a move.

"No matter how difficult the circumstances or how remote from civilisation, the colonel believed in keeping up appearances. To insure a decent turnout, his mule carried starch and an iron. He was first-class at his job, demanding yet efficient, cool and precise. He never showed fear or worry. He was able both to intimate genuine interest in the welfare of the men and to remain sufficiently aloof to keep respect. With his junior officers he seldom unbent.

"Our Colonel Walker, too, was not one to sit still and wait. It would have been preferable to roll up in one's own blanket and sleep under the brilliant stars, but Walker ordered patrols out every night. And over the next few weeks we made a number of punishing attacks designed to keep the Japanese off balance, kill as many as possible, and return with prisoners and captured weapons.

"On the day before the raid the CO held a briefing around a sand table. The 'table' was a patch of natural sand under a palm tree. Walter Walker brimmed with enthusiasm as he drew diagrams with his stick and efficiently put into operation so many staff college lessons and his battle experience from the North West Frontier and elsewhere. He had to integrate our Gurkha infantry, the attached machine gunners, the Gordon Highlander tanks of 116th Regiment, and Royal Armoured Corps, together with a bombardment by Hurricane fighter bombers; by our own three-inch mortars, and by the faithful supporting artillery of 136th Field Regiment. This collection of arms and armour had no common language."

This so called 'raid' turned into a battle, for the Japanese had brought up reinforcements, and as captured documents revealed, they had intended to launch an attack on my battalion at 0900 hours. I launched my attack at 0800 with the support of Hurricane aircraft, Sherman tanks, artillery fire from the ever faithful 136th Regiment, and machine gun fire. Scotty's company was in the thick of the fighting. This was also the second battle of Milaungbya referred to in the citation of my first DSO.

"After six hours of fighting in the hot sun and through burning houses and smouldering vegetation, the Japanese were eliminated from base, the northern section of Milaungbya.

"The BRO (battalion routine order) next day summing up the battle read in part:

"The commanding officer heartily congratulates Lt. S. Gilmore, the Gurkha officers, NCOs and all ranks of 'A' Company on the overwhelming and crushing defeat which they inflicted on the enemy yesterday, 18 March 1945 ... The brigade commander has sent his personal congratulations to all ranks of 'A' Company who have killed more Japs in one battle than any other company or battalion in the brigade ... Killed (actually counted) – 94."

"The above casualties do NOT include enemy wounded nor those enemy who were buried in bunkers or blown up by artillery and tank fire. The brigade commander considers that the total of casualties inflicted on the enemy was between 150 and 200.

"Our own casualties including No 11 Platoon of D Company who co-operated in the attack were: killed 6, wounded 13."

Chapter 10

FERRET FORCE – FAR EAST LAND FORCES (FARELF)
TRAINING CENTRE (FTC)

At the outbreak of the Malayan Emergency in June 1948, my wife and I with our children were on long overdue leave in Malaya's main hill station, the Cameron Highlands, in the State of Perak. I was not surprised when, on 16th June, I received an urgent telephone call summoning me to report to the Army District HQ at Kuala Lumpur. I was told that three English rubber planters had been killed in cold blood by the Chinese Communist terrorists (CTs) and that a State of Emergency had been declared in the northern State of Perak. An armoured car would escort me to Kuala Lumpur where I would be briefed on an important role that I was to assume as a matter of urgency.

Why was I not surprised at this urgent summons? Because I had been studying the internal security situation in Malaya in the light of the violent labour and industrial unrest in the mines and rubber plantations and the frequency of rioting, all of which had been stirred up by the Chinese Communists, who had wormed their way into key positions in the trade unions. Above all were the six hundred thousand discontented landless Chinese squatters living off the edge of the jungle. These were ripe for subversion by the Chinese communists.

It was the high commissioner, not the army, who was responsible for internal security. Why did he not ban the Communist Party? Because he was acting under instructions of Britain's Labour Government, and a low profile was the order of the day. His police force was only ten thousand strong and lacked a special branch responsible for counter-subversion duties.

On arrival at HQ Malaya District I was told that I had been selected to train and equip a special force consisting of former non-Regular British officers of Force 136 which had operated in Malaya against the Japanese in World War II. This Force would consist of civilian volunteers most of whom were now rubber planters. They would lead small formations of British and Gurkha regular soldiers. I was given three months to accomplish my task.

These amateur soldiers did not take favourably to the professional jungle warfare tactics that I had devised as a battalion commander in Burma against the Japanese and which I had now adjusted to suit a guerilla type enemy, namely the CTs. I had to impress upon them that not only would they be responsible for the lives of regular British and Gurkha soldiers, but also that there was the world of difference between operating as guerillas mainly against Japanese installations and communications and leading regular soldiers in counter insurgency operations against Chinese Communist terrorists.

I had been training Ferret Force for only about a month when I was told that General Sir Neil Ritchie, Commander-in-Chief, Far East Land Forces, wished to see a demonstration of my jungle warfare doctrine. Accordingly, I demonstrated a silent approach to a terrorist camp, a silent killing of the sentries followed by an attack on the camp itself. He said he was most impressed and now wanted me to put my training doctrine to a far more important role. I was to open a Jungle Warfare School at the Far East Land Forces Training Centre, to teach jungle warfare techniques to the major reinforcements being sent from England. The first to arrive would be the Guards Brigade.

I was immediately appointed commandant of the Far East Land Forces Training Centre (FTC) and raised the Far East Jungle Warfare School, where I evolved the tactical doctrine for counter-insurgency and guerilla warfare operations and taught them to the reinforcements and then to all units in the theatre. This was from October 1948 to November 1949.

If I was to convert Guardsmen into jungle fighters in the short time available to me, I had my work cut out. My first task was to reconnoitre the surrounding jungle terrain and choose the areas where I would be giving all the various jungle warfare demonstrations. Then I had to write the instructions on how to fight every possible event; from silent approach to attacking terrorists camps, and how to lay an ambush and remain silent for days on end, and then spring it; and many other jungle warfare 'drills', including tracking.

I ran numerous courses during the year, October 1948 to November 1949, when I was commandant of the FTC. These courses included officers and NCOs from Thailand, Indonesia and Malaya. I 'fielded' many VIPs, not only British, but also from the Commonwealth and from Far Eastern countries.

I struck up a close rapport with Sir Malcolm MacDonald, the Commissioner-General for South-East Asia. One of the VIPs he brought to witness my demonstrations was Britain's Minister for Foreign Affairs, Sir Anthony Eden. He paid very close attention to my training techniques and in my hearing told Malcolm MacDonald how impressed he was with what was being achieved.

I was awarded the OBE, the citation for which read as follows:

"OPERATIONAL AWARD – OBE
"This officer has commanded the FARELF Training Centre at TAMPOI since October 1948.

"He took over at a very difficult time when things at the FTC had not been going at all well. He quickly improved matters and the centre now is a very live and going concern.

"He is an officer of the highest principles, who will only

accept the best, and drives himself and his staff hard to achieve it.

"No work is too much for him and he has worked at continuous high pressure ever since taking over command without sparing himself.

"Besides the normal courses, i.e. jungle warfare, weapon training and services NCOs, he has had to undertake the training of federation police, Thai officers and all incoming units.

"In addition he is required to arrange, often at very short notice, demonstration days for distinguished visitors of all services, for civilian and high ranking foreign officers and officials.

"All these have gone without a hitch and have inevitably entailed a very great deal of preliminary planning and preparation.

"As well as the FTC, Lieut. Colonel WALKER is responsible for the administration of the GURKHA Divisional Provost Company, the GURKHA Education and the GURKHA Signal Squadron, all of which are located within the FTC grounds.

"It is a large and complex command and it might be fair to say that an officer of less merit than Lieut. Colonel WALKER could not have competed with the task nor have overcome the various set-backs and vicissitudes which he has undoubtedly experienced."

Chapter 11

In May 1990, Charles Allen sent me an autographed copy
of his book, *The Savage Wars of Peace* for which he had
interviewed me at length. He wrote these words in the flyleaf:
"To the 'Fighting General' in admiration and gratitude from
the Author, Charles Allen. May 1990."

He reproduces the recorded words when he interviewed
me. This is what I told him:

"On my way up to the 1/6th Gurkhas base in Bahau to
assume command, I was told by the divisional commander,
General Headley, to call on him at Seremban where his
headquarters were, and he said to me – a lot of people won't
like this: 'You are going to take over one of the smartest
battalions in the Gurkha brigade, but they can't kill Communist
terrorists – and I don't know why. Their kill rate is very low,
and yet their men are bloody good. You have got to find out
the reason and you have got to make them as good in the jungle
as they are smart in appearance.' "So I went out with each
company in turn to see what was wrong and I found them too
noisy. I found their tactics were shoddy and we missed a lot of
communist terrorists in the ambushes, which we had laid down
as a result of good information."

Charles Allen wrote: "Walker was no newcomer to jungle
warfare. He came to 1/6th GR with a reputation as a ruthless
disciplinarian and as a man who got results. In Malaya he was
to become the supreme exponent of the ambush, using skills
that he had first acquired a decade earlier in Waziristan on India's

North West Frontier. 'I suppose I really learned the technique on the North West Frontier', he asserts. 'When we went out of our perimeter camp to ambush the tribesmen who were sniping at our camps at night, you had to be an absolute adept at concealing yourselves and making certain that if they entered your ambush they were killed.' These skills had been further refined in Burma."

I then said to Charles Allen: "I tried them out in training to see why was it that the Japanese did not walk into this ambush? Why was it that when the Japanese did walk into this ambush they were not all killed? What were the mistakes? And I therefore laid down the technique of how an ambush should be laid, so that you didn't fire until the enemy had entered your ambush, that you had stops to get the people who might not have been immediately in the ambush, and stops to make certain that those who retreated from the ambush were also killed. And this technique, which I learned and taught in Burma, I carried forward to the Malayan Emergency."

To quote Charles Allen again: "On taking over command of his new battalion Walker set about retraining it to his requirements, which were set out in the form of a series of 'Golden Rules' that had to be learned and followed to the letter. After two months of so-called rest and retraining – 'mighty little rest and a helluva lot of retraining' – 1/6 GR went back into action." 'We were then sent down to Johore where we started to knock off communist terrorists,' Walker recalls. 'I went out with my troops and I don't suppose the company commanders particularly liked me for being there but I was determined that my soldiers would be led in the way I wished them to be led. And I was determined that my company commanders would adopt the policy I had laid down.' "Walker's methods worked", and 'when we were eventually sent from Johore elsewhere the brigade commander, Brigadier Pugh, had me up and said, "You have killed more communist terrorists in my brigade than any other battalion and I am very sorry to lose you.'"

Charles Allen describes the vital importance that I paid to battalion commanders establishing a close relationship with their local Special Branch officers.

"Learning to trust and to act on information from their local Special Branch officers did not come easily to all commanding officers, but where a good working relationship was established it often paid dividends. By 1953 when Walter Walker took his 1st/6th Gurkhas to Perak he had learned to 'put my faith entirely' in the Special Branch. 'There were those who thought that the army should be in charge of intelligence and that the police should be subordinate to the army intelligence. I did not agree with that because the Malayan police were living in the country, spoke the language, knew the terrain, knew the habits of the people. Some were not as good as others but I had a very, very close liaison and friendship with Special Branch. I trusted them and they trusted me and if I failed to pull off an ambush on their information then, of course, they were very upset and so was I.' "There were disappointments to begin with but as the Special Branch began to penetrate the local terrorist network, so harder information began to come in. This culminated in a meeting between Colonel Walker and a 'turned' terrorist at an agreed rendezvous in the jungle at which Walker learned of a meeting of local terrorist leaders to be held at a certain location within a four day period. Walker was determined that the ambush should be a complete success and drew up meticulous plans involving the full battalion.

'It meant a night march so that no one in the village would know we were moving. These six leading terrorists were due · to arrive at this particular hill-top and I got the whole battalion round the camp. I had one man actually on the hill-top hidden

117

in foliage with a light machine gun and orders to fire as soon as he got a target of all six of them, and the signal for the attacking platoon would be that burst of fire. I went round and allotted every company its place and we wiped out all our footsteps with branches and twigs. I remember so well how on this burst of fire the Gurkhas rushed forward – I was just behind the leading six, I suppose – and those who were not killed by that light machine gun were killed when they ran into the cordon. I got a very nice signal from Templer saying, 'Terrific!', because we killed six out of six.'

The secret meeting with the turned terrorist which had led to this success was, in fact, quite a 'hairy' experience. I had to obtain the prior approval of my brigade commander to undertake such a dangerous mission. The brigadier knew me well for pre-World War II he had joined my old regiment, the 1/8th Gurkha Rifles, as a captain, having transferred from the Sherwood Foresters. I was adjutant at the time. The brigadier agreed on condition that I took every possible precaution for my own personal safety, and that the mission was to be top secret and strictly on a 'Need to know' basis. He asked me if I had made a will and where was it. Also did I require a 'pill' in case I was captured. I was accompanied by the Head of Special Branch and a Gurkha signaller who was in touch with a stand-by company, which would be able to rush to our assistance in the event of us walking into an ambush. I hid the signaller on a convenient hillock from where he could see both of us at the agreed rendezvous.

I was out in the jungle with my battalion when I received a signal to say that Brigadier Lewis Pugh – who had been the brigade commander when my battalion was operating with such success in Johore – had been appointed one of the Deputy Directors of Military Operations at the Ministry of Defence and had asked for me as one of his senior staff officers. I was to take over the appointment on arrival in England.

Malaya

Alor Star
KEDAH
Sungei Patani
Kulim
Penang I.
Grik
Lenggong
KELANTAN
Sungei Siput
Gua Musang
Kuala Kangsar
Ipoh
Cameron Highlands
PERAK
Bikam
Slim River
Jerantut
Fraser's Hill
PAHANG
SELANGOR
KUALA LUMPUR
Kajang
Titi
Kuala Klawang
NEGRI
Jelebu
Pass
Bahau
Seremban
SEMBILAN
Port Dickson
Segamat
Labis
MALACCA
JOHORE
Muar
Kluang
Yong Peng
Kota Tinggi
Johore Bahru
SINGAPORE

THAILAND
TRENGGANU
SOUTH CHINA SEA

Miles
0   100

I refused the appointment saying that I had been commanding my battalion on exceptionally strenuous jungle warfare operations for three years and was entitled to six months home leave. Furthermore I had already filled this appointment at GHQ New Delhi, India, and knew how exacting it was. I insisted on my entitlement to six months leave. Also, to pull me out of the jungle in the middle of a vital operation was tactical suicide. I added for good measure that I still had two months left before completing my tenure of command.

The brigade and divisional commanders, and also the commander-in-chief, himself, supported my plea. Back came a signal saying that Colonel Walker had been offered a plum job and to refuse it could affect his future prospects. This angered me and steeled my resolve to stand my ground. I told my superiors that I regarded such a pronouncement as military blackmail. Again my superiors, except for the commander-in-chief, supported me. My reaction to my brigadier was that I told him in confidence that I would seek redress from General Sir John Harding, Colonel of the 6th Gurkhas, and now Chief of the Imperial General Staff. Meanwhile I said I was adamant that I would not accept the appointment.

I then received a direct order to hand over command of my battalion, pack our family belongings with all speed and proceed with my wife and children to Singapore and embark on the troopship shortly to sail for England.

I wasted no time in writing to General Sir John Harding and enclosed copies of the signals sent by his military secretary's branch. I asked him to intervene on the grounds that on his recent visit to the battalion he had remarked that I looked tired and thin and was due for a rest. "After three years on jungle operations", he said, "any battalion commander has been under great stress and strain and is due for a rest. You now need some long leave."

General Harding had told me to be careful always to go through the correct channels before addressing him direct. Well, I had done precisely this.

During my almost three years of commanding the 1/6 Gurkhas, I was awarded my fifth Mention in Dispatches, promoted to Brevet Lieutenant Colonel and awarded a Bar to my DSO. The citation for this second DSO read as follows:

"Lieutenant Colonel Walker has on all occasions shown outstanding devotion to duty, drive, and operational ability as a result of which his Battalion has eliminated fifty-three Communist terrorists in PERAK and thereby almost completely disrupted the enemy organisation along the entire sixty mile length of the road GRIK-KUALA KANGSAR. His relentless and aggressive determination has been the finest possible example and inspiration to all ranks of his unit.

"On 6th May 1952, in the GRIK area of PERAK, Lieutenant Colonel Walker personally led a platoon which guided by an SEP took up its ambush position. Eight armed and uniformed bandits entered the ambush. Fire was opened killing three and wounding four who tried to escape. Prompt aggressive follow-up action was successful in killing three of these. Amongst those killed were the Political Party Representative and Commander 1st Company 12th Regiment, the Secretary to the Regimental Commander 12th Regiment, and his bodyguard and a Section Leader; the State Committee Member and Regimental Commander 12th Regiment were wounded.

"On 22nd May, 1953, in the LENGGONG area of PERAK, Lieutenant Colonel Walker was present with a specially selected assault platoon which had the task of attacking a camp where six Communists were expected to arrive. After an arduous two days approach march the platoon took up its position and, in spite of the earlier than expected arrival of the terrorists, assaulted the camp under close automatic fire and in five minutes killed all six enemy.

"Both these actions owed their success to meticulous planning and able execution under the direct control and personal leadership of Lieutenant Colonel Walker.

"By his outstanding leadership and determination his battalion has become one of the best operational units in Malaya."

When the troopship anchored at Southampton, I was called on the tannoy to the ship's orderly room. There a military policeman handed me an envelope addressed to me and typed in green ink. It was marked Personal and Confidential and was from the Chief of the Imperial General Staff (CIGS) – General Sir John Harding – Colonel of the 6th Gurkha Rifles. In his letter to me, General Harding apologised for the manner in which I had been treated, said that I was to proceed on six months leave, and that he had given instructions that I was to be appointed to an equally plum first grade job on the termination of my leave.

A few weeks later while we were staying with my parents, I received a telephone call from the military assistant to the military secretary – a three star general – asking me if it would be convenient for me to meet the military secretary in four days time. I agreed that I was free on that day.

I duly reported to the military secretary. At first he was abrupt and unfriendly. He started off by saying: "Must you take advantage of the fact that the CIGS is colonel of your regiment and therefore you saw fit to address him direct?" I replied: "Must your staff resort to sending me a signal amounting to military blackmail? Obviously you are unaware of this. Allow me to give you a copy." The military secretary was aghast when he had read the signal and said: "No wonder the CIGS had expressed his annoyance to me. All I can say is that I apologise to you that this should have been perpetrated. I will make it my personal responsibility to ensure that after your well earned six months leave you will be appointed to an equally key first grade appointment."

During my leave I received a posting order as the senior staff officer (Operations and Staff Duties) at Headquarters Eastern Command at Hounslow to the west of London. Married accommodation had been allocated to us at Cheam in Surrey.

Farewell visit to Gurkha families 1/6GR, 1960

Chapter 12

GENERAL STAFF OFFICER FIRST GRADE (GSO1)
HEADQUARTERS EASTERN COMMAND, 1954-1957

In November 1954, I assumed the appointment of Senior Staff Officer, Operations and Staff Duties (GSO1, Ops and SD), in Headquarters Eastern Command at Hounslow. The time had come for me to do a stint at a desk job and I did not relish the thought of churning out bumph. The general officer commanding-in-chief was General Sir Francis, later to become Field Marshal Festing and Chief of the Imperial General Staff (CIGS). He was renowned for being the untidiest general in the British Army and often appeared at the headquarters rather late in the morning, wearing a scruffy shooting jacket and ill-fitting breeches and hob-nail boots. On his very first day he arrived unobtrusively wearing this outfit and walked straight across the immaculate bowling green which was opposite the front entrance of the headquarters. The groundsman shouted at him: "Get of my f...g green." The General stopped and said: "Do you know who I am?" He received the reply: "I don't care a b...r who you are, get off my f...g green." The General complied. This incident was being watched by the headquarters sergeant major, seconded from the Brigade of Guards. He suggested that the groundsman could hardly be blamed, with which General heartily agreed.

Each Friday he would leave his official residence for his home in the North of England. I would prepare a list of territorial army centres and other establishments that he could visit en route, thus authorising the use of his official car and driver.

The Chief of Staff (COS), a Major General John Cowley

was a mad-keen golfer so spent as little time as possible in the headquarters. This suited me well because with him and the army commander away on long weekends, I could really get down to the mass of paper work. I served directly under the Brigadier General Staff (BGS), Brigadier "Tottie" Anderson. We knew each other well for he had been the army instructor at the Joint Services Staff College when I was a student in 1950. I served under him for only three months because he was to be promoted to major general and fill the appointment in Malaya of General Officer Commanding 17 Gurkha Infantry Division and Major General Brigade of Gurkhas. We spent a great deal of time together for he asked me to brief him on Gurkhas in general and the current state of play in the Malayan Emergency. As I had recently been commanding the 1/6th Gurkha Rifles for three years during the Malayan Emergency, I was able to put him in the picture and answer his string of questions.

Little did I know that in less than three years time I would be commanding a Brigade under him in Malaya. Before leaving HQ Eastern Command, he wrote me a very complimentary interim Confidential Report, in which he graded me "outstanding, and fit now for promotion to brigade commander or brigadier general staff".

He was succeeded by a brigadier who was essentially a staff officer rather than a commander. I was responsible for briefing the army commander and all the senior members of the staff every Monday morning on the situation overseas, the changes taking place in the UK Order of Battle, and our commitments for aid to the civil power in the light of the industrial unrest then taking place in the form of strikes prejudicial to the safety and economy of the realm.

After one year the time arrived for the BGS to be promoted to major general and a key intelligence appointment in Whitehall. He was required to write an annual Confidential Report on me for the year 1955. He also graded me as "An officer of outstanding all round ability who has clearly shown that he is fit now for promotion to brigade commander or brigadier general staff."

My next boss was a brigadier who was quite a different character. He was a horse gunner, and one of the best and most successful point-to-point riders in the country. He gave me a completely free hand. Shortly after his arrival I received an unexpected assignment. I was told that I had been selected as one of about two hundred British and Commonwealth officers to attend the British nuclear weapon tests in the Maralinga Desert Range in South Australia. For obvious reasons, only those officers were chosen with characteristics which should bring them to the highest positions in the army. We were to be away from the UK for forty days, which was long enough for those who were holding key appointments.

On the first day of our arrival at Maralinga we were given a series of lectures by the British Chief Scientist, Sir William Penny. Then came the bombshell. Work on the preparations for the firing were so behind schedule that it would not be possible to meet the time factor of forty days. Therefore the two hundred selected officers would have to be formed into manual working parties to prepare the range, or what was called the 'Target Response Area'. This meant pick and shovel work digging slit trenches – preparing the ground for all the various 'targets' such as tanks, bridges, dummy buildings, military dispositions and so on. I happened to be one of a working party digging slit trenches when Sir William Penny came up to me and said: "Would you like to convert yourself into an amateur scientist and fit strain gauges and cameras on all the equipment, buildings and dummy soldiers etc. in the whole of the target response area?" I jumped at this proposal for it would absolve me from the hot and dirty pick and shovel work.

After forty days all was ready with all the targets – tanks, dummy buildings, bridges, dummy soldiers, and so on – all in their correct positions. I had spent all day and every day fitting strain gauges on every item of equipment and every target in the response area on the range. Suddenly it was announced that the wind was blowing from the wrong direction and would have blown the fall-out over cultivated land. This was not the only false alarm, for quite obviously the wind direction had to be spot on because of the danger of fall-out reaching inhabited areas.

At last the wind was exactly right and we were suitably dressed and assembled for the first test to take place. We stood three miles from 'Ground Zero' with our backs to the blast. We heard the count-down, felt the blast of heat and the scorching wind on the back of the neck and after a short pause were ordered to turn round. We saw and watched the impressive sight of the fireball rise into the mushroom cloud. When the radio activity had fallen to a safe level, we toured the target response area. An amazingly and impressive sight met ones eyes. Houses had disappeared, steel bridges were buckled, tanks completely wrecked. Dummy soldiers standing in slit trenches were no longer there. This, then, was a salutary lesson. I recorded the readings on all the strain gauges that I had fitted and in every case tanks, steel bridges and all the other targets had not only been wrecked but bodily lifted and blown considerable distances.

Unfortunately I was only able to witness the first of the four tests because the new army commander who had succeeded Festing – Lieutenant-General Sir Charles Coleman – had grown impatient at my long absence and recalled me. I was by no means the only senior staff officer to be recalled for our absence had well exceeded forty days.

On my return to duty I was ordered to give a lecture to

128

the headquarters staff, including the army commander himself, on the qualities of nuclear weapons and their value and limitations on the battlefield. As a result of my talk I was told to tour the whole of the command area and give similar lectures in order to spread the gospel.

It was during this time that I was informed that I was to be promoted to brigadier and return to Malaya to take command of the 99 Gurkha Infantry Brigade Group, which, by the time of my arrival, I knew would be poised to fight the most important and hopefully final battle of the twelve year Malayan Emergency.

On leaving HQ Eastern Command I received yet another Confidential Report, which again graded me as 'outstanding'. Obviously three such reports were to stand me in good stead.

Chapter 13

Early in 1957 I was promoted to brigadier and took over command of 99 Gurkha Infantry Brigade Group in Malaya. I was given the task of fighting the battle against the most formidable remaining communist terrorists in the southern state of Johore. I was told that if I could win the Battle of Johore decisively, I would have succeeded in administering the *coup de grace* to the terrorists in Malaya. This, indeed, was a challenge which I relished.

I decided to give my offensive the code name 'Operation Tiger'. In my initial briefing of my battalion and subordinate commanders, I emphasised that every unit was to show 'the cunning, stamina and the offensive spirit of a tiger'. Until I was ready to launch the offensive I ordered every battalion to select its own ambush range in the jungle and train to the highest possible pitch; far higher than hitherto. I made it crystal clear that I would not accept failure whenever they were acting on Special Branch information.

Meanwhile I had important business to perform with Special Branch (SB). I asked the head of SB these questions: first, what was his assessment of the situation; second who were his secret agents; three, where were they located? Marked maps were produced from their secret safes at police headquarters. I was absolutely amazed and shocked at the small number of red pins indicating agents in CT areas of operation. I made it clear that I was not prepared to launch such a major offensive on such flimsy intelligence. SB would have to increase considerably the number of trustworthy agents, and provide me with the necessary reliable information to enable me to mount the offensive with every prospect of success.

I warned all battalion commanders and SB that I intended to hold a two-day study period during which I would ask each battalion commander in turn to give his detailed appreciation of the situation, and his plan for the overall conduct of Operation Tiger. I would want to know where they considered the approximately one hundred CTs were located in the twelve hundred square miles of jungle, and how they could be eliminated, captured or forced to surrender. Also what restrictions would have to be enforced to deny the CTs their sources of food. I required their plan to include the best means of waging psychological warfare to enable a first class propaganda campaign to be launched.

The study period was attended by the executive secretary of the Johore War Executive Committee, John Davis, who was an old acquaintance of mine having been the commanding officer of Ferret Force. In fact, during World War II he was a close friend of the present leader of the communist terrorists, Chin Peng, when they had both served in Force 136 against the Japanese. After the study period John Davis said to me that he had been dubious about the necessity for having such a study period, but now that it was over he could understand how valuable it had been. This was a typical example of the attitude of those irregulars who had been fighting behind the Japanese, as opposed to the professionalism of regular soldiers who had fought the Japanese head on and were masters of their craft.

I was particularly pleased that each battalion commander had caught my enthusiasm and produced a first-class appreciation of the situation and a sound, imaginative and aggressive plan. Special Branch had also come up trumps and I found a Chinese officer who was on a par with Cyril Keel, in not only having now enlisted a network of reliable informers, but who would obviously be as successful in 'turning' captured and surrendered CTs.

Operation Tiger was to prove the importance that the ambush plays in jungle warfare. I laid down that when acting on SB information every soldier must be prepared to lie in ambush for at least ten days, with two teams alternating every two hours. In one case, namely that experienced by 2/2 GR whose ambush was on a trail along which SB were convinced that a party of CTs were due to travel, the most suitable locations were in a swamp. When the ambush had been in a position for two weeks without any sign of the party of CTs, hints reached me from members of my staff and elsewhere that the mental and physical strain would take their toll, and that if the ambush was sprung, the CTs would probably not be hit. I ignored such hints, for SB information was such that I was convinced that the party of CTs would eventually appear.

When the Gurkha ambush had been lying in swamp for twenty-seven days, the Commanding Officer appealed to me for permission to withdraw it. He put forward his main reasons: first, the longest lasting ambush ever known; second, the appalling conditions of the swamp; third, the ordeal being suffered by his men was beyond the power of human endurance. I told him that I was one hundred percent certain that the CTs would definitely come along the trail and that zero hour was fast approaching. Meanwhile he must buoy up the morale of his men with this certainty.

The very next day three CTs appeared in the killing zone. Two were killed outright and the third had his rifle shot out of his hand. He screamed and turned to run away, but he must have been so shocked by the springing of the ambush and the killing of his two comrades that he surrendered. A surrendered CT meant more to me and SB than any number of dead CTs, for the information that he could provide would be vital to the immediate conduct of my operation.

I had been receiving visits by the Commander-in-Chief Far East Land Forces, General Sir Richard Hull, his chief of staff and a number of other potentates. They were fascinated by my 'reading' of the battle and how I was reacting to vital information as and when I received it throughout the day, and sometimes at night. On one such visit the C-in-C brought with him Mr. (the late Lord) Julian Amery, then Army Minister, who showed tremendous interest. Many years later, after my retirement, he was to write a forthright foreword to my two books – *The Bear at the Back Door* and *The Next Domino*. "We shall ignore its warning, and its message, at our peril." was what he wrote.

There was increased urgency for Operation Tiger to succeed in eliminating lock, stock and barrel, the ninety-five or more CTs in South Johore, because events in Johore had an immediate impact upon Singapore across the Straits, and their elections were due before the end of the year. By the beginning of November 1958, my brigade had accounted for ninety of the enemy. The terrorist organisation in South Johore had been shattered, but the most important prize had yet to be eliminated. This was the terrorist leader, Ah Ann, who had held sway for ten years and foiled every attempt to track him down. Now he was on the run with his wife and four others. He was one of the most formidable CTs remaining in Malaya. He might try to vanish across the Straits into Singapore or escape with the aim of fermenting another insurrection. He was a ruthless man who had ordered the execution of five of his men that year, and was known to have large sums of money with him.

On 6 November I held a press conference and said, "I will stick my neck out and say that South Johore should be declared 'white by Christmas'. I now relied once again on special branch to bear fruit as, indeed, I had throughout the operation from the very beginning. My faith in them was not to be misplaced at this vital juncture. A special branch Chinese officer went to visit Ah Ann's mother on the chance that she might receive word from him, if not a visit. He waited there until a visitor did arrive. It was a message from Ah Ann. With the skill that had become routine, the SB officer persuaded the messenger that the war was over and that information leading to the arrest of Ah Ann could make him rich for life. The terrorist agreed.

For the mission to his mother, Ah Ann had lent the messenger his own pistol. So it was arranged that the traitor should return it to him, unloaded. This he did and, a moment later, a police raiding party burst into the camp. Ah Ann raised his empty pistol and squeezed the trigger. Instantly he was shot dead. With him died his wife and another district committee member. Two others surrendered and the sixth escaped into the jungle – the sole survivor of the terrorists who had dominated South Johore at the beginning of the year. My brigade's triumph was complete.

On the last day of 1958, South Johore was declared 'white' and the last major campaign of the Malayan Emergency had ended in the defeat of the insurgents.

I now quote from Tom Pocock's biography of me – *Fighting General*: "Praise of Brigadier Walker was the talk of Kuala Lumpur, Singapore and Whitehall. To Walker himself success had not come as a surprise. Methodically, he had assessed the problem, judged what action had to be taken and then carried this out. His genius for training, inspiring confidence and enthusiasm, which he had applied to the 8th Gurkhas in Burma, had been stretched to embrace a complete brigade. Knowing what he could do with potentially satisfactory material had given him an invincibility.

"At the press conference he held in November, Walker reminded his audience that at his first press conference back in April he had forecast this success. 'Our pursuit of the CTs is going to be ruthless, relentless and remorseless and when we meet them we will hit quick, hit hard and keep on hitting,' he had said. But he did not claim the credit for himself. He praised, in this order, the War Emergency Committee of South Johore, the special branch, the information services, the police, the airmen and finally the soldiers themselves, whose tenacity, enthusiasm and skill had, he said, been the greatest factor of all.

"Walker's achievement was recognised by his appointment as a Commander of the British Empire. This was followed by a warm congratulatory letter from the Commander-in-Chief Far East Land Forces, General Sir Richard Hull. Praising Walker's drive and initiative, Hull laid particular stress on the close co-operation he had established with the police and the civil authorities."

The citation for my award of the CBE covered the period from November 1957 to December 1958, and read as follows:

"For the past year Brigadier Walker has been in command of 99 Gurkha Infantry Brigade in Johore, one of the most troublesome and 'black' areas of Malaya. He set about the task of eliminating the 234 strong terrorist organisation in his area with resource, drive and initiative. By his tact, perseverance and personality he ensured the complete cooperation of the civil authorities, the police and other services.

"His plan of campaign has been imaginative and soundly conceived. It has been pursued with relentless energy under conditions varying from a slow war of patient attrition (during which vital information was collated) to a series of cleverly conceived moves and counter-moves employing all the resources and materials at his disposal.

"He has done far more than is normally expected of a brigade commander. He sought, found and applied new combat measures, using new techniques and tactics to outwit, fight, defeat and then hound to surrender the hard-core terrorists in South Johore.

As a result, by the end of December, 1958, the complete communist terrorist organisation in South Johore had been eliminated, and, on 31st December 1958, the whole state was declared a 'white' area.

"It is very largely due to Brigadier Walker's first class planning, efforts and the close knit combined control which he established with the civil authorities, the police and other services, that this outstandingly successful conclusion of operations has been achieved."

LESSONS OF OPERATION TIGER

1. The clear proof that well-trained, observant troops, ably led, can track through the most difficult jungle, without the aid of dogs or Ibans (Sarawak trackers). From 4 to 16 Oct., three Gurkha battalions in turn tracked the terrorists for nearly 40 map miles through hilly jungle country, a distance probably equal to 70 miles on the ground.

2. The light aircraft flights have a major part to play because they can provide quick intimate support in a multitude of different tasks – locating lost patrols, air supply, visual reconnaissance, guiding helicopters, dropping leaflets, roving loud hailers, and dropping rifle and LMG simulators as deception. In the visual reconnaissance role 11 Liaison Flight's accurate reporting of terrorist camp-fire smoke on three occasions played a decisive part in the operation when tracks had been lost. There is little doubt that the light aircraft flight is an indispensable asset to the brigade group in jungle operations.

3. Helicopters are vital in operations in deep jungle, but the location (or lack) of jungle LZs is bound to dictate deployment. To maintain surprise, speed must often be sacrificed by flying troops into LZs well short of their objective.

4. Without air supply the operation could not have been launched at all.

5. Psychological warfare must be employed to the full even though at the time it is often hard to gauge its effect.

6. Above all the discipline, physical fitness, determination and self-reliance of the soldier in the jungle on the operation were quite outstanding. Troops, travelling light, patrolled daily right up to last light in their efforts to pick up tracks. Three-man patrols spent many nights away from their platoon bases without an evening meal, and slept where they were in their wet clothes when night made the jungle impenetrable. Platoons in every battalion went without food on occasions for as long as 48 hours. In 60 days of intensive operations from 28 Aug. to 28 Oct. the soldier on an average spent 50 days in the jungle.

CONCLUSION

At the end of his book *Defeat into Victory*, Field Marshal Lord Slim has this to say on the value to be derived from anti-terrorist operations in Malaya, in the nuclear age:-

"Dispersed fighting ... will have two main requirements – skilled and determined junior leaders and self reliant, physically hard, well-disciplined troops. Success in future land operations will depend on the immediate availability of such leaders and such soldiers, ready to operate in small independent formations. They will have to be prepared to do without regular lines of communication to guide themselves and to subsist largely on what the country offers. Unseen, unheard and unsuspecting, they will converge on the enemy ... Stalking terrorists in a

138

Malayan jungle is today, strange as it may seem, the best training for nuclear warfare. The use of new weapons and technical devices can quickly be taught; to develop hardihood, initiative, mutual confidence, and stark leadership takes longer."

Before closing this account of Operation Tiger I must pay tribute to the outstanding effeciency of my brigade staff officers. No brigade commander could have been served and supported by such a loyal and first-class team. Chief among them was my extremely astute and brilliant brigade major, Ronnie McAlister, later to become Major General Brigade of Gurkhas.

He was ably supported by a young captain in the Royal Artillery, Stewart Cox by name, of the Army Air Corps. It was he who commanded 11 Liaison Flight and, at a later date, was the author of the foregoing Lessons of Operation Tiger. By his own flying skill and example he was brilliantly successful in giving me the location of the CTs resting places and camps. He too, went on to become a major general.

INTERNAL SECURITY

My next assignment could not have been so totally different to that of hunting and fighting the CTs in the dense jungles of Malaya. At long last General Sir Richard Hull's mind could be put to rest about the internal situation in Singapore prior to and during the forthcoming elections when unrest was forecast. My orders were to move my brigade on to the island of Singapore and assume direct command of internal security throughout the length and breadth of the island.

The sharp weapon that I had forged in the shape of soldiers who had been taught to fire like greased lightning and with deadly accuracy at a fleeting target, namely the CTs, and when in ambush or when attacking a CT camp, to hit quick, hit

139

hard and keep on hitting, and be ruthless, relentless and remorseless; all this had to be cast aside.

At that time there was a fire-brand in Singapore in the shape of a young Chinese politician named Lee Kuan Yew. He was regarded as being a communist in all but name and one who was capable of stirring up anti-British rioting. There was also the danger of communal friction.

Internal security was not new to me for I had not only witnessed it but taken an active part in suppressing inter-communal riots in Multan, in India – now Pakistan – and Bombay, when I was a 2nd lieutenant. Indeed, I had been the target of a soda water bottle which was thrown at me and drew blood on my forehead. My immediate reaction was to draw my pistol from its holster, but as quick as lightning my platoon sergeant was by my side – not to mop up the blood, but to jog my memory with the words: "Minimum force, sir." I remember this sergeant to this very day. His name was Sergeant Green, who held my hand throughout my one year's attachment to The Sherwood Foresters.

Under my command in Singapore I had five battalions, three of which were Gurkha. I had compiled and issued on a wide scale an outline of the "Principles of Internal Security in a City". After giving my unit commanders and sub-unit commanders sufficient time to absorb my directive and put the various 'drills' into practice, I decided to launch a large-scale exercise in the city. I had anticipated that the exercise would prove to be a complete flop. Such was the case, for my troops had been living in the jungle for so long against a ruthless enemy who presented only a fleeting target, that they now had to learn to live in a city and be confronted by screeching mobs and yet withhold their fire. Furthermore they were told never to allow themselves to come into close contact with a screaming mob, whatever the provocation.

I allotted to each battalion its own slice of the city and the commanding officer was given the following instructions:

First, to achieve an intimate knowledge of every road, alleyway, footpath, traffic light, flow of traffic, open space, flat roof-tops, type and customs of the inhabitants. Second, these details were to be portrayed on a sand or cloth model. Third, each battalion was to have such an accurate knowledge of its particular slice of the city that it could move to any target area as quickly by night as it could by day. Fourth, peaceful crowd dispersal was to be rehearsed again and again until every soldier was thoroughly au fait with the drill and able to react without hesitation to the unexpected. Fifth, liaison with every helicopter pilot was to be so close that soldiers could be winched on and off flat roofs with the minimum of delay. Sixth, each battalion was to be trained to such a pitch that it could completely dominate its slice of the city. Seventh, to rehearse every eventuality and, in doing so, to identify themselves so closely with the inhabitants of the island that they would come to be treated as friends, and thus win the hearts and minds of the inhabitants.

Once I had given each battalion sufficient time to dominate its slice of the city, I pitted battalions against each other and, in doing so, judged them on speed and efficiency in dealing with one or more serious incidents. These exercises were carried out by day and night and they were closely watched by every household – rich and poor – and, I hoped, by Lee Kuan Yew himself. The 'picture' I intended to leave them with was that I held in my hands the complete domination of the city.

I had briefed each battalion commander on the vital necessity of compiling a manual on internal security in a city, and that they were to produce their own version to cover every eventuality as they progressed with their training, and while the lessons learned were fresh in their memories. My Brigade HQ would then pool the lessons learned and produce a manual entitled *Internal Security in a City*.

In the event, the elections in Singapore passed off without any sign of trouble and Lee Kuan Yew was elected Chief Minister. We had won the hearts and minds, the friendship and respect of a previously hostile Chinese population.

The correct standard of treatment towards the public is one of the first principles of internal security duties. Rough handling and bad manners towards the public are quite unnecessary, alienate feelings and make the task doubly difficult. Commanders must bring home to all ranks that there is a world of difference between quick and effective action against terrorists and a bullying attitude towards a person held for checking or screening. The former is efficient, the latter is the very opposite.

Chapter 14

HOW BORNEO WAS WON

When I was general officer commanding-in-chief, Northern Command, British Army, with my headquarters at York, 1967-69, I was asked by the then Minister of Defence, Mr. (now Lord) Denis Healey, to write my account of *How Borneo Was Won*.

It was in December 1962, at the outbreak of the Brunei Revolt, that I was appointed commander of all British and Commonwealth Forces in Borneo, and a short time later Director of Operations, Land, Sea and Air.

After my account had been submitted for strict scrutiny by Whitehall, it was published in the journal *The Round Table* in 1969. It was called *How Borneo was won* – The Untold Story of an Asian Victory". The Editor had this to say about it:

"The story of one of the most remarkable Commonwealth achievements of recent times is told for the first time in this issue of *The Round Table*. This is the defence of Malaysia from Indonesian attack by Malaysian, British, Australian and New Zealand forces. The descriptions by General Walker of how he trained and used his troops will strike anyone with a knowledge of the Vietnam tragedy as a classic use of the minimum necessary force combined with an understanding of the mentality of peasant and tribal peoples. General Walker points out that the experience which went into this operation is in danger of being lost. That experience is concentrated at present in the British Army, which is trying to convert itself into a purely continental force at a time when it has unique political relations and military skills for handling world wide threats of another kind. This is a serious problem which ought to be faced."

The account could not mention the fact that I was the architect of my secret 'knock-out weapon' – CLARET – cross-border operations, because at that time it was closely guarded as Top Secret. It was not made public until 1973, when Tom Pocock, the eminent journalist, war correspondent and author, published his biography of me in his book called *Fighting General – The Public and Private Campaigns of General Sir Walter Walker*.

The photograph on the dust cover of this book is, in fact, a snap shot of me turning round in the front seat of my staff car to talk to Mr. and Mrs. Armstrong of *The Round Table*, when they visited me in Borneo. It was Christa Armstrong who took the snap shot without me knowing.

I must emphasise again that my article is far from complete because at the time I could not mention my top secret 'battle winner' – CLARET – cross border operations. Operation CLARET is fully explained by me in the following chapter.

BRUNEI

0 10   50 miles

—————— DIVISIONAL BOUNDARY
—·——·——· INTERNATIONAL BOUNDARY
———— BRUNEI BOUNDARY

N

SOUTH
CHINA
SEA

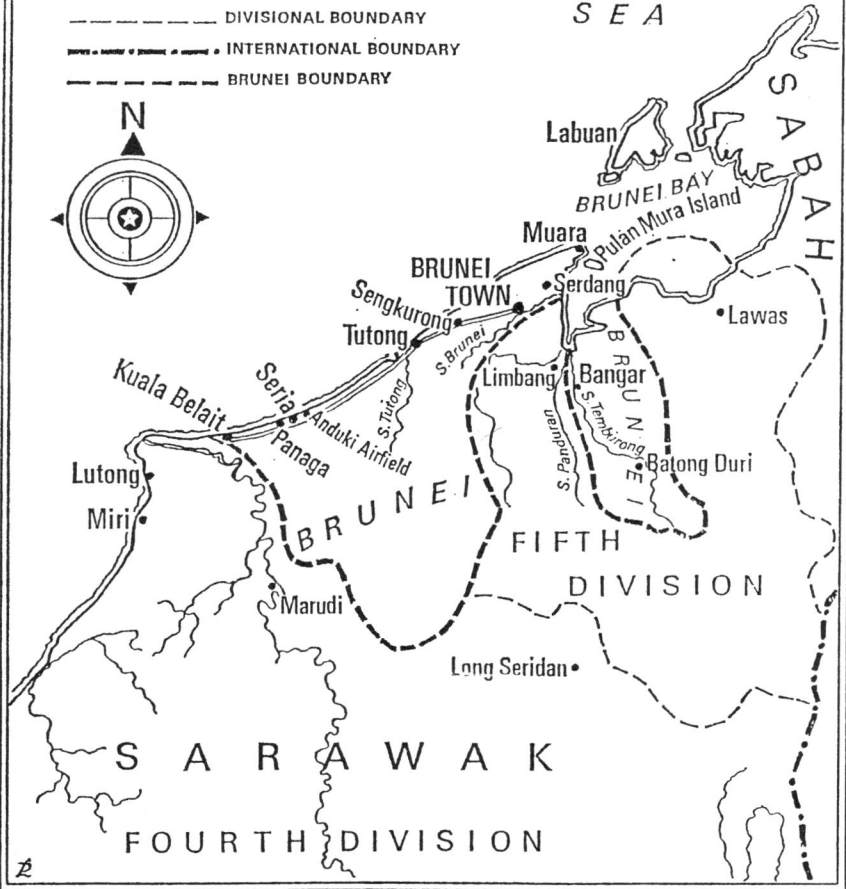

Labuan

BRUNEI BAY

Muara

Pulau Mura Island

BRUNEI
TOWN

Serdang

Sengkurong

Tutong

S.Brunei

Limbang

Bangar

Lawas

Kuala Belait

Seria

Anduki Airfield

Panaga

S. Tutong

S.Padungan

S.Tembirong

Batong Duri

Lutong

Miri

B R U N E I

FIFTH

DIVISION

Marudi

Long Seridan

S A R A W A K

FOURTH DIVISION

145

Chapter 15

THE INGREDIENTS OF SUCCESS IN COUNTER-INSURGENCY JUNGLE
WARFARE, WHETHER AGAINST A TERRORIST TYPE ENEMY, OR A
MORE WELL-ARMED AGGRESSIVE ENEMY.

No one in his right senses would expect me, of all people, to indulge in whitewashing or to conceal the truth. My aim, therefore, is to highlight the lessons to be learned from the twelve year Malayan Emergency and the four year Borneo campaign in the hope that those who follow, and who undoubtedly will find themselves involved in future similar contests, will be able to profit from the successes and failures of their predecessors.

On almost every occasion that a crisis has broken out since World War II, the 'powers that be' have been caught with their trousers down. By indulging in wishful thinking, they have underestimated the situation and in so doing those at the 'sharp end' have been obliged to play themselves in with inadequate equipment and training. In future we shall not be afforded such breathing space either by the enemy without or within. The only safe prediction today is that, in spite of the spies in the sky, the unexpected *is* to be expected.

We should learn our lessons from what went wrong at the beginning of a campaign, and not from what went right at the end of it.

The British Army's fundamental trouble was that within two years of defeating the Japanese in Burma in World War II, all our military training and thinking had become focused on nuclear and conventional tactics for a European theatre against a first-class enemy. So, when the Malayan Emergency broke out in 1948, we had forgotten most of our jungle warfare

147

techniques and expertise learned the hard way at such high cost in the Burma Campaign against the Japanese in World War II.

The authorities fell into the same trap in the short interval between the end of the Malayan Emergency and the outbreak of the Brunei Revolt in 1962, followed by Indonesian Confrontation, 1963 to 1966.

The 'Whitehall Warriors' imagined that 'Jungle Exercises Without Trees' on Salisbury Plain were a suitable rehearsal for jungle operations, forgetting that the jungle is such that if a soldier loses sight of the sweat-stained back of the man in front, he loses his way.

The military tactics of guerillas is something quite new within the accepted pattern of warfare – surprise attack by the enemy against soft targets – withdrawal in the face of opposition to the sanctuary of the jungle.

Although Borneo was mainly the platoon and section commanders war, nevertheless, it was the company commander who had to be able to set the example and do everything that his men could do, do it better and do it for longer.

Unlike the American policy in Vietnam of 'Search and Destroy' and then return to base, our technique in Borneo was 'clear, hold and dominate'. Results could not be achieved merely by attacking and shooting the enemy and then returning to base.

He had to be played at his own game, by living out in the jungle for weeks on end, by winning the hearts and minds of the people and by planting our own agents in villages known to be unfriendly.

In these conditions, the soldier carried his base on his back, and it consisted of a featherweight plastic sheet, a sackful of rice, and a pocketful of ammunition. The jungle belonged to him; he owned it, controlled and dominated it day and night for months on end. What, then, was the technique of domination of the jungle?

We gradually devised tactical techniques and battle skills which would have done credit to a cat-burglar, gangster, gunman or poacher. The soldiers were able to live in the jungle as close to the animal as it was humanly possible to do so, and became so well trained that they were able to fight the guerillas both in the jungle and out of it, and to kill and harry them until they were utterly exhausted.

The type of fighting, the type of country and the climate called for individual stamina and fortitude, stout legs, stout hearts, fertile brains and the acceptance of battlefield conditions almost unimaginable in their demands on human endurance.

The soldiers made great use of deception and guile, never doing the same thing twice. Their objective was to dominate and own the jungle and the frontier, week in, week out, day and night. Unlike the Americans in Vietnam, there were no 'Prince Rupert' tactics of galloping over the jungle canopy in helicopters. Company and platoon commanders used all their cunning and guile (for example, contour flying) to get within striking distance of the enemy by helicopter, but without being seen or heard. Then the soldiers tracked him down, stalking and closing in on their feet for the kill. The sure way to beat a guerilla is to operate more quietly, smoke less, and talk less to possible enemy agents before an operation.

Victory in guerilla warfare goes to the tougher, more resourceful soldier and the more gadget filled our life becomes, the harder it is to produce him. Fortunately in the Gurkha soldier the British Army has an ever-ready crack force, if only they would use them in time and not dive for cover at the very mention by the Whitehall political pundits of the same old words – 'political objections'.

Even long after the successful conclusion of the Borneo

campaign, a great deal of unnecessary secrecy was still attached to the cross border operations that took place, code named 'CLARET'. We cannot afford to forget the art of hitting an enemy by methods which neither escalate the war nor invite United Nations anti-colonialist intervention.

Offensive action is the very essence of successful military operations when faced with guerilla or terrorist forces, whether in the Far East, the Middle East, Western Europe, which includes the United Kingdom, of course – yes, and Ulster too. A policy of containment is the passport to failure.

Defensive thinking is now such a national as well as a NATO disease that plans are based on appeasement, and when this fails on the assumption of an initial retreat and even surrender.

The Helsinki fraud was a typical example. This propaganda exercise was a vital step forward for the Russians in their long term strategy for disarming Europe by first inducing a spirit of neutralism. The will of western nations to provide for their defence was further sapped and Russia's military might further increased.

The lesson to be learned from counter insurgency operations is that terrorists fighting a guerilla-type war can tie up lavishly equipped modern regular forces ten times their number in strength.

Moscow and Peking represent but two of the countries who have never underestimated guerilla and terrorist power. The money spent arming nationalist, neutralist and terrorist movements across the world has paid tremendous dividends, for they have enmeshed too many countries in their communist web.

Their financial outlay that is incurred by the systematic arming of rebel terrorists is certainly money well spent.

The ill-informed British public did not, and still do not

realise that it is the hands of so many countries which are pulling the strings of terrorism. Revolutionaries everywhere are all in someone's net. This is what is called 'revolutionary war by proxy' – getting the local extremists to do their dirty work for them.

The lesson of Cambodia, of the French in Indo-China, of the Portuguese in Africa, the Americans in Vietnam – the list is endless – is crystal clear. It is that well equipped modern armies, sophisticated military operations, and air power, are no protection against guerilla tactics.

By contrast Britain's counter-insurgency operations in Malaysia and Borneo were a complete success. Indeed, unlike the Vietnam fiasco, we were so successful that we avoided a tragedy that could have fallen on a whole corner of a continent.

In Vietnam an over-sophisticated American Army and an Air Force which dropped four times more bombs than they did in the whole of World War II, failed to win a limited guerilla war against puny men of a puny nation.

That phoney and infamous 'peace with honour' – which earned a Nobel Peace Prize – amounted to nothing more than a fig-leaf to cover a scuttle. They were outfought and outwitted not only in battle but also at the Paris peace negotiations and in their evacuation plan with their mighty rescue armada. And in Washington they were divided and paralysed as well.

The United States poured into the Vietnam War eight years of effort, the lives of 50,000 young men, the good health of another 300,00, $150 billion of their hard-earned tax money and the honour and prestige of their nation.

It is easy to see why the Soviets wanted to keep the war going. While America spent $150 billion on weapons that are now down the drain in Vietnam, the Soviets spent an equivalent amount on nuclear weapons to control the world.

History will be left to explain America's decision to fight

a costly no-win war (or could it not have been won?) that left South-East Asia in far worse condition than it was before American intervention began.

In both Malaya and Borneo the enemy was at least as formidable as the Vietcong in the early 1960s, and Indonesia just as strong militarily as North Vietnam. If either campaign had been mismanaged, the British too could have had a Vietnam on their hands.

The Borneo campaign stands out as being a notable example of how highly trained professional infantrymen can achieve a decisive victory against a well-armed, aggressive and unscrupulous enemy with little bloodshed to themselves, little destruction of the countryside and with so little disruption of the normal life of the civilian population, that reversion to peacetime conditions at the end of hostilities was virtually automatic.

There was no area bombing or interdiction, no napalm or defoliation of the jungle. Indeed, during the whole campaign not a single bomb was dropped nor rocket fired. No wonder the Commonwealth Forces were welcomed for the social and economic benefits they brought to the jungle villages.

By mastering the physical conditions, by securing the willing help of the inhabitants, and by the highly skilful use of thoroughly trained infantrymen, the Borneo campaign was won without the people at home or the world at large realising the extent of the fighting soldiers' achievements.

The reason why the fighting was poorly reported was not the fault of the war correspondents who either were not allowed to see what they wanted, or tell all they had learned.

With Commander Royal Marine Commando Battalion, 1962

Briefing officials on Hearts and Minds Campaign, 1963

Flying over Borneo Jungle, 1963

Visit of Peter Thornycroft as Minister of Defence to Brunei and Borneo, 1963

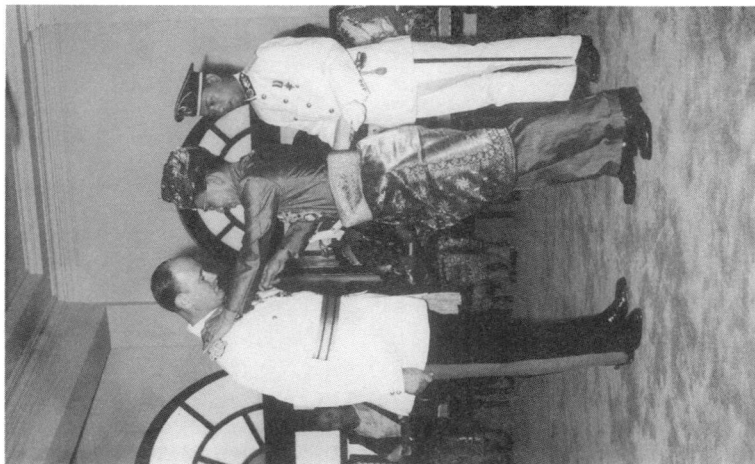

Investiture of the PSNB by His Highness The Sultan of Brunei, January 1964

Visit of Mr Fred Mulley, Army Minister, Borneo 1964

With Headman of a village deep in the jungle, Borneo 1964

Chapter 16

It has been said that: "There is no doubt that General Sir Walter Walker's greatest military success on the battlefield was as Director of Operations, Borneo, 1963-65, during the Borneo Campaign – Confrontation with Indonesia."

It was while I was on one of my treks in Nepal in December 1962, that the Brunei Revolt blew up. As I was General Officer Commanding 17th Gurkha Division as well as Major General Brigade of Gurkhas, I was thousands of miles out of place just as my troops were about to emplane in Singapore to Brunei.

A Dakota aircraft was sent for me and I flew to Singapore at about 100 knots an hour! After being quickly briefed, I flew by night to Serembam to say goodbye to my wife and to pack. I flew the next day to Singapore, and then from Singapore to Brunei by jet bomber, arriving at midday, and immediately took over the reins.

When the Commander-in-Chief Far East Land Forces said goodbye to me, he said, "I will see you back in three months, after having quashed the rebellion." I replied, "It is going to be more like three years." I had been studying the aspirations of President Sukarno of Indonesia, whereas my superiors' ideas were firmly fixed on the internal security situation in Singapore.

When the Commander-in-Chief, Far East Land Forces, paid his first visit to Sarawak, he told the Resident of the Fourth Division, my brother-in-law, John Fisher, and next in seniority to the Governor of Sarawak, that "no other General in the

British Army could match my experience of counter-insurgency operations in the jungle, and that I was an inspired trainer and outstanding leader," John Fisher replied: "Oh, that bloody man who quarrels with everyone. As far as I am concerned you could not have made a worse choice!" The Commander-in-Chief was aghast and struck dumb. When later in the day, John Fisher, accompanied by his wife, my sister, was saying goodbye to the Commander-in-Chief at the aircraft steps, he said: "I am absolutely delighted that you have sent my brother-in-law, Walter. We can now all sleep safely in our beds!"

It was in December 1962, at the outbreak of the Brunei revolt that I was appointed commander of all British and Commonwealth Forces in Borneo, and when Indonesia embarked on active Confrontation in April 1963, I was appointed Director of Borneo Operations, and remained as such until March 1965.

I now quote from one of the many books written about the Borneo Campaign – confrontation with Indonesia: "If one had to choose an expert General of the British Army to start off as Director of Operations, Walter Walker would have been the best choice. In the Burma campaign against the Japanese, he had won the first of three DSOs, commanding a battalion. In the Malayan emergency he again commanded a Gurkha battalion and then a brigade, winning a second DSO. So he knew a lot about counter-insurgency in jungle environments and, in the opinion of his superiors, he was the ideal choice."

The importance of the Brunei revolt was that well before the time I handed over command there was a very efficient Joint Headquarters on Brunei soil. I, as the Director of Operations, had a Tri-Service Operational Headquarters working very efficiently and was also bringing the civilian authorities into it. I was quite convinced in early 1963, that the trouble was going to spread in Sarawak and North Borneo (now Sabah) and although I was under pressure from the Army Commander-in-Chief stationed in Singapore to cut my headquarters down and move my troops back to Singapore and Malaysia, I was absolutely certain from intelligence reports and from the vitriolic anti-Malaysian and anti-British propaganda on Radio Jakarta, that this was madness and a prime example of under-estimating the real enemy, and that it was going to become a very serious problem. I was the commander on the spot and could 'read the battle'.

Although under great pressure I stuck to my guns, which was just as well because in April 1963, the first raid came across the border in Sarawak against a police post. It was but a foretaste of what was going to happen in the future. Gradually, the Indonesian based terrorists camps all along the border began to be built up and incursions started.

With a 1,000 mile border in such rugged territory, I faced a big problem. I had five regular battalions only under my command at that stage in 1963, so it would have been madness to put them in penny packets along the border. I therefore held them back and relied on small surveillance groups on the most likely incursion routes. These surveillance groups were formed by SAS four-man patrols with long range wireless sets and by the Gurkha Parachute Company which was operating in a SAS type of role, and eventually, a new concept, the 'Home Guards' – the Border Scouts which were formed in a hurry. Border Scouts were the local tribes who lived on or astride the border. The aim of using them was in an 'eyes and ears' role 'without a sting', and wearing their native clothes. I definitely relied on these small groups to get information back to the battalion and brigade commanders.

Repeatedly I emphasised through Admiral Sir Varyl Begg, the overall Commander-in-Chief, Far East, to the National Defence Council (NDC) in Kuala Lumpur in Malaysia that the initiative had to be wrested from the Indonesians, that the Indonesian bases just over the border had to be pushed back further into Kalimantan and not left as they were, literally yards from the border. But my urgings were all to no avail, although strongly supported by Admiral Begg. As usual the politicians were afraid of their own shadows and dragged their feet.

In the Acknowledgements to his book: *Counter-Insurgency Operations: 1, Malaya and Borneo* published in February 1985, Brigadier 'Birdie' Smith singles out, in particular, the many people who gave him advice in many ways. He ends with these words: "In the bibliography I have mentioned certain articles on both these campaigns which have been most useful. If I single out those written by Gen. Sir Walter Walker, KCB, CBE, DSO, it is because he played an important part in the Emergency and was the true architect of victory during the Confrontation. There was no officer then serving with a greater knowledge of counter-insurgency in a jungle environment than General Walker. Those of us who served under his command know what a debt Malaysia and Great Britain owe to him."

In certain parts I quote from this book, for as Birdie Smith says, the book contains articles written by me.

On more than one occasion President Sukarno of Indonesia prepared a political offensive and stated he was prepared to negotiate a cease-fire. One of these occasions was in January 1964. U Thant, the Secretary of the United Nations, had appealed to both the Governments of Indonesia and Malaysia to meet for peace talks rather than continue shooting. His efforts led to an official cease-fire being announced on 23 January 1964. This did not stop the Indonesian Border Terrorists (IBTs) from making incursions across the border, nor did it influence the CCO into abandoning its training and anti-Government propaganda. Although I knew perfectly well that it was a trick, on orders from the NDC, I was told to prevent further infiltration from Kalimantan but to allow insurgents already inside Borneo to return peacefully; operations that had already been mounted were to attempt to capture rather than kill the Indonesians. It was one thing to issue such instructions, another for the security forces to carry them out; challenging any suspicious intruder before shooting meant that the situation became farcical and was open to ridicule, especially when the Indonesian Government made it clear that the 'volunteer' terrorists, sponsored by them, were not bound by any rules whatever.

Ministerial delegations from Malaysia, the Philippines and Indonesia met in Bangkok during February, 1964, but these sessions consisted of much bombastic posturing which served only to harden attitudes on both sides. It was at such a time that Indonesian Mustang fighters and B-25 Mitchell bombers began to 'buzz' towns in Sarawak, and the situation became even more impossible especially when a group of insurgents, which had penetrated Sarawak, was told by the Indonesian National Army (TNI) to stay put and await developments. On the Indonesian Government being asked when these invaders were to be withdrawn, its reply was that these men, and any other incursion parties, would stay, and, adding arrogance to intransigence, Sukarno demanded the right to re-supply all those troops by air. Not unnaturally, Malaysia's reply was a firm 'no' and for the first time an Air Defence Identification Zone (ADIZ) was set up supported by Royal Air Force fighters: nothing more was heard about any projected Indonesian airdrops over Sarawak thereafter.

On 4 March 1964, full-scale operations were resumed when for the last time Indonesia firmly refused to withdraw its insurgents. Undoubtedly, as I had suspected, the undeclared war was now resumed and Indonesia went about proving it with a series of raids into Sarawak by strong forces of well-trained regular troops. By this time the planning and execution of such incursions was far more professional; Indonesian soldiers often fought with skill and tenacity and for the Security Forces the campaign became less like fighting the terrorist in Malaya and more like the jungle war that took place against the Japanese in Burma. It became clear to me that overall direction of operations had been taken over by the TNI, with complete units being deployed as such rather than being split up into groups or as individuals leading half-trained gangs of volunteers. From spring 1964 Sukarno put his insurgence strategy into top gear in the knowledge that his opponents were forced to keep a wary eye on the potential fifth column in their rear, the Chinese Communist Organisation (CCO), as well as attempting to guard against possible incursions from across the long border. The sanctuary of camps just out of reach of the security forces was for us an insuperable problem and as long as the Indonesians retained this immunity, they could strike at will knowing that an escape route nearby was assured: the outlook for the Borneo territories, and for Malaysia as a whole, was grim indeed. But the Indonesians made one very big mistake. Their cold-blooded murders, coupled with the looting of the villages resulted in the news of their brutality being passed from longhouse to longhouse. This meant that I had won the hearts and minds of the border villages – in fact of all the people of Borneo.

During this period, I had to rely on my thinly-spread surveillance screen giving early warning, and thereafter, by using my air transport to its maximum, deploying troops in an attempt to stop and harass the Indonesian invaders. As long as the Indonesian incursions came singly or on occasions overlapped, then I was able to cope by switching my forces rapidly to the area threatened. But if, as seemed increasingly likely, three or

162

more incursions occurred at the same time, then a situation would develop which would be beyond the capacity of the forces under my command. In the short term many more helicopters were required, but if the campaign was to be won, more than that was needed. I had to be allowed to force the enemy's base camps away from the border, back into Kalimantan, or if political clearance for this proved impossible then at least my forces had to be allowed to cross over the unmarked border when in 'hot pursuit' – but my request even for this limited concession was firmly refused by the NDC.

In June 1964, after military pressures had built up and the scale of fighting escalated, once more Sukarno deemed it an opportune moment to go back to the conference table in the hope that these threatened incursions would induce the Malaysians, in particular, to give in. The Presidents of Indonesia and the Philippines met the Malaysian Prime Minister in Tokyo to resume the talks that had been broken off earlier that year. While this was happening, Sukarno asked for a Thai mission to visit Sarawak in order to witness the apparent withdrawal of his forces from Sarawak back to Kalimantan. It was a carefully rehearsed operation with smart, well-equipped soldiers being filmed and photographed marching out of Sarawak; in fact, they had crossed over a little way along the border earlier that day. On 20 June the Tokyo negotiations broke down and it was back to the war.

By now the Commonwealth land forces in Borneo had received reinforcements, and as a consequence, a full divisional organisation was set up under a land forces commander. The three subordinate service commanders moved out of Brunei to the island of Labuan, leaving me with a small staff free to concentrate on the conduct of operations. It was a typical British compromise because my superiors – but not Admiral Begg, who pressed for it – were reluctant to give me an appropriate

163

higher rank commensurate with my duties, so that both I and the Land Forces Commander, Major General Peter Hunt, were of the same rank. Fortunately, we were old friends which meant that we made an untidy organisation work to the best of our ability.

By this time each of the eight Gurkha battalions was serving a series of six-month tours in the Borneo territories. The Gurkha infantrymen had been quick to learn how to dominate the jungle and thus to own their particular part of the frontier. The ambush became the key operation both for the guerillas and the security forces. In ambush, the Gurkha lay in wait for the dangerous Indonesian raider whose own sense of smell and keen eyesight was remarkable.

In the jungle operations the Gurkhas bore the brunt at this stage of the confrontation because it was to take some time for the British battalions to acclimatise to the terrain and the humid climate. Moreover, after serving so long in Europe, they had forgotten how to fight in the jungle. The majority of the British infantrymen did not reach the necessary peak of efficiency until the unit concerned came for its second tour in Borneo. Obviously, there were exceptions, and some notable ones at that – the SAS and 40 Commando, in particular – but few British units had any veterans from the Malayan Emergency, unlike their Gurkha counterparts.

The troops had become so well trained that they were able to fight the guerillas both in the jungle and out of it, and to kill and harry them until they were utterly exhausted.

The Indonesians held the initiative because they could attack from safe bases in Kalimantan, the majority of which were conveniently close to the border. They knew that the bases were safe from attack because there had been no official declaration of war and, not unnaturally, the British Government was anxious to avoid taking any steps that would be presented

164

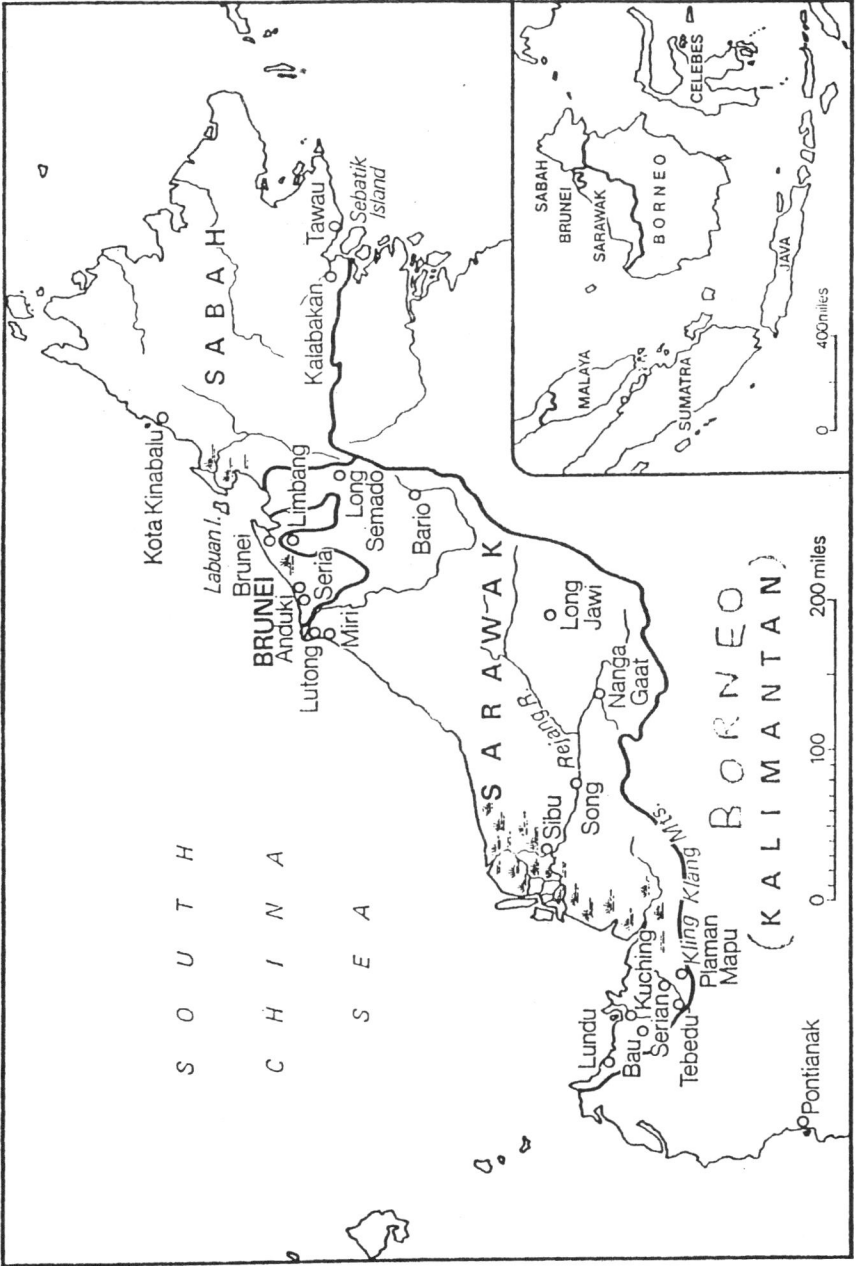

to the Third World element in the United Nations Assembly as being 'Imperialist aggression'. Thus, with one arm tied behind my back, I had little chance of forcing the Indonesians to go on to the defensive. As if to emphasise that this was a Commonwealth operation, the lst Royal New Zealand Infantry Regiment had arrived.

As a result of Indonesian sea and parachute landings on the mainland of Malaya (now Malaysia) the Malaysian Government in Kuala Lumpur thoroughly alarmed at Sukarno's latest actions, now supported my continual requests that cross-border operations should be approved up to a depth of 5,000yds inside Kalimantan. Faced with this request from its Commonwealth ally, the British Government gave its approval, stressing that there was to be no public announcement and that the operations were to be carried out under conditions of maximum secrecy.

Fortunately I had previously briefed Mr. Fred Mulley, Healey's Deputy Secretary of State for Defence and Army Minister, when he visited me in Borneo, of the vital need of limited and secret cross-border operations and convinced him of their necessity. In fact he had already been briefed by Admiral Begg, who sent me a secret coded message saying: "It only requires a push from you to convince Mulley of the vital necessity for cross-border operations."

It was vital that the SAS should cross the border, because it was and is part of its role to probe deeper into enemy territory than the conventional forces, reconnoitring and disrupting potentially dangerous enemy dispositions. This would be done in its normal clandestine manner: its four-man patrols searching for tracks of raiding parties and watching rivers which were the main highways on both sides of the rugged and, in many places, undefined border.

In addition to their watching and reporting role, the SAS

patrols would begin interdiction, such as ambushing tracks and rivers and setting booby traps where it was known that only Indonesian raiders would pass. On occasions, their ambushes would be sophisticated affairs using the electrically-detonated Claymore mines at both ends of prepared ambush positions, while in the middle the troopers raked the killing ground with automatic fire. Such activities would suit the SAS well, and, when this role was activated, they, with typical wry humour, called such groups 'The Tiptoe Boys', because after a sudden sharp little action by the ambush parties, they vanished into an apparently empty jungle.

Shortly afterwards I decided that infantry attacks could be launched in order to pre-empt any suspected or anticipated Indonesian attack. These operations were given by me the code name of 'Claret' and all were graded 'top secret', to be handled with the greatest care by the minimum number of officers, on a 'need to know' basis. 'Claret' operations changed the fortunes of war for both the Indonesians and their Commonwealth opponents. No longer could the Indonesians feel secure in the border bases and camps even if they were within Kalimantan territory, nor would the Security Forces ever feel as frustrated as they had been earlier in the campaign.

Initially, these raids were confined to a penetration depth of 5,000yds but eventually this was increased, for a few specific raids, to as much as 20,000yds. There were a set of definite, clear and detailed orders governing 'Claret' operations which I called the 'Golden Rules'. In time these were amended as the situation changed but, initially, my guidelines were as follows:

1. All Raids had to be personally authorised by me as the Director of Operations.

2. Only tried and tested troops were to be used – in other words, no soldiers were to be sent across into Kalimantan during

their first tour in Borneo. This meant that only Gurkha battalions were used initially, apart from the SAS, but this was changed after the British infantry units had gained the requisite experience in jungle fighting.

3. All raids were to be made with the definite aim of deterring and thwarting aggression by the Indonesians. No attacks were to be mounted in retribution with the sole aim of inflicting casualties on the foe. Civilian lives must not be risked.

4. Close air support could not be given except in an extreme emergency and then only authorised by me.

5. The depth of penetration had to be carefully controlled, initially up to 5,000yds, eventually reaching a maximum of 20,000yds but only for one or two special operations.

6. Every operation had to be meticulously planned with the aid of a sand-table and thoroughly rehearsed for at least two weeks. I always went to the battalion headquarters and to the headquarters of the company that was actually going to carry out the raid. I visited the company first, listened to the company commander's briefing, watched him do a rehearsal on a sand-table or cloth model, and so was in it right from the beginning.

7. Each operation had to be planned and executed with maximum security. Every man taking part must be sworn to secrecy; full cover plans must be made and the operations to be given code names and never discussed in detail on telephone or radio. Identity discs must be left behind before departure and no traces – such as cartridge cases, paper, ration packs etc. – must be left in Kalimantan.

8. On no account must any soldier taking part be captured by the enemy – alive or dead.

The control and power of veto remained with the Director of Operations: by holding the reins tightly in my hands, I and my successor, Major General George Lea, were able to diminish the possibility of escalation. Minimum force was to be the principle used, rather than large scale attacks which would have invited retaliation and risked turning the border war into something quite different, costly in lives and fraught with international problems.

An American general commented that only the British could have conceived 'Claret' operations and devised the masterly 'Golden Rules' that governed them: later he was generous enough to add that only well-disciplined troops such as the SAS and Gurkhas, under their experienced, capable leaders, could have won the successes that were obtained.

Perhaps the most remarkable aspect of these 'Claret' operations was the security and secrecy that was maintained at all levels. It is doubtful whether the Indonesians realised that they were seeing the beginnings of a new Commonwealth strategy. This was partly because the new series of actions took place so near to the border which was, in any case, badly defined, and partly because their communications and administration with Kalimantan could not cope with the flow of reports and assess them quickly and accurately – as was happening in my headquarters.

British Intelligence at the time considered that there might be some 24,000 Chinese sympathizers giving moral support to the 2,000 CCO terrorists within Sarawak, while dotted along the border were over 22,000 TNI troops, supported by an unspecified number of volunteers.

To meet these threats, the forces available within Borneo under me were pathetically small. At this time the total number of soldiers under my command within the Borneo territories was little more than 10,000.

In the end my strong protests did produce three more

infantry battalions, bringing the total up to 13, but my urgent plea for helicopters only produced another 12 Whirlwinds for the whole theatre.

As a result of these reinforcements, by January 1965 the British and Commonwealth forces in Borneo totalled some 14,000 soldiers supported by 29 guns, two squadrons of armoured cars and four field squadrons of Engineers, with less than 60 troop-carrying helicopters to help me deploy and switch my troops over an area the size of England and Scotland together. I was convinced that the only way I could throw the Indonesians off balance was to increase the number of preventive, cross-border operations, and the Labour Government in London showed its trust in me by allowing 'Claret' raids to increase until the depth of penetration reached first 10,000 and then 20,000yds. In addition, the Royal Marine Special Boat Sections were authorised to make small-scale amphibious raids round either flank on the coast.

My participating soldiers bitterly regretted the heavy loads they were forced to carry. Weapons such as the SLR and GPMG were heavy and unwieldy, wireless sets were cumbersome, and rations in their packs were unsuitable and bulky for the climate, terrain and role the infantrymen had to play. The plea for lightweight equipment, radios and rations was one that did not meet with a quick response by Whitehall, which failed to appreciate that victory in guerilla warfare goes to the tougher, more resourceful soldier, one who can remain for longer periods at peak physical condition in the jungle – which means that the load he has to carry on his back must be cut down to the minimum. An important lesson this, and one that was only resolved in the late autumn of the campaign, thanks to Lord Mountbatten and his Chief Scientific Adviser, Sir Solly Zuckerman, when they visited me and listened to what the troops in the jungle had to say.

170

The 'undeclared war' was in many respects an unknown one because the fighting was not reported and few pictures of any significance reached the television screens in the United Kingdom or elsewhere in the world. I gained from this silence which enabled me to mount the 'Claret' cross-border raids without news-hungry journalists breathing down my neck, and in a rush to 'scoop' their fellows, breaking security. In complete contrast, the Falklands War was invariably fought before the eyes and ears of the world so that the Government and senior Service officers were constantly seeking to tread a difficult path to ensure the necessary security for operational reasons, while satisfying the desire by everyone in the UK to know what was going on. Although the 'undeclared war' never hit the headlines, certainly it was a campaign that, in the words of Denis Healey, "witnessed one of the most efficient uses of military force in the history of the world".

The helicopter proved to be a real battle winner. Operationally, I reckoned that one minute in a helicopter equalled a day's march in jungle; that one hour equalled five days; and that one battalion with six helicopters in direct support was equal to a whole brigade. So you can see how much I depended on them.

It was a strange war, an undeclared war and an unknown war. Nevertheless it was a most successful one. It showed that the British Army, and the British Gurkha Infantry in particular, could fight as well as anyone else in the jungle providing they had time to re-adjust. They had to forget their gadgets and learn to live and fight in the jungle. Confrontation lasted three years and nine months. At the height of Confrontation there were 17,000 Commonwealth Forces, as the Australians and New Zealanders came in near the end, plus 10,000 in support. The security force casualties were 114 killed and 200 wounded. It is difficult to say what the Indonesians lost. We know that they lost at least 600 killed and 700 captured, but as things started to go wrong for them towards the end of confrontation, when our raids across the border were breaking their logistic chain, we know that hundreds more died of malnutrition and starvation.

I realised that I was a very controversial character and in fact I got on far better with my Royal Air Force and Royal Navy comrades than I did with my immediate Army Commander in Singapore. He and I were fighting each other a good deal of the time. The blurb of Tom Pocock's book, *Fighting General*, says that, "I fought many wars and I also fought my superiors." Well I did.

Unlike my superiors in Singapore, I believed profoundly in the unified system of command (land, sea and air), then recently introduced in the Far East Command by Lord Mountbatten. As Director of Operations in Borneo, I insisted on dealing direct with the overall Commander-in-Chief Far East in Singapore, Admiral Sir Varyl Begg, thereby by-passing the Land, Navy and Air Force Commanders, all of whom outranked me. It is hardly surprising that the latter took grave exception to this. When visiting military and civilian potentates came to Singapore to discuss the Borneo situation, they were told rather ruefully that Walker's 'bamboo curtain' effectively kept them out of Borneo, and that they would be obliged to discuss the situation with the Commander-in-Chief Far East.

When the Chief of Defence Staff, Admiral of the Fleet Lord Louis Mountbatten visited Borneo, accompanied by the Commander-in-Chief Far East – with whom I got on extremely well – landed at Kuching airport, I was about to hear some interesting news. As they were coming down the aircraft steps they stopped and I heard Mountbatten say to Begg, "Have you told General Walker that our recommendation that he should be awarded a Knighthood has been turned down?" Begg answered, "No. I thought it would come best from you." When

Mountbatten had shaken me by the hand, he said: "I want to thank you as the architect of success for having fought a brilliant campaign. In recognition of what you have achieved, Admiral Begg and I recommended you for a knighthood, but your ungrateful army hierarchy in Whitehall rejected it. You were then recommended for Commander of the Order of St. Michael and St. George, but again this was rejected. The highest Award that the Chief of the General Staff (CGS) and the Army Board would sanction was a second bar to your DSO. Never mind, I am sure that the accolade of a Knight Commander of the Bath will 'come up with the rations' in due course."

Standing immediately to the left of me in the receiving line was my friend, Major General Peter Hunt, who had only recently arrived in Borneo with his Division Headquarters to relieve me of much of the more mundane work, thereby leaving me free to fight the battle against the Indonesians. Of course, he overheard all that Mountbatten had said.

Much later when I was serving in NATO, Peter Hunt was staying with Beryl and me at Fontainbleau, when the New Year's Honours List for 1967 was published. It was announced that Major General George Lea, who had inherited my policy of fighting the campaign against the Indonesians, had been appointed a Knight Commander of the Bath. Peter Hunt expressed his indignation to me in no uncertain terms. "How can anyone stoop so low and hit you below the belt in such a vengeful way?" he said.

Several years later Peter himself was to become the CGS. When he had completed his tour of duty, he was so outraged at the way his political masters were treating the Army and what their future policy was, that he refused promotion to Field Marshal on his retirement from the army. This courageous sacrifice of his went largely unnoticed for it was not 'hot' news for the media.

When I was awarded a second bar to my DSO, I received

many letters not only of congratulations, but also of anger from serving officers. One of them wrote, "I find it difficult to congratulate you on receiving an award which I consider to be meagre and shaming. I thought a year ago that you had been shamefully treated but hoped that the CB was only a necessary preliminary. Now I feel, as will so many others, humiliated and degraded on being connected, in however small a way, with those who have seen fit to recommend this miserable token of recognition."

I had been invested with a knighthood by the then Sultan of Brunei and shortly after my return to England, I was invested with a knighthood by Tunku Abdul Rahman, the Paramount Ruler of Malaya. The Tunku had asked the powers that be if I could stay on as Director of Operations, but was told that in the interests of my career it was necessary for me to gain experience of NATO, where I was to be appointed to an important post on the staff.

Before Lord Louis Mountbatten left Borneo, he and Admiral Sir Varyl Begg told me that, "In spite of the magnitude of your achievement you will receive little recognition for it and are going to be scurvily treated. There is little we can now do about it because of the attitude of the army hierarchy in Whitehall, where you have made powerful enemies. However, you are to be given an important NATO appointment, which is essential for your future prospects, because you have never been in a NATO appointment before."

This warning proved to be only too accurate. On my homecoming on leave to England I was not summoned to Whitehall for a thorough debriefing, I was simply ignored. Churchill learned after the war that gratitude is not a natural instinct of the British.

This was in stark contrast to a telegram I received some years later from a Malaysian Minister which read as follows:

174

"To: General Sir Tan Sri Walter Walker, KCB, CBE, DSO, PMN, PSNB. Please accept my heartiest congratulations on the auspicious and happy occasion of your 80th birthday. Through your great ability and leadership Sarawak was saved from the enemy. You did more for Malaysia than anybody else we can think of. May God Bless you and your family always."

Before my departure to England, the Sultan of Brunei arranged a farewell official reception for my wife and myself, which was attended by all the Brunei potentates and selected Brunei civilians. He made certain that I was given a copy of his speech. I now reproduce extracts from it:

"Speech by His Highness the Sultan of Brunei at a farewell reception to General Dato Seri Setia Walker on Wednesday, 10th March 1965.

Honoured Guests

It is now over two years since General Dato Walker arrived in the State to take over the control of the operations then proceeding against the rebels. So successful were his efforts that the forces under his command were quickly able to restore law and order and thus the State and its inhabitants were happily preserved from a long internal conflict with all the suffering that would have entailed for innocent people. It might at first have been hoped that with the restoration of peace and tranquility to Brunei, General Dato Walker would have fulfilled his mission. Unfortunately that was not to be the case. The deliberate policy of hostility towards the concept of Malaysia, a "confrontation" which resulted in increasing aggression towards our neighbour Malaysia resulted in a military threat from Indonesia which called for the most determined counter measures. It was here that General Dato Walker, as Director of Borneo Operations, took command of the situation and the manner in which these operations were conducted cannot be

175

too highly praised. The area for which he was responsible is large, the communications difficult and the initiative remained with the aggressor. I do not need to emphasise the difficulties facing General Dato Walker. I would however wish to pay tribute to the manner in which he has dealt with them.

"General Dato Walker has often told me that he is a soldier and when I have had the advantage of hearing his views on current problems he has stressed that his opinions are based on military considerations. No doubt this is true but General Dato Walker does not do justice to his own skill as a diplomat. Throughout his service as Director of Borneo Operations he has maintained close relations not only with my Government here in Brunei, but also with the Governments of our neighbouring States and the Government of the Federation of Malaysia.

"I take this opportunity therefore on my own behalf and on that of the people of Brunei to thank General Dato Walker for all that he has done for us and to wish him and Datin Walker every happiness in the future. This period in his distinguished military career General Dato Walker will not readily forget and he will follow with keen interest events in this part of the world. I look forward to the day when General Dato Walker and Datin Walker will visit the State again, they are assured of a ready welcome from us all."

Before the Sultan departed we had a short private tête-a-tête when he asked me if I had any suggestions for the future security of his State against future internal trouble. I suggested to him that it might be a good idea for him to raise a special force of retired or redundant Gurkha soldiers. But I gave him my solemn warning and this was that there must be a strict proviso that only those Gurkha soldiers with a completely stainless character in their previous Regiment should be eligible. Even then, I said, "it would be vital that the senior Gurkha Officer must have his own intelligence network and thus be in

176

a position to nip in the bud the slightest whiff of disloyalty to him and his State". I added for good measure that the Communist Party in the capital, Kathmandu, and the plains of Nepal was growing in strength and could constitute a threat. My final word of warning was that there were elements in Nepal who were stirring up trouble about Gurkhas serving a foreign power as mercenaries.

Malaysian gratitude was expressed when I received the award of Honorary Penglima Mangku Negara (PMN) – the Malaysian equivalent to a Knighthood – from the Tunku Abdul Raham in London in June 1965. I was presented with the following citation:

CITATION FOR THE AWARD OF PANGLIMA MANGKU NEGARA MALAYSIA
(TAN SRI) – PMN – 1965
MAJOR GENERAL TAN SRI SIR WALTER COLYEAR WALKER,
KCB, CBE, DSO**, PMN, PSNB

"Major General Tan Sri Walker commanded the Malaysian and Commonwealth Forces in East Malaysia since the inception of Malaysia in September 1963 and was made Director of Operations for this region in February, 1964.

"During this period of Indonesian confrontation, Major General Tan Sri Walker, with tireless energy and professional skill of the highest order, led this operation so successfully that every enemy incursion had been thrown back across the border and the territories of Sabah and Sarawak have been held intact.

"In co-ordinating the efforts of the three armed services, the police, and the civil administration, Major General Tan Sri Walker never spared himself. He toured the country extensively, often over inhospitable country.

"It was very largely due to his drive and determination that Indonesian confrontation failed militarily in East Malaysia.

"In recognition of his excellent service to Malaysia His Majesty the Yang di-Pertuan Agong has been graciously pleased to confer upon him the award of the Order of Panglima Mangku Negara (Honorary)."

On my return to England, I was soon summoned by Lord Mountbatten himself and asked to report direct to him at the office of the Chief of the Defence Staff. First, he congratulated me on what I had achieved in Borneo. He then asked me for my views on a unified command structure in the light of my practical experience of having made such a success of it in Borneo. I gave it to him in full measure and emphasised that all three Services were grossly top heavy with far too much 'top brass', at the expense of the front line soldiers, sailors and airmen. He asked me for my opinion about the calibre of young officers; those trained at the Royal Military College, Sandhurst, compared to those trained by the Royal Marines. I replied that the latter were superior, particularly the Royal Marine Commandos. The same applied to Royal Marine helicopter pilots compared with RAF helicopter pilots. As an example I told him that when I had to land on particularly 'hairy' helicopter pads deep in the jungle, I insisted on a Royal Marine helicopter pilot – such helicopter pads were known as 'pirate pads'. Often it meant descending straight down a jungle 'tunnel' with the helicopter blades almost nicking the leaves of the trees as the helicopter descended and ascended.

Next I was asked to see Healey in his office as Minister of Defence. I seemed to have made a deep impression on him when he visited me in Borneo, for he said that several important points from my briefings in Borneo had stuck in his mind. The first was that in the type of operations I had fought in Borneo, a battalion with six helicopters to hand was worth a brigade without. The second was that the army should be organised from front to rear and not from rear to front which was the present organisation. In this way the front line fighting troops and formation headquarters would receive top priority and be given the best commanders and very best equipment. What was left over would be available for static headquarters including the Ministry of Defence. This would automatically reduce the number of static headquarters and the number of 'desk warriors'. He then turned to my experience of the success of unified command in Borneo. He showed great interest and asked me to discuss the matter in detail with Fred Mulley, Minister of the Army.

I spent one and a half hours with Fred Mulley, whose questions ranged far and wide, and so interested was he in my detailed replies that he asked me to commit them to writing and produce a strictly private and confidential report for the eyes only of Mountbatten and himself. I explained to him that this would present difficulties because, strictly speaking, I should submit the report through the Army Board. However, I told him that, as Lord Mountbatten had warned me before he left Borneo, I would be shabbily treated on my return to England. His warning had proved to be only too correct, in that so far the Army Board had shown no inclination to debrief me. I would comply with his wishes. Mulley smiled and said, "We will by-pass the Army Board. I want your views, not a sanitised version."

I had my report typed in private by my daughter, who was at a secretarial school in London. I had explained to Fred Mulley that because the army hierarchy had ignored my return from Borneo, I could not be seen in the corridors of the Army hierarchy. It was therefore arranged by Mountbatten and Mulley for me to hand two copies of my report to an officer on Mountbatten's staff in the entrance hall of the Ministry of Defence. I duly carried out this mission.

Field Marshal Sir Gerald Templer contacted me and asked if I would be good enough to brief the Board of the Company, which he had joined, on my views of the situation in Borneo, Malaya, Singapore and Indonesia, from the military and political points of view and what the future prospects were likely to be.

The Field Marshal later contacted me again and said he was conducting an enquiry into the rationalisation of air power and had told the CGS, General Sir James Cassels, that he wanted my personal views on the command and control of aircraft, particularly helicopters, in Borneo. The army then acknowledged my presence in England for the first time. I received a personal message that the CGS had instructed that I was to read the directive from the Army Board on air policy. My reply was terse. I replied that Field Marshal Templer had told me he wanted my personal views in the light of my practical operational experience as Director of Operations, Borneo. Back came an official order that the CGS had directed that I was to read the army directive and an office had been set aside for me to read the directive. I knew exactly what it would contain, and having skimmed through it, I ready my newspaper.

I told Templer privately how I had employed the aircraft and helicopters under my command in Borneo, and that the key to success in the type of jungle fighting in Borneo against the Indonesians was decentralisation and flexibility and immediate availability. Often this entailed helicopters being deployed with the forward troops and maintenance carried out in forward company bases.

In the same way I broke one of the Royal Artillery sacred cows by deploying guns singly and flying them strung under helicopters to give immediate support to forward troops against a threatened invasion by the Indonesians.

There was no doubt that the Field Marshal did not require any convincing in the light of his experience of High Commissioner and Director of Operations, Malaya during the Malayan Emergency.

In my briefings to Mountbatten, Healey and Mulley and

in all my lectures, I emphasised the vital importance of the SAS and how they should and should not be deployed. Their morale, *esprit de corps* and discipline were phenomenal. To me they were worth their weight in gold and deserving of the very best equipment and training facilities. Again and again I repeated that in the type of warfare we were fighting and against the type of enemy – the Indonesians who had defeated the Dutch – and in jungle conditions over such a wide front, one SAS squadron with helicopters was worth seven hundred infantry to me.

Although the Army Board ignored me and had decided that they could do without a debriefing, I found it difficult to compete with all the invitations I received from many quarters, such as the Imperial Defence College, the Joint Services Staff College, the Army Staff College, and many study periods of the four Army Commands in the UK. There was no doubt therefore that my voice was being heard loud and clear.

My wife and I had some well earned leave to come. After leave in London, and having made this successful contact, at their request, with the then Minister of Defence, Denis Healey, and the Minister for the Army, Fred Mulley, off I went with my wife to my NATO posting at Headquarters, Allied Forces Central Europe, at Fontainbleau in France. I was appointed Deputy Chief of Staff, Plans, Operations and Intelligence.

It was while I was in AFCENT that two events occurred that could have brought my army career to an abrupt halt, had I not taken the bit between my teeth.

In July 1966, I received a letter from the Military Secretary, who informed me with some reluctance and embarrassment that No. 1 Selection Board had decided that I would have to retire from the army between March and September 1967. It was obvious to me that 'The Establishment' of the army was determined to get rid of me despite the assurances from Mountbatten, Begg, Healey and Mulley. I decided to throw down the gauntlet. It so happened that I'd read in a newspaper report that Fred Mulley was shortly to visit Paris for a military conference. I asked Mulley's Ministry if, as the senior British Army officer in the Paris area, I might pay a courtesy call on the Minister at his hotel. Mulley was only too pleased to meet me again and invited me to have coffee with him after breakfast on 27th July.

We had a pleasant and friendly conversation during which Mulley asked me if I had yet heard of my next appointment. I told him that the Army No. 1 Selection Board had decided that I was not to be promoted, and that the Military Secretary had warned me officially that I would probably have to retire from the army between March and September 1967. I showed Mulley the Military Secretary's letter. Mulley was horrified and asked if he could borrow the letter to show Healey. I had taken the precaution of making a photocopy for, if I succeeded in enlisting Mulley's support, my decision to submit a formal representation against the decision of No. 1 Selection Board, would be immensely strengthened.

I soon received an acknowledgement to my letter with the assurance that my representation would be considered by the Board at their meeting at the beginning of October. Meanwhile Mulley wrote to me in his own handwriting to confirm that he had spoken to Healey, who had promised to pursue the matter.

Healey had not only been surprised by the army's decision but shocked. In September, he informed the Army Board that my future was to be reconsidered. In October the Military Secretary informed me that I was to be considered for promotion.

I was duly promoted to Lieutenant General and appointed General Officer Commanding-in-Chief, Northern Command, England, with my Headquarters at York.

Director of Operations. Climbing into my helicopter, 1964

In helicopter with Harry Tuzo, Brigade Commander, 1964

Working in my office, Borneo, 1964

Visit to 1/7GR Kuching, with Lt. Col. Carroll, Major Kelly
and Mr Henry, Commissioner Sarawak Constabulary, 1964

With my wife and daughter, official residence, Brunei 1964

Meeting with PM of Malaysia (Tunku Abdul Rahman), 1965

Farewell visit to 7GR, Borneo, 1965

Chapter 17

HAROLD JAMES, MC, AND DENIS SHEIL-SMALL, MC,
Authors of *The Undeclared War*. Published in 1971

I must digress for a short while in order to introduce Denis Sheil-Small.

Denis won his spurs in Burma shortly after my battalion had crossed the River Irrawaddy during the pursuit of the retreating Japanese. I was expanding the bridgehead, and advancing by careful bounds in the knowledge that the Japanese would also be retreating by similar tactical bounds.

On reaching an obvious tactical feature, I deployed Denis Sheil-Small's company to reconnoitre, occupy and consolidate a ridge on my left flank. This was to prove to be the first battle of Milaungbya, referred to in the Citation of my first DSO.

A short time later I set forth on foot with my escort to check Denis Sheil-Small's company dispositions. As I was returning to my battalion HQ, Japanese artillery shells and machine gun fire struck his exposed platoons which, of course, had not yet had time to dig in. About three hundred Japanese broke out from their concealed and natural cover and assaulted Denis's company. His wireless set was smashed so he could not call for artillery close support.

However by this time I had already reached my headquarters and had been watching the Jap assault. I immediately called for artillery close support fire to break up the Jap assault. I had to take a calculated risk and the artillery battery in my support responded. Some of their shells burst on my Gurkhas who, of course, had not yet been able to dig in, and sadly several were killed and wounded. But all three platoons stood steadfast while the artillery shells struck immediately in front of Denis's company position, and enough Japs were killed and wounded to force them to retreat. Their assault had been repulsed with significant losses.

The Brigadier had been watching the battle and was as pleased as I was at the steadfastness, stubbornness and courage of my Gurkhas.

I wasted no time in submitting citations for gallantry, including an immediate Military Cross for Denis Sheil-Small and another for one of his Gurkha officers.

Now to concentrate on the subject highlighted in the heading of this chapter.

In the Acknowledgements of *The Undeclared War*, the authors stated:

"This book could not have been written without the most generous help and encouragement from a great number of people. We should first of all like to thank most warmly General Sir Walter Walker, KCB, CBE, DSO, for letting us have a great deal of information and for introductions to numerous contacts."

In introducing me, the authors wrote: "Walker is probably the greatest jungle fighter of the post-war period. He is also a man of considerable energy, insisting on hard and imaginative work from his officers and men. His Military Intelligence Officer once remarked: 'I used to be rather ashamed, as a much younger man, of feeling tired after a hard day flying with the General all over Borneo. He would visit various commands, making suggestions, listening to problems, then back to headquarters for a cocktail party with local politicians to play his diplomatic role. He still would look remarkably fresh. And after the party, back to work with his light burning well into the early hours.'

"In April 1963, one of General Walker's Staff Officers telephoned him at dawn: 'Tebedu Police Post has been captured, sir, and all the police taken prisoner.' First reports in this type of campaign are often inaccurate and make the situation seem a lot worse than it really is. The General was fully committed at the time to a big hunt for Affendi, leader of the Brunei Revolt. His only reserve was B Company, King's Own Yorkshire Light Infantry, but he decided to take a calculated risk and send it to Sarawak. The company was in the jungle, and an Auster was flown to the area to summon the troops by loud-hailer to a rendezvous on a main track.

"Walker also decided to send 846 Royal Naval Squadron to Kuching, but the Staff Officer told him that the squadron was carrying out aircraft maintenance, and in fact one helicopter's engine had been removed for a check. 'How long will the squadron take to get operational?' asked Walker. 'It will take a week, sir.' 'Make it a night', said Walker.

"Undeterred, the Naval ground crews did a quick change and all six whirlwinds flew down to Kuching the next day, deliberately flying over the town in display formation to boost morale.

"A third and unique intelligence source was initiated by Mr. Fisher, resident of the Fourth Division, and Walker's brother-in-law. The use of irregular forces in the later stages of the Brunei Revolt had brought the whole problem of border surveillance into focus. Fisher convinced the General that a force could be raised of 'one thousand pairs of eyes and ears', but Walker suffered innumerable frustrations at all levels of government, police, and GHQ before he was able to persuade Sarawak to raise the Border Scouts. The Sarawak Government had to sell some shares to finance the project, and an order was promulgated on 10 May 1963.

"A force of this nature required a commander with unusual talents and with experience in dealing with indigenous tribes. Walker decided that Major John Cross was the man for

189

the job. He had already proved himself in the Malayan jungle during the Emergency. Walker impressed on Cross that if civilian morale broke down confrontation would succeed. If the Border Scouts were effective, however, civilian morale would not break down, and confrontation would fail. 'That is why I called you to take on this post' Walker concluded. 'Now get on with it'.

"The badge devised for the uniformed Scouts was a Hornbill, worn on the left arm. Cross put new words to the Scarlet Pimpernel jingle:

> He wanders here, he wanders there,
> The Hornbill wanders everywhere,
> So seldom in, so often out,
> That damned elusive Border Scout."

An uneasy truce ended the first year of 1963 of operations in Borneo. The authors of this book reproduced the statement I made: "'A year', wrote General Walker at the time, 'which began with the end of a revolution and ended with the beginning of an undeclared war. No one knows where this exercise in brinkmanship will end. We are sure only of one thing: we have set our faces to the enemy, and until more reasonable counsels prevail, we shall not look back.'

"March 1965, saw the end of General Walker's tour as Director of Borneo Operations. It was a sad moment for troops and civilians. In those first years of confrontation he had been the prime architect of the solid resistance built up by the Security Forces, and the instigator of the aggressive spirit which was apparent in all engagements fought against the Indonesians. He was a soldier's general, with the knack of endearing himself to the local people as well. It was due to his drive and determination above all that confrontation had so far failed."

Admiral Sir Varyl Begg paid frequent visits to me and he and Lady Begg always stayed with my wife and me for several days at a time. He and I spent each evening and late into the night sitting on the verandah discussing every aspect of the operational situation. We became firm friends and Varyl Begg never failed to show that he had complete confidence in me and gave me his constant support. This was in sharp contrast to my other superiors in Singapore and London, who had no jungle warfare operation experience and never failed to accuse me of 'crying wolf'. Of course they did not know that I already had my own secret sources of information in the form of the matchless SAS patrols across the Indonesian side of the border. My intelligence of the enemy's movements was therefore far more up to date than the information passed to me by 'Signal Intelligence' (SigInt). Varyl Begg visited each brigade in turn and expected to be given a briefing by the brigade commander himself and then by each battalion, company and platoon commander. He soon became extremely well versed in the tactics of jungle warfare.

I well remember the occasion when a certain brigade commander, who had assumed command about a month before but nevertheless had had enough time to play himself in, turned to his brigade major and said: "You can now brief the Commander-in-Chief on the up-to-date situation." Varyl Begg snapped back: "I want your personal and verbal up to date assessment of the situation and not that prepared by your staff." The brigadier gave an unconvincing and mediocre performance and was unable to answer Varyl Begg's searching questions. By this time Varyl Begg had paid me a number of visits and toured the whole length and depth of the one thousand miles of my frontier of responsibility. Accordingly he had become completely au fait with all the jungle warfare techniques that had been evolved.

A great supporter of mine and an old friend was Admiral Begg's Chief of Staff – Major General Brian Wyldbore-Smith. He never said no and always cut through the bureaucracy in Singapore to accede to my requests in double quick time.

At the beginning of 1964, I was visited by Mr. Peter Thornycroft (later Lord Thornycroft), the Secretary of State for Defence and Mr. James Ramsden, the Secretary of State for War. After taking them for a day's tour of my operational area, I gave them a detailed briefing in view of the fact that it was obvious to me that what they had been told in London and Singapore bore little resemblance to the true and up-to-date operation situation, and I also spelt out my deficiencies of manpower and equipment on land, sea and in the air. I particularly emphasised that unified command had been established in the nick of time, and explained why this was so. I received a smile of approval from Admiral Sir Varyl Begg. To rub it in I said that all I had to do was to deal direct with Admiral Begg through his Chief of Staff, Brian Wyldbore-Smith, and my requests were dealt with by return. This cut out having to deal with three separate headquarters, army, navy and air, and achieved speed of action instead of interminable delays.

I emphasised the vital role being performed by the SAS, who, I said, were in a class of their own and must not be denied their essential requirements of equipment; nor should they ever be lacking in manpower. As far as I was concerned they were worth their weight in gold, and no economies should ever be exercised at their expense. Their present strength should never be subjected to manpower cuts.

At the end of my briefing Thornycroft said to me: "You have given me a detailed and clear briefing and explained what your deficiencies are, for which I am most grateful. But you have not said what your own personal deficiency might be. I am sure there is something which you must lack." I looked at Admiral Begg who nodded his approval for me to speak out. I said that there were no hotels in Brunei and consequently all visitors were accommodated and fed by me and the High Commissioner. The latter received a handsome entertainment allowance whereas I did not receive one penny piece in spite of repeated requests through army hierarchy. The reply I had received was that the appointment of Director of Operations did not exist in the army establishment. Thornycroft said: "How scandalous. Please give me a message pad and I will draft a personal signal to London immediately. You can rest assured that there will be no delay in your receiving an entertainment allowance compatible with your vitally important appointment, and backdated from the day you assumed command."

At this time I was visited by Denis Healey who was the Labour Party Opposition spokesman on defence. Varyl Begg accompanied him throughout his visit. I gave him a detailed briefing in my headquarters and was impressed with his questions which was somewhat of a change. I said to him "You are coming to dinner tonight and will meet my wife and Lady Begg. There will be ample opportunity for more talk with the Commander-in-Chief and myself." After dinner we all sat on the outside verandah and Admiral Begg said to me: "You take Healey into a corner of your verandah and let him ask you anything he likes. I will stay with your other guests. Unless I am mistaken you have made a great impression on him." I replied that he had obviously done more homework than most.

Healey's opening gambit to me was, "Leaving aside the bullshit you gave me at your briefing today, I would like to get down to the facts." I thought to myself – here comes another ignoramus. My immediate response was, "Those were the facts and nothing but the facts. I will be accompanying you and the Commander-in-Chief on a helicopter tour of the frontier tomorrow and you can land anywhere you like and check the facts for yourself with the commanders on the spot of any rank – senior or the most junior." Healey asked me many searching questions which I made no attempt to shirk, but gave him the truth, the whole truth and nothing but the truth. He seemed well satisfied and also converted.

The following day we visited the forward troops and I gave Healey a free hand to question whoever he wished to grill. By the very nature of his questions, there was no doubt that Healey had a good grasp of the nuts and bolts of the defence implications as they existed in the jungle. At the end of the day, Varyl Begg remarked to me: "I think you impressed Healey with the extent of your expertise, and he will return to London well versed in your conduct of the war and the problems involved."

Some time later he was to prove a great ally when my future was in the balance, and he was Minister of Defence in a recently elected Labour Government. This relationship continued when I arrived home on leave and called on him at his office. We next met on his visit to Northern Command, York, when I was General Officer Commanding-in-Chief. Healey asked me if I had any particular points that I wished to bring to his personal notice as Minister of Defence. I replied that I had a number of points, particularly recruiting. We went into the control tower at the airfield and he asked me to speak while he jotted down notes. The substance of this meeting is recounted in Chapter 20 headed "Northern Command".

This camaraderie lasted until shortly after I assumed the appointment of Commander-in-Chief Allied Forces Northern Europe in 1969. The rupture occurred over a documentary film that I made with Tyne Tees Television about NATO, which is recounted in the chapter, 'A Day in the Life of a General'. Healey objected to it on phoney political grounds. In doing so he showed himself to be a most sensitive and thin-skinned politician. My warning in the film was too strong meat for him.

The next time I 'fell from grace' with Healey was after I retired when I found the country in such an appalling mess that I wrote to one of the tabloid newspapers and expressed my views. As a result I received an enormous amount of fan mail – each letter enclosing money – asking me to give a lead. With the urging and backing of some prominent figures, I set up a country-wide organisation to anticipate and prepare for various eventualities. I was smeared, particularly by the trade unions and left wingers, with the accusation that I was establishing a 'private army'.

Later Healey was promoted to the House of Lords and it was in late March 1995 that he took part in a televised discussion with the Minister for Foreign Affairs – Douglas Hurd – and others. He showed his left wing colours when he criticised the amount of money being spent on sophisticated armaments now that the Cold War was over. The Cold War may be over but new threats – including nuclear and chemical warfare – are appearing over the horizon in the shape of Iraq, Iran, North Korea and the Islamic Fundamentalists, to mention but a few. Furthermore, Russia would certainly become a potent threat again if the fanatical extreme nationalist, Valadimir Zhirinovsky, were to come to power. He regards as his destiny ruling the Kremlin as a dictator and would control the world's second largest nuclear arsenal, still targeted at cities such as London, Paris and Washington.

Healey's memory is short and he has no sense of history.

My first official visit from a minister of the new Labour Government was Mr. Fred Mulley, Healey's Deputy of State for Defence and Army Minister. I gave him a detailed briefing during which I explained and emphasised that the time had come for the British Government to give a lead to the National Defence Committee in Kuala Lumpur, Malaya (now Malaysia) by authorising me to conduct carefully controlled and limited cross-border operations against the TNI. Following Admiral Sir Varyl Begg's instructions I gave him my appreciation of what the future situation would be were I not to be given such authority.

Fred Mulley was a wartime sergeant and prisoner of war, whom I found intelligent and certainly able to ask me searching questions. At firs he argued against my proposal but I did not find it too difficult to state bluntly what the penalty would be in the short and long term future were I to be denied my request, which was supported to the hilt by the Commander-in-Chief, Far East. Mulley, of course, could not commit himself for he had to make a full report to Healey who, in turn, would put the proposal to the Cabinet.

I was careful not to reveal the fact that SAS four-man patrols were already across the border in a reconnaissance role and for several months had been sending back vital information. The TNI used rivers as their main highway so these were being watched with particular care, as were all the tracks.

I gave Mulley a fairly comprehensive tour of the operational area which enabled him to meet commanders at all levels and get a feeling of the jungle conditions. I liked him immensely and we got on very well indeed. He, like Healey, was also to prove a staunch ally in the days to come.

Peter Dickens sent me an autographed copy of his fascinating and brilliant book, with this inscription: "General Sir Walter Walker – with deep respect." He also enclosed a letter saying: "I send you this book with profound respect for your great achievement, but also with apologies and regret for not having obtained your help in writing it." In fact his letter was returned to him because my wife and I had moved from Somerset to Wiltshire.

Peter Dickens deserves the highest accolade for having written such a masterly book which succeeds in penetrating the innermost recesses, not only of the matchless SAS, but also of the conduct of the Borneo Campaign. It takes the Senior Service to produce such a remarkable achievement! As the blurb on the dust cover relates, his book "brings vividly to life the danger, tension and elation of jungle fighting". He has a rare perceptive insight into what motivates the sheer innate quality of this very rare breed of elite fighters – the SAS – a regiment without equal, a squadron which I had the honour to have under my command when I was Director of Borneo Operations. Their long-term future must never be in lingering doubt, as it was at one time by the 'ceasefire soldiers' in the corridors of power in London.

In my briefings of visiting potentates I sang their praises and stressed the vital importance of providing them with the best possible equipment not only to provide me with information, but also to enable them to carry out their demanding role of living amongst the local tribes and performing their skills of medicine, language, diplomacy and improving their quality of life in the remote jungle. Until top secret 'CLARET' cross-border operations were sanctioned, I could not, of course, reveal that I already had four-man SAS patrols across the border in an 'eyes and ears' role.

Peter Dickens pays me a handsome tribute in his book:

"Major General Walter Walker was appointed Director of Operations and rarely can a general have been so absolutely right for a task and been given it. He was a fighting general who won his battles, fierce and aggressive like his Gurkha soldiers with most of his active experience having been in the jungles of Burma and Malaya. Walker was also a soldier's general, that high accolade which meant, in his case, that he drove his men hard but himself harder and that they mattered to him and knew it. With those at the head of affairs such as governors, administrators, police chiefs of the three territories he could be embarrassingly terse when they failed to see things his way. Yet he was also essentially an English gentleman: polite, interested in others' opinions and capable of inspiring that cooperation among his colleagues which was vital in the circumstances."

It was my original intention to parachute SAS to secure those vital airstrips that were vulnerable to Indonesian airborne assault. This would entail parachuting into trees to restore the position. But their highly professional Commanding Officer, Lieutenant Colonel John Woodhouse, persuaded me that if I was to dominate the jungle over such a long frontier, he suggested that I should give him the role of deploying the SAS into four-man patrols on the frontier itself, where they could stay for long periods. He went on to explain that they would befriend the local tribal villagers, whose land extended across the frontier, and thereby obtain early warning of the movements of the Indonesians. In other words the tribal people, carefully briefed and guided by the SAS, would become my eyes and ears.

I had no hesitation in agreeing one hundred per cent with John Woodhouse's proposal, for it fulfilled four of the six ingredients of success that I had already promulgated, namely: unified operations; timely and accurate information, which meant a first-class intelligence machine; speed, mobility and flexibility; and hearts and minds, namely winning the local people's trust, confidence and respect.

I was not at all sceptical about launching the SAS Squadron deep into the jungle on such a wide front to fulfil this role, because I could judge a true professional commander when I met one, and John Woodhouse was such a soldier to his finger tips. Furthermore, when his squadron finally returned to base, I addressed them in these words: "I should like to congratulate you on your excellent performance. You have been deployed in your classic role over a 900-mile front to provide me with my eyes and ears. Above all the work of your signallers and medical orderlies has been quite outstanding and they have made a significant contribution both to our Intelligence sources and to our efforts to win the support and loyalty of the tribes. We have enjoyed having you with us and hope, should the need arise, that you will come back."

When the Defence Minister, Peter Thornycroft, visited Borneo, I made sure that he saw for himself the value of the SAS in at least one of their roles. His attention had been carefully drawn to the matter lest it should escape him; and I voiced a much quoted tribute, which, because it is often misquoted, is given here in full:

"I regard 70 troopers of the SAS (one squadron) as being as valuable to me as 700 infantry in the role of hearts and minds, border surveillance, early warning, stay behind, and eyes and ears with a sting."

"If an SAS trooper takes that to mean that he is as good as ten private soldiers, even he would be well advised to say so with caution, but it was certainly true that infantry skills did not match those concentrated in just one four-man SAS patrol. In the First and Second Divisions, where the infantry were watching the border, many more men were needed. But there they were also guarding it, which the SAS could not do. The equation fitted better in the wilder parts, where if the infantry had been strung out along the border, they would not have been strong enough to defeat a determined probe at one point; it was the SAS who enabled them to remain in reserve, fully mobile and ready to move in sufficient force against a known threat. The SAS knew perfectly well that they were only part of a team and, while being trained to a pitch that gave them calm self confidence in performing their own tasks, were not given to idle boasting that they could outdo, or even equal, those of others; besides they never knew when they might need the others' help. Still, it was pleasant to have such a compliment on the record, and from a man whom they had learnt to respect very highly indeed.

"General Walker's good opinion also had practical effects. He continued to press strongly for a third squadron to be formed, but that would take time. The limitless Borneo frontier could absorb more SAS or SAS-type men than would ever be available, so it was also decided to train the Guards Independent Parachute Company in the SAS jungle role, with the wild Third Division particularly in mind. Later, the Gurkha Independent Parachute Company too was retrained and added to the strength."

I have dealt with cross border operations, 'CLARET' in some detail elsewhere in this book. But I must give John Woodhouse the credit which is his due. When I was in a position to expand and extend the tri-Service operations, the time came when there was less need for the SAS on the British side of the frontier. It was John Woodhouse who was quick to suggest to me that the correct deployment of his SAS was now on the Indonesian side of the border where, he said, they could harass the enemy and disrupt incursions before they started. I knew only too well the political obstacles that would have to be overcome before such a role would ever be sanctioned. But, I thought to myself, there was the world of difference between harassing and disrupting the enemy, as opposed to lying doggo on the other side of the border and blending with the jungle, in an eyes and ears role, but without a sting. Furthermore, small parties of SAS, each equipped with their own sophisticated wireless sets, would be able to transmit vital intelligence reports swiftly to their own headquarters, and thus give battalion and brigade commanders – not to mention Woodhouse and me – early warning of the movements of the enemy.

What now follows shows that Peter Dickens had a clear and astute instinct into the ramifications involved if political approval of limited cross border operations was ever to be obtained. "The successful defence of Malaysian Borneo depended on the Step-Up drill for flying infantry in quickly when an incursion was detected, and it was constantly practised and improved. But a still more effective way of achieving security was indicated by a glance at the map of the two main rivers. General Walker saw clearly that if the enemy were to be hit in his own bases and have his supply route constantly interrupted, he would be kept busy defending himself and have little inclination for raiding across the border. That, however, would be a bold political as well as military move which excited shock and dismay at all levels up to the highest. But nobody could deter Walker when he knew he was right, and he pressed the case with importunate vigour. Woodhouse, quietly gratified, ordered the SAS to make all preparations now."

During a redeployment of the SAS, Peter Dickens relates an amusing incident: "Daubney's patrol, staging through an up-country airstrip, arrived by chance just before General Walker himself and were hustled behind a hut by local officialdom as being no fit objects for a discriminating and potentially critical eye and nose. But the General had already spotted them from his helicopter, for they were undeniably conspicuous, and Hartill relates, 'He got out and made a bee-line for us, asked who we were and what we'd been doing, listened to what we told him and then went to meet the officers. A really nice fellow.' A soldier's general; and an effective one too, for 1965 had come and Malaysia was far from crushed."

Peter Dickens concluded his description of my tour of duty as Director of Operations with these words: "The decisive period began with Major-General Walter Walker's relief by Major General George Lea as Director of Operations. This event was hard luck on the former because it was he who had launched the offensive policy in principle and achieved the means for implementing it; political backing, reinforcements, the initiation of cross-border operations, and, above all, bringing his troops to such a pitch of professional excellence and morale that Lea was amazed and delighted when he met them.

"Walker had successfully defended Malaysian Borneo, but left under a cloud nevertheless; mainly because of his efforts as Major-General, the Brigade of Gurkhas, in trying to save them from the economic axe. His bitterness at that threat was not founded just on sentiment but on a lifetime's experience of their enormous value to Britain, culminating right here in Borneo, where he put them in the forefront of the battle and they well repaid his trust. He was allowed to creep home without the knighthood which precedent should have accorded him, despite the enthusiastic backing of important people such as Healey, Mountbatten and Begg without whose help he might even have been retired."

What Peter Dickens and others did not know was that

John Woodhouse presented me with a silver statuette of a fully equipped SAS trooper mounted on an ebony plinth with a silver plaque inscribed as follows:

To Combritbor
Borneo l963
(HQ 17 Gurkha Div)
From All Ranks
22 Special Air Service Regiment

In presenting this to me in front of his troopers, he said: "I know generals are not supposed to accept presentations. But we have noted that you, like us, do not always abide by rules and regulations. We have been careful, therefore, not to include your name in the inscription."

It was a moving moment.

Peter Dickens concludes with these words: "Lieutenant Colonel John Woodhouse left the Army in the New Year for other activities. The General tried hard to persuade the powers that be that they could not afford to lose Woodhouse. His advocacy was ineffective, perhaps because he too was a man who did his duty as he saw it, without fear, favour or affection; a fine moral principle but one that is often too disturbing for establishments to live with."

I tried my level best to recommend John Woodhouse for the award of the DSO, but the powers that be ruled that the SAS were a separate entity and that such a recommendation had to be initiated and processed through quite separate channels.

"Walker said on leaving: 'It is true that we have imposed the present lull on Sukarno and that the Borneo frontier is under our control. I don't think the Indonesians will risk all-out war, but I am sure they will increase the scale, tempo and intensity of raids and terrorism, and it will be a major tragedy if a complacent mood that the crisis is passing develops. We must not underrate the Indonesian soldier, who is tough and well trained, and the threat of the Clandestine Communist Organisation though now controlled could explode if a large-scale Indonesian incursion succeeded in setting up a puppet regime in a pocket area.'

"As October 1964 drew to a close, a gradual turnover of SAS Squadrons took place. During it Lieutenant Colonel John Woodhouse went on his last operational patrol before leaving the SAS and the Army at the end of the year. Sadness was evident then, despite the boisterous fun enjoyed at a hail and farewell party for those of the two Squadrons not in the jungle. No one could fully believe that the man they all regarded as the father of the modern Regiment would soon be gone."

Before John Woodhouse left Brunei, I visited his headquarters to say goodbye to him. Peter Dickens recounts this occasion: "General Walker thanked Woodhouse for his great contribution to the Borneo campaign and the border peoples, 'among whom you and your men are worshipped'. And he added: 'You enjoy a unique, unchallenged reputation as an expert in counter-guerrilla warfare and it is my hope, shared by many others, that the powers that be will recognise this and continue to employ you in this sphere'."

Talk about Whitehall bureaucracy at its worst! I would dearly like to have some of those Whitehall 'desk wallahs' under my command in thick jungle against a first class cruel and savage enemy such as the Japanese, or even against barbaric and highly trained guerrillas. It is like night fighting – unseen and unheard.

In August 1964, I was recommended by Lieutenant Colonel John Woodhouse for the honour of being made an Honorary Member of the SAS Association. I reproduce his letter verbatim:

"Major T. Burt, MBE, TD
Secretary
SAS Regimental Association,
Officers Mess, 22 SAS Regt. Hereford
Agenda: Honorary Membership SAS Association
Major General W. C. Walker, CB, CBE, DSO.
Ref: Your letter of 24 August 64.

1. In 1962 22 SAS Regt. proposed that Maj Gen. Yarborough Commanding General US Special Forces was made an honorary member of the SAS Association. This proposal was approved and I have no doubt has done much to assist the close liaison we continue to maintain with Special Forces. Gen. Yarborough is still in the same appointment and may well achieve higher rank in due course.

2. I now wish to propose a second name for this honour – Major General Walter Walker Director of Operations in Borneo. He has since Jan. 1963 when SAS troops first came under his command consistently supported the Regiment to an extent much beyond what we would expect as a right. When we have asked from time to time for unusual concessions which have caused extra work for the Staff or MOD he has always taken our side, and when necessary argued our case with higher authorities with a zeal which has probably made him unpopular with everyone except ourselves. He has shown quite exceptional interest in the welfare of all SAS troops.

3. On the operational side he was the first to appreciate the value of 22 SAS in the roles we have developed and he has consistently, forcibly, and cogently argued and put over the importance of the SAS to Cabinet Ministers, and senior officers of all the Services. The expansion and increased importance of 22 SAS Regt has been due in no small measure to this support. Last and not least General Walker together perhaps with General

Sir Charles Harington are the only Generals all ranks in 22 SAS whole-heartedly respect and like!

I realise the importance of restricting this honour very severely but request the Committee to consider this proposal favourably.

Lt. Col. J. Woodhouse
Commanding."

BRIGADIER E. E. SMITH, CBE, DSO.

Brigadier 'Birdie' Smith, was the author of the book, *East of Katmandu – The Story of the 7th Duke of Edinburgh's Own Gurkha Rifles, Volume II 1948-1973*, published in 1976.

I had the honour of being Colonel of this Regiment for eleven years, 1964-1975. At his request I took over the colonelcy from Field Marshal Sir Gerald Templer.

A helicopter crash during the campaign in Sarawak, Borneo, threatened to end Birdie's life and his career as a soldier. Although he lost his right arm and had to be evacuated to England where he had to spend many months in hospital and at the rehabilitation centre, Headley Court, through sheer guts and typical courage he pulled through, passed the medical board, and was rewarded with the appointment of Commanding Officer of the 1/2nd King Edward VII's Own Gurkha Rifles in Borneo, Brunei and Hong Kong. He succeeded me as Colonel of the 7th Duke of Edinburgh's Own Gurkha Rifles, by which time he had been promoted to Brigadier.

The flyleaf of his book has this to say: "General Sir Walter Walker, a former Colonel of the Regiment and Commander British Forces Borneo, has contributed a characteristically hard hitting foreword that bears full testimony to the valour and achievement of the 7th Duke of Edinburgh's Own Gurkha Rifles."

The Chairman of the History Committee ends the Preface with these words: "The Foreword has been written by the Colonel of the Regiment whose own service during the period of this history included, in Malaya and Borneo, command of a Gurkha Battalion, a Gurkha Brigade, the Gurkha Division and the appointment of Director of Operations Borneo. Later he was to become Army Commander Northern Command in the United Kingdom and to conclude his thirty-nine years' service in one of the key NATO appointments that of Commander-in-Chief, Allied Forces Northern Europe. It is a generally accepted fact that there is no officer serving or retired who has a greater knowledge and experience of the type of active service operations upon which the Regiment has found itself engaged during most of the twenty-five years covered by this story, than General Sir Walter Walker."

I started off the Foreword to this book with these words:

"My last and pleasant task after eleven years as Colonel of the Regiment is to write the Foreword to this latest edition of the Regimental History. It is fitting that my successor, Brigadier 'Birdie' Smith, should be the author. The Regiment and the Regimental Association owe him a debt of gratitude for the way he tells the story and the stirring story he tells.

"Not many officers, one month after their twenty-first birthday, have been awarded the Distinguished Service Order and few have won it on the same day as their Commanding Officer in a battle, moreover, which was awarded to the Regiment as one of its Battle Honours – 'Tavoleto' – one of the few in any war to be earned by a single Battalion. This was thirty-one years ago, in Italy, during the assault on the Gothic Line held by the Germans. Since then the Regiment has continued to distinguish itself and has played a leading part in operations which, unlike the Vietnam fiasco, were so successful that they avoided a tragedy that could have fallen on a whole corner of a Continent."

207

In his chapter on the confrontation in Borneo, the text has this to say: "On 19 December 1962, Major General Walter Walker was appointed Commander British Forces Borneo, an appointment that was greeted with joy and acclaim by all, and by the Brigade of Gurkhas in particular. No General in the British Army had so much experience of fighting guerrillas in the jungles of south east Asia and if anyone was going to clear up the situation in Brunei, and probably neighbouring Sabah and Sarawak where rumblings of revolt were beginning to be heard, then it was General Walker. He made his intentions clear from the start: Brunei was to be rid of the TNKU rebels before the official formation of Malaysia, planned for August 1963."

As the first year of the campaign drew to a close, the author wrote: "At the end of 1963, the Director of Operations, General Walker, wrote: 'A year which began with the end of a revolution and ended with the beginning of an undeclared war.'

As the end of my tour of duty came to a close, the author wrote: "The fortunes of the combatants had changed and the Indonesian border terrorists, supported by their armed forces, could no longer probe into Sarawak or Sabah with impunity, nor indeed could they expect to be left alone in their bases and camps if these were located near the border. The man who had done most to bring this change (CLARET) was the Director of Operations, Major-General Walter Walker. It was time now for him to hand over after two arduous and exacting years in the appointment: two years during which he had not spared himself in any way or at any time, working long hours at his desk, probing for new solutions to the 'undeclared war', making regular visits to the many units and sub units dotted around North Borneo, attending numerous conferences in East and West Malaysia, briefing the stream of important visitors who by their very presence added to his considerable burdens and, occasionally, helped to resolve the difficulties that beset him.

There was never any let up for the Director of Operations nor did he expect there to be.

"General Walter Walker had laid the foundation for the final victory that was to come under his successor, Major-General George Lea. Not unnaturally, the Regiment had taken great pride in the Colonel's achievements in Borneo and were disappointed when he had to wait a further two years before official recognition of his leadership was forthcoming in the shape of a much deserved but belated KCB.

"It was typical of General Walker that his farewell message to his troops contained a warning as well as expressing his gratitude to the Security Forces who had served him so well. 'I caution you to be on your guard. Do not slacken. Our best contribution to peace is to convince the Indonesians that aggression will fail, no matter in what form it may come. This requires the best efforts of everyone of you. I hope you will succeed. Good luck to you all.'

MAJOR GENERAL CORRAN PURDON
Author of *LIST THE BUGLE – REMINISCENCES OF AN IRISH SOLDIER* published in 1993.

The author of this book was one of my best Battalion Commanders in Borneo, a charming man and a great soldier, who was absolutely without fear. Few, if any, can match his active service experience in so many corners of the world.

He sent me an autographed copy of his fascinating book, with this inscription:

"General Sir Walter Walker, KCB, CBE, DSO.

Remembering great times under your inspiring leadership in Borneo, your victorious campaign.

The Commanding Officer of your 'White Gurkhas', with warmest good wishes. Corran"

We first met when he was a Major on the staff at GHQ Far East Land Forces, Singapore, filling the appointment of DAAG (Deputy Assistant Adjutant General). He describes this occasion as follows:

"Another interesting assignment I had was to organise under the direction of Brigadier Walter Walker, the equivalent of the Westbury Regular Commissions Board for Gurkhas and Malays. This was the first time that I met the dynamic fighting soldier who was to be my General eight years later during confrontation with Indonesia in Borneo. Among the successful candidates was a young Rifleman Lalbahadur Pun who, after completing his course at Sandhurst, went on to receive a Regular Commission into the 2nd (King Edward VII's Own) Gurkhas (The Sirmoor Rifles). He was to be decorated with the OBE, the Military Cross, be ADC to General Walker in Borneo and become Commanding Officer of the Brigade of Gurkhas Depot as a lieutenant colonel.

"Before I left England for Hong Kong, arrangements had been made for my battalion to be trained, a company at a time, at the Jungle Warfare School at Kota Tinggi in Johore, Malaysia.

"Shortly after my arrival I went off to the Jungle Warfare School in Malaysia to get back into the operational groove and to see my boys learning all the jungle techniques and tactics.

"I attended an official cocktail party where I was talking to Lady Walker, wife of Major General Sir Walter Walker. When Lady Walker heard that I and my battalion were training for the war in Borneo she took me along to her husband whom I had not met since the Malayan Emergency. General Walker has always been a hero of mine. He is a tremendous leader. All he wanted from the units he commanded was efficiency, no bluffing and a bit of dash and personality, and regiments that provided that mixture were sure to find his approval. General Walker was Director of Borneo Operations and I asked him

210

where we were to serve. Was it to be Sarawak, Brunei or Sabah? The General told me that he had not yet decided for various reasons but he then and there wrote me a chit authorising me to fly out to the theatre of operations and to visit certain battalions, which he specified, and which were operating in each of the three main states, Sabah, Brunei and Sarawak.

"Prior to our arrival in Borneo, and because in all the towns of Sarawak there were known to be cells of the Clandestine Communist Organisation, all licences for twelve-bore shotguns had been cancelled – all 8,500 of them – and most of these weapons had been successfully collected by the Security Forces. This process was code named Operation Parrot. In the Third Division these shotguns and other recovered weapons were held in corrugated buildings separated from the main road only by a single-strand barbed-wire fence about ten feet in height. Special Branch told us that the CCO were very much alive in our area and I wanted these weapons out of the way before they tried to get hold of them. Our police chief was away and I could get absolutely nowhere in persuading the police to move them.

"I decided to take responsibility myself. However, General Walter Walker was paying us one of his welcome visits so, to salve my conscience I told him my problem and what I intended to do. It was typical of him that he immediately and wholeheartedly supported me.

"General Walter Walker came to see us and I took him to see Niall Ryan's platoon, then stationed at Tepoi. Niall had been at Sandhurst with one of the General's sons and rather to my surprise, on being introduced to our awe-inspiring Director of Operations said, 'How is he, Sir? Is he still bluffing his way?' However, the General loved it and was much amused by this fine, big, soft-spoken southern Irish boy – one of my very best platoon commanders.

"By now my time in command was coming to an end and I felt very, very sad at the thought of leaving my wonderful battalion.

"I said my farewells to everyone. This I found very hard, more especially when old friends took me by the hand and said, 'We hate to see you go, Sir.'

"Before I went to board the aircraft from Singapore, I was handed the following message from General Walker:

"From D of Ops. On relinquishing command of your white Gurkhas I would like you to know that you and your distinguished battalion have exceeded my expectations and added great renown to your already high reputation. Thank you for everything. Bon Voyage and best wishes for the future. I rely on you to spread the gospel in the UK."

GENERAL SIR PETER DE LA BILLIERE, KCB, KBE, DSO, MC.

His Autobiography *LOOKING FOR TROUBLE – SAS TO GULF COMMAND* was published in 1994.

He very kindly autographed my copy with these words:

"To Walter Walker
To a great Commander, leader and solder.
Thank you for your support of my Regiment.
Peter de la Billiere."

His 'A' Squadron SAS arrived in Borneo in June 1964, to take over from 'D' Squadron, who had had a gruelling six months tour and operated brilliantly, as I have described earlier. At that time his Commanding Officer was John Woodhouse. I now quote from his book.

"As soon as I arrived in Brunei I therefore went to see the Director of Operations, Major-General Walter Walker, at

212

his headquarters on Labuan Island, off the coast of Sabah, just north of Brunei. A remarkable Gurkha officer, Walker was tall, spare, dark-haired and energetic, with a tongue as sharp as his mind, but always prepared to hear what one had to say. At that date he was one of the few senior officers who did understand the SAS: having seen how effectively our people could operate, he had become a stalwart supporter, and consistently battled with the system to obtain everything we needed. He it was who made the famous remark, towards the end of the campaign, that in Borneo one SAS squadron was worth ten infantry battalions, because the intelligence which we provided enabled him to make full use of his other forces."

Peter's first tour with his 'A' Squadron ended in October 1965. At that time he was still a bachelor but very much in love with a girl in England. He describes his feeling as follows: "I headed home in a fever of anticipation, not even sure that she would be prepared to see me; but I was winged on my way by a general personal signal from the Director of Operations, Walter Walker, praising the contribution of the Squadron and sending 'thanks for a job most splendidly done'."

Peter's 'D' Squadron returned to Borneo for their second tour in May 1965. By this time I had handed over my appointment of Director of Operations to Major General George Lea, who had commanded 22 SAS during the Malayan Emergency. It was an easy hand-over for I suggested to him that he should visit the whole of the area of operations before he took over from me. When he returned he said to me that he was so impressed that he had every intention of adhering to my policy with which he thoroughly agreed.

Peter de la Billiere describes his return to Borneo in these words: "In Brunei again, we found many changes in key personnel. Walter Walker had finished his tour without the recognition that he deserved, returning to the United Kingdom with a Distinguished Service Order, but not the knighthood with which a less outspoken officer in his position would surely have been rewarded. He had defended Malaysian Borneo with rare vigour, managing the difficult political side of his command no less skilfully than the military operation; but the exceptional directness with which he championed his forces – not least his beloved Gurkhas – had made him unpopular in high places. In his determination to secure what we needed, he had never hesitated to confront his superiors head-on. Helicopters were a prime example: he saw that without more helicopters we could not fight the war properly, and when the system would not provide enough aircraft, he attacked Whitehall and Headquarters, Far East like a tiger, even going so far as to make a public protest – and in the end he got what he wanted, though ultimately at his own expense."

BRIGADIER CHRISTOPHER BULLOCK, OBE, MC.
Author of *JOURNEYS HAZARDOUS* published in 1994.

His book is the story of his Gurkha Company's clandestine operations – CLARET – in Borneo in 1965. I read the book with absorbed interest for, having been Director of Operations in Borneo, I was able to see how the implementation of my Top Secret weapon – CLARET cross-border operations – was being executed at battalion, company and even lower level.

In his Introduction, Christopher wrote: "In mid-1964 the decision was taken to allow offensive operations against Indonesian military targets within Indonesia. They were to be known as 'Claret' operations and were to be politically deniable. In this way it was hoped to put the Indonesians on the defensive and wrest the initiative away from them. The architect of this strategy was General Walter Walker, a very experienced and able Gurkha officer who was fortuitously in command of the Borneo operations."

CHARLES ALLEN
Author of *THE SAVAGE WARS OF PEACE* 1990

I have already quoted from this book in a previous chapter – Commanding 1/6 QEO Gurkha Rifles.

Prior to the publication of his book, Charles Allen produced a programme which was broadcast on BBC Radio 4 in November 1988, entitled *The Savage Wars of Peace*. Part of his interview with me was broadcast on this programme which was presented by Major General Sir Jeremy Moore, KCB, OBE, MC and bar, who introduced me with the following words:

"But perhaps the last word should come from the man who never received much public acclaim but whom we all know to have been the architect of our victory in Borneo."

MAJOR GENERAL JAMES LUNT, CBE, MA.
Author of *JAI SIXTH! – THE STORY OF THE 6TH QUEEN ELIZABETH'S OWN GURKHA RIFLES 1817-1994* published in 1994.

The author has not written the conventional kind of regimental history but rather does it tell in a superb manner, the story of the regiment from its raising in 1817 to 1994.

I have extracted those parts which affect me.

"One of the Brigade of Gurkhas' most distinguished officers, Lieutenant Colonel Walter Walker, took over command of the 1/6th in 1951. Originally an 8th Gurkha, he had commanded the 4/8th with great distinction in Burma. He was an inspired trainer and an outstanding leader who went on to achieve Four Star rank in the British Army with no less than two bars to his DSO.

"No other general in the British Army could match

Walker's experience of counter-insurgency operations in the jungle. He had served in Burma both during the retreat and afterwards, winning the DSO in command of the 4/8th Gurkha Rifles. At the beginning of the Malayan Emergency he raised and trained Ferret Force, intended to operate in small groups for long periods in the jungle. From 1951-54 he commanded 1/6th GR in Malaya, making it one of the best Gurkha units, but not without a good deal of blood, sweat and tears.

"During the Malayan Emergency he realised that continuous patrolling in small numbers in the jungle, month in and month out, might have adverse effects on both discipline and morale, particularly for those who had had no let-up since Burma and he instituted a very intensive training programme whenever he managed to get the battalion together in Sungei Patani with, undoubtedly, excellent results.

"Hot foot after the TNKU rebels (North Kalimantan National Army) went Major General Walter Walker, GOC 17th Gurkha Division, from Seremban, Malaya, who assumed the appointment of Commander British Forces Borneo (COMBRITBOR) on 19 December 1962. His brief was to clear the TNKU from Brunei before Malaysia was established in August 1963. This he accomplished by April in the same year.

"When the Author visited Singapore in 1965 on a mission from the MOD, he stayed with General Jolly, whose GSO 1 he had been in BAOR. When discussing the Borneo situation with Jolly he recalls him saying rather ruefully, 'Walter Walker's 'bamboo curtain' effectively keeps me out!'

"Although the abortive rebellion in Brunei received considerable sympathy in Indonesia, President Sukarno, did not intervene on the rebels' side, or at least not openly. However, the Tunku's (Tunku Abdal Rahman, Prime Minister of Malaya) announcement of the intention to incorporate the Borneo territories as 'East Malaysia' in a wider confederation with

Malaya, enraged him. He regarded it as a British neo-colonial plot and set about disrupting it, both politically and militarily.

"General Walker recounts the story of a Gurkha battalion which was celebrating its forthcoming departure from Borneo by one of two hectic parties in the British Officers' Mess. A newly arrived rifleman on guard for the first time, was being instructed in his duties by the guard commander, a Sergeant. After the sentry's knowledge of the password and other procedures had been carefully checked, the Sergeant said, 'You are a sentry. It is one o'clock in the morning. Suddenly you see a figure crawling towards you through the long grass over there. What would you do?' Without a moment's hesitation the sentry replied, 'Show him the way to the Officers' Mess!'"

Chapter 18

THE GURKHA SAGA

It was on my last trek in Nepal in late 1962 as Major General Brigade of Gurkhas, that after having my annual audience with the King, I asked him if I could speak on another matter. The King readily agreed. I asked him if he had been informed by the British Government that they intended to cut the Brigade of Gurkhas by more than half. The King replied that he had not been so consulted.

The British Ambassador was present, and as events proved, he reported the audience to Whitehall.

It was a short time later and while I was on this trek in Nepal that the Brunei Revolt blew up.

As soon as I had been informed of the intention of reducing the Gurkhas to 10,000, I had already circulated two signals. One, for the benefit of the Gurkhas, so breaking the news as gently as possible, and asking them to accept it with their customary loyalty. The other was to the Chief of Staff, Far East Land Forces, stressing the damage and stating vehemently that the affair had been handled quite disgracefully.

I had also written a directive to all Gurkha Brigadiers and Commanding Officers, both to warn and encourage them. It warned of the British Government's duplicity in proposing to cut the Brigade savagely and secretly, so presenting it to the Government of Nepal as a *fait accompli*. Once the directive had been circulated, I realised that I had done all that I could for the time being.

I had not become the Major General Brigade of Gurkhas in order to preside over the liquidation of the Gurkha soldiers.

As the Major General Brigade of Gurkhas, it was my

duty to fearlessly advocate the policy I considered to be right. When a final decision was taken by the highest authority I had to carry it out, whether I agreed with it or not.

Only one exception was possible. If the question was a continuing major issue, such as the future of the Brigade of Gurkhas, in which I myself was directly involved as Major General Brigade of Gurkhas, then I had the right to say, 'I'm sorry, I cannot do it'. I maintained that it was not only a right: it was my duty. It would have been dishonourable for me to have allowed my name to be associated in the carrying out of a policy which was repugnant to my conscience and contrary to my expressed opinion.

The future of the Brigade of Gurkhas had to be built on consultation and cooperation and could not be built on the dictatorship of the Defence planners or the domination of Great Britain over Nepal. To me consultation meant the taking of counsel one with another and the mutual exchange of views, information and advice. Could it possibly be twisted to mean that the Government of Nepal should be consulted only after it was far too late for their views to have any effect at all?

The Gurkhas have always had to suck on the hind tit and I was determined to put a stop to this.

It was the Prime Minister of Nepal who, when asked for an additional 20 battalions of Gurkhas after the fall of France in 1940 said: "Does a friend desert you in time of need? If you win, we win. If you lose, we lose."

At a time when I was up to my eyes and ears in conducting the fighting in Borneo, I received a signal from the Ministry of Defence summoning me to London. So regretfully, but with confidence, I left the war in Borneo in the capable hands of my senior brigadier, and flew to London.

On arrival at the Ministry of Defence, I was met by my old friend, General Sir William Pike, who was Vice-Chief of the Imperial General Staff. He said: "I can read you like a book,

Walter. You are a fighter and you are fighting for your Gurkhas with every weapon you can find. You cannot fight the CIGS, General Sir Richard Hull. Unless you apologise he will court-martial you. Then what would happen to your Gurkhas? And what would happen to the campaign in Borneo which you are fighting so successfully? You have achieved your aim. Now you can afford to say you are sorry and make a handsome apology."

So I did just that, with my tongue in my cheek, and returned to Borneo!

Shortly after I retired from the army, I was invited to a Conservative Party dinner sponsored by Lord Salisbury, which was also attended by Lord Thorneycroft, who was Secretary of State for Defence when I was Director of Operations, Borneo, 1962-65. While we were all having coffee, Lord Thorneycroft came across to me and said, "I have always wanted to meet you again and apologise for the shameful way Field Marshal Sir Richard Hull treated you. Had I known in advance that he intended to recall you from the middle of a battle which you were fighting brilliantly, and that he was going to threaten you with a court-martial, I would have put a stop to it. To relieve you in the middle of a battle, which you were winning with such conspicuous success, was bad enough, but to threaten you with a court-martial, without first consulting me, was beyond belief."

These were not Commonwealth soldiers but Gurkhas, the loyal subjects of an independent sovereign country, who had poured their blood voluntarily for Great Britain in two World Wars, saved Malaya from going Communist, and Borneo from being taken over by President Sukarno of Indonesia.

In spite of this, the government and Army Council were prepared to break faith with, and betray the trust of these gallant men, and our staunchest ally – Nepal. I argued that Britain's oldest ally, excluding Portugal, had been betrayed by politicians.

In doing so, they were trading on the Gurkhas' incredible loyalty and remarkable discipline; at the same time taking advantage of the absence of their leader – me – while I was Director of Operations in Borneo.

I was accused of betraying a confidence, but the fact that the government and Army Council were themselves breaking confidence with the Gurkhas and the Nepalese Nation did not enter their reckoning.

Such nefarious designs and behaviour on their part automatically absolved me from extending to my superiors the customary degree of loyalty.

As the senior officer of the Brigade of Gurkhas, it was my duty fearlessly to fight, particularly as Nepal was being denied any prior joint consultation. To me joint consultation means taking of counsel one with another and the mutual exchange of views.

Instead the whole procedure was conducted in a clandestine manner so that Nepal was not consulted until it was too late for her views to have any effect at all.

The government and the Army Council showed themselves as being callously unconscious of the feelings, the spirits, the traditions and the loyalty of the Gurkhas.

The 'powers that be', who up till then the Gurkhas had trusted, ratted on them and slashed at them like runts in a Soho gang.

I had also been fighting for the SAS, who were doing a marvellous job in Borneo with their four-man patrols over a frontier of 1,000 miles. In Borneo one SAS Squadron with helicopters was worth ten infantry battalions to me.

After I retired, I was made an honorary member of the SAS. There had been only two honorary members – Winston Churchill and myself. Now there was only one. There will never be another, so I had been told.

After I retired in May 1972, I continued to argue that the

most effective deterrent to terrorism would be a Division of Gurkhas. I foresaw that the Brigade of Gurkhas, and indeed the whole of the Armed Forces, would be cut to the bone as soon as the Cold War ended.

In 1988, I wrote to Field Marshal Lord Bramall, and to the then CGS, General Sir John Chapple, himself a Gurkha, and said that Gurkhas should become a United Nations Force for which they had no equal.

They both disagreed with my proposal.

However, five years later, Field Marshal Lord Bramall had changed his mind and in a letter to the Daily Telegraph in June 1993, he proposed a world role for Gurkhas in the form of a United Nations permanent standing force.

Then in March 1994, Dwin Bramall said in the House of Lords that the Brigade of Gurkhas would be an ideal addition to the UN peace-keeping force in Yugoslavia. Why? Because they could be trained quickly, turn their hands to anything, and there was no one better than a Gurkha for taking up a neutral, well-ordered and disciplined stance in any conflict, whether it be motivated by ethnic, political or religious considerations.

As I am engrossed in writing this autobiography in 1995, in the midst of the biggest shake-up of the Gurkha soldiers for 35 years, the Brigade of Gurkhas were to be cut from 6,500 to 2,500. This compared with 120,000 Gurkhas in the Indian Army. How can a subsidised country afford this number when we have to cut them to the bone?

Of course, we shall live to regret this, as we will the emasculation of British regiments, for we are living in mortal danger. Few are aware of this – perhaps fortunately. The black market in nuclear and biological materials is now a very serious threat. If they fall into the wrong hands we may not survive. Our politicians, few of whom, if any, fought in World War II, have short memories and no sense of history. Then there is the ever-growing threat of world-wide Islamic Fundamentalism.

Nepal is the world's seventh poorest country. Now there will be even fewer Gurkha soldiers to send money home to buy farms or businesses when they retire. Previously about £30 million a year came to Nepal from British military funds, a fifth of their national income.

The Ministry of Defence attempted to soften the blow with retraining and resettlement projects, providing 18,000 pensioners and redundant soldiers with some £4.8 million a year. But our government's record was quite appalling. For 22,000 Gurkhas made redundant after the Second World War and in the late 1960s who did not get pensions, £1 million a year was coming from the Gurkha Welfare Trust. The Gurkha Welfare Trust (GWT) was providing a monthly welfare pension of £8.50 to no less than 609 of my previous regiment, the 8th Gurkhas, or their widows, who were destitute without a service pension, and totally reliant on this monthly sum. Their average age was over seventy. The Trust was, therefore, having to find over £60,000 each year for the 8th Gurkhas alone.

The British Army regards the Gurkhas as among their very best soldiers: adaptable, tough, skilled at arms, willing, loyal, bravest of the brave, and cheap. If recruiting was to be turned off and Gurkhas removed from the British Army – which God forbid – we might never get them back. Therefore if ever Britain were to require a resurgence of the finest fighting soldiers, for whatever role, the Gurkha source might not be available.

"It's Tommy this, an' Tommy that, an' 'Chuck him out the brute!' But it's Saviour of 'is country when the guns begin to shoot ..."

Kipling wrote that in 1892. Men in the services go through these vicissitudes. I remember one of them after the First World War – "the war to end all wars" – when we blithely stripped down our defences; then rightly blamed politicians for not restoring them fast enough when Mussolini and Hitler struck their almost mortal blow, followed by Japan. This country stood alone until Japan struck at Pearl Harbour, which brought America into the war.

It is an axiom that "if you wish for lasting peace, then prepare for war". We in Britain should remember 1938's appeasement and the price we paid for not being prepared.

With British Regiments finding it so difficult to attract recruits, it would be no surprise to me if a third Gurkha Regiment had to be raised.

VJ Day, the commemoration of the end of the war with Japan, and also the 50th Anniversary of the end of the 1939-1945 War, was held on 19th and 20th August 1995. The Gurkha veterans, led by four Gurkha VCs, received the loudest, spontaneous and prolonged acclamation from the crowds lining the Mall in London during the march past the Queen on the 19th August. Again at the Beating of Retreat at Horse Guards Parade on the evening of the following day, the Gurkha contingent of Pipes and Drums received the loudest applause. There was no doubt that the nation had taken the Gurkhas to its heart. I had to watch the proceedings on both days from television coverage, lying on my bed. I felt very proud of my Bravest of the Brave, whose motto is: "It is better to die than be a coward."

"Bravest of the Brave.
Most Generous of the Generous
Never had a country more faithful friends than you."

This quotation is taken from an officer who served in the First World War, Professor Sir Ralph Turner, MC, who wrote:
"As I write these last words, my thoughts return to you, my comrades, the stubborn and indomitable peasants of Nepal.

Once more I see you in your bivouacs or about your fires, on forced march or in trenches, now shivering with wet and cold, now scorched by a pitiless and burning sun. Uncomplaining you endure hunger and thirst and wounds, and at the last, your unwavering lines disappear into the smoke and wrath of battle. Bravest of the brave, most generous of the generous, never had a country more faithful friends than you."

It was entirely as a result of two successive articles and appeals published in the Sunday Express on the 9th and 16th July, 1995, that the British public were made aware of the miserable annual pittance paid to holders of the Victoria Cross – VC. These two articles concentrated on but one Gurkha VC, Havildar (Sergeant) Lachhiman Gurung of the Regiment I commanded in World War Two, in Burma against the Japanese, the 4th/8th Gurkha Rifles. He won his VC at the ferocious battle of Taungdaw on the 13th May 1945, and in his citation I described the amazing valour that he performed even after losing an arm and an eye, and in the process killing thirty-one Japanese soldiers. The pension that this hero received was a meagre £21 per month, the extra £1 being in recognition of his VC.

After reading this newspaper's graphic description of the squalor and poverty in which he had to live, the British public's response was spontaneous with its generosity and gratitude. The Sunday Express article of 9th July produced donations amounting to £39,000, and by the time the article of 16th July was published this sum had grown to £79,000. The day before the VJ Commemoration on 19th July, there appeared a picture of the Prime Minister and Lachhiman Gurung outside number 10 Downing Street holding between them a large banner in the form of a cheque for no less than the magnificent sum of £100,550.

As I was having my enforced afternoon bed rest on 18th August, a representative of the editor of the *Sunday Express*, Mr. Brian Hitchen, called at my house. He said he had come with an invitation from Mr. Hitchen to be his guest at the VJ Commemoration on the following day, Saturday, 19th August. Unfortunately I had to decline this very kind invitation because of the persistent severity of my chronic disablement.

The letters published in the Sunday Express from readers were very poignant. One of them compared the meagre £21 a month with the thousands of pounds in compensation paid to women who became pregnant while serving in one of the armed forces and are forced to leave their arm of the service. This becomes even more scandalous when one considers that the combined number of VC and GC holders is only 83. The powers that be should be ashamed of themselves and rectify forthwith this scandalous and disgraceful state of affairs.

In conclusion the magical relationship between the Gurkhas and Great Britain has survived the eclipse of empire, and may it endure into the 21st century. It is a relationship based on mutual admiration, something approaching love and an extra dimension whose chemistry has never been explained.

The world in which the Gurkha soldiers live alongside their British officers is one in which Rudyard Kipling would feel at home.

Yet remarkably, the Gurkhas have never been branded lackeys of the British ... probably because they retain a self-respect and dignity that is as old as the Himalayan valleys from which they hail.

Finally, it is all too apparent that it is the Gurkha Welfare Trust, not the British Government, on whom those thousands of poverty stricken ex-Gurkha soldiers and widows, without pensions, have to rely for their livelihood. Hence the frequent appearance in the newspapers of the illustrated Gurkha Welfare Appeal, with the heart-rending caption:

"TOO OLD TO FIGHT
TOO PROUD TO ASK"

Visit to Italy when Deputy Chief of Staff, AFCENT 1966

NATO Senior Officers Advanced Weapons Orientation
Course 24-28 January, 1966

Chapter 19

In 1965 I was appointed Deputy Chief of Staff in charge of Plans, Operations and Intelligence, Headquarters Allied Forces Central Europe (AFCENT). The main headquarters was in the Chateau de Fontainebleau, France. Beryl and I moved into an extremely nice house in Fontainebleau, with a complete RAF staff consisting of house sergeant, cook and two other ranks. I had my own staff car with British driver. Our daughter, Venetia, was also with us and working for the Base Commander.

The staff in the headquarters was multi-national and consisted of British, American, French, German, Dutch, Belgian and Canadian officers and other ranks. The Commander-in-Chief, Land Forces, was the German General Graf Johann von Kielmansegg. Kielmansegg's Chief of Staff, under whom I worked directly, was the Belgian Lieutenant-General Jean Ducq. He arrived shortly after me. I had already agreed with General Kielmansegg that the best way for me to get myself properly and quickly in the picture was by visiting all the subordinate headquarters, to be briefed by my opposite numbers, to meet the Formation Commanders and tour the respective battle areas. Only in this way could I get a proper feel for the whole of the command area, get to know all the personalities with whom I would be dealing and be known by them. Having received the personal and enthusiastic agreement of the Commander-in-Chief himself, I agreed a tour programme with all the subordinate commands.

Then along came General Ducq as the new Chief of Staff, who disagreed with this whole concept on the grounds that there was far too much paperwork pending for such a tour. I told him that the tour plan had already been agreed by the Commander-in-Chief himself and the programme agreed with the subordinate commands. I told him outright that we would be made to look extremely stupid by all the subordinate headquarters by putting paperwork of more importance than personal liaison and an intimate knowledge of the various battle areas. There was a tense confrontation and relations between us were strained for four months. I had informed the Military Assistant to the Commander-in-Chief that General Ducq had cancelled my tour and that we had lost face with subordinate commands who had already drafted tour programmes for my visit. General Kielmansegg was extremely annoyed.

It took about four months before normal relations with General Ducq were restored. Meanwhile relations between General Kielmansegg and General Ducq were becoming extremely strained and it was obvious that they disliked each other intensely. I soon found myself being consulted by the Commander-in-Chief, thereby bypassing his Chief of Staff. But I made a point of always telling General Ducq what had transpired between the Commander-in-Chief and myself. From then onwards General Ducq and I became firm friends, but the enmity between him and General Kielmansegg persisted. For General Kielmansegg to have relieved his Chief of Staff of his appointment would have caused an international furore, so he remained, while I found myself dealing more and more directly with the Commander-in-Chief and was virtually becoming his Chief of Staff in all but name. General Kielmansegg and I became firm friends, a friendship which lasted until after I had retired from the British Army in 1972.

Likewise General Ducq and I eventually became good friends and he and his wife came to stay with us at Claxton Hall, when I was General Officer Commanding-in-Chief, Northern Command, York. Beryl and I had enjoyed a pleasant weekend with Jean Ducq and his wife at their seaside holiday home in Belgium and also at their flat in Brussels. By then I had learnt how to steer a somewhat tricky course between the most senior Generals at HQ AFCENT. Fortunately I had a very efficient military assistant, by name Major Barry Pollard, who was a fluent French speaker and an accomplished staff officer with an exceptionally good brain. He vetted all the incoming mail and when papers and letters reached me they were accompanied by a short brief pointing out the pros and cons and a suggested course of action. He and I used to spend Saturday mornings going through and pruning very long-winded papers submitted by the heads of the three departments for which I was responsible, namely Plans, Operations and Intelligence. Barry, who was a sapper (Royal Engineers) went on to become a Major General before he retired from the Army. Beryl and I kept in touch with them after I retired and I still meet them at my house from time to time.

I was appalled by the peace time tempo of the very First exercise, FALLEX 67, in which, by virtue of my appointment in the HQ, I took a leading part. One of the objects of the exercise was to test the speed of reaction to urgent requests from Army Groups in the field to resort to the use of tactical nuclear weapons. Such urgent messages were taking on an average of four hours to reach my desk in spite of our sophisticated electronic systems. I told General Kielmansegg that I had better and speedier communications on the North West Frontier of India by using semaphore flags and heliograph reflectors by day and morse lamps by night.

I asked him for a free hand to reorganise our battle communications. Using my experience of having been General Staff Officer First Grade at Headquarters 7 Indian Division in Burma, I designed a mobile caravan in which maps were properly displayed, communications were at my elbow and radio contact constantly maintained with the commanders in the field and with the main headquarters. By ruthless cutting out of all unessentials and superfluities and the number of stages through which messages had to pass, I reduced the four hour delay to twelve minutes and was able to contact General Kielmansegg within seconds.

By now General de Gaulle had become a thorn in the side of NATO. He objected to American dominance of Western Europe, and announced that French forces were to be withdrawn from NATO by 1st July 1966. Furthermore all NATO forces, including headquarters and all infrastructure, had to be withdrawn from France by 1st April 1967. This meant uprooting of all headquarters, elaborate communications, airfields, stockpiles, fuel dumps and pipelines, all of which had been installed in great quantities during the past twenty-five years.

SHAPE was to move to Casteau near Mons in Belgium, while AFCENT would move to the Netherlands at Brunssum in the northern province of Limburg. The only possible accommodation that the Dutch could offer was in the buildings which housed the large complex of offices of a coal mine at Brunssum. An advance party commanded by a Dutch general was sent to set up AFCENT headquarters.

When General Kielmansegg decided to visit Brunssum to check the progress that had been made so far, he was horrified to find that little progress had been made, that there was no sense of urgency and that there was not a hope of AFCENT headquarters and all the appendages being moved and functioning by the 1st April 1967 – a time factor of three months. Kielmansegg called me to his office and said that if anyone could adopt a proper sense of urgency and achieve the almost impossible it was the British, and of the British element in the headquarters the one person who had the practical experience and the necessary qualities of command and leadership was me. He there and then appointed me his Director of Movement Coordination with the powers of complete control of the move from Fontainebleau to Brunssum. He gave me a free hand to choose my own staff from every branch of the headquarters and to report direct to him any incident of non-cooperation. He told me to ride rough shod over any hurt feelings and to disregard the difficulties that the various branches would undoubtedly encounter in the rearrangement of their staffs.

When I arrived at the office complex of the coal mine at Brunssum I was horrified to find that coal trains were still running, that the miners were still using the showers and changing rooms, and some of the offices had not been vacated. I realised immediately that I would have to be completely ruthless in exercising command and that my staff would have to be driven with an iron fist. I summoned my staff immediately and made it crystal clear that there would be no working to rule and that the working day would be from dawn to well into the night. Every office would have to be gutted and refitted and certain new buildings constructed. The Dutch authorities did not know what had hit them, such were my constant demands. At the same time I had to maintain cordial relations. I was not concerned with who would have to foot the bill. It did not take long for me to earn the nickname, 'The Dictator'. Those who did not make the grade were returned to Fontainebleau as soon as their replacement had arrived.

In addition to organising the layout of the office blocks, I was responsible for finding accommodation for a staff of about six hundred and their families. An added responsibility was to evacuate the headquarters at Fontainebleau and hand it back to the French in good order. Then there was the mass of hired accommodation in and around Fontainebleau.

I worked to a strict timetable and had to move my own office almost every day as the buildings were converted, offices gutted and refitted and new buildings constructed. Within less than the stipulated three months and well before the end of March, AFCENT had the new headquarters at Brunssum. There had not been one gap when AFCENT headquarters had been unable to operate at peak efficiency to meet any emergency.

The inauguration ceremony took place on the 1st April 1967, in the presence of General Kielmansegg, his subordinate formation commanders and VIPs from Holland. Kielmansegg called me to his office and in congratulating me said: "You have achieved the impossible. I shall personally ensure that your achievement is immediately brought to the notice of the Supreme Allied Commander Europe and to the British Chief of the Defence Staff."

Shortly before I heard that I was to be appointed the next General Officer Commanding-in-Chief, Northern Command in the United Kingdom with my headquarters at York in 1967, the British Chief of the General Staff (CGS), General Sir James Cassels telephoned me from London. He said that as a result of the Mountbatten Report on the prisons in the United Kingdom, I had been recommended as the most suitable candidate for the new post of Director of Prisons. It stood out a mile that the CGS was very anxious that I should be selected for the appointment. Why? Because it would mean that I would have to leave the army with the rank of major general, thereby solving the vexed question of my future promotion in the army. Later I was told that it was Lord Louis Mountbatten himself who had recommended me as the ideal choice as Director of Prisons.

My own superior in NATO, General Graf von Kielmansegg, expressed to me his utter amazement in no uncertain terms that I might be forced to leave the army, particularly as he had only recently brought to the notice of the highest authority, including those in London, my recent performance of "having achieved the impossible".

General Cassels asked me to fly to London immediately because the Home Secretary would like to see me in two days time. On arrival in England I was told that after my interview with the Home Secretary, the CGS wished me to telephone him personally to say whether I thought I had made a good impression on the Home Secretary. Why the hurry? It was only too obvious to me.

I found the Home Secretary a "cold fish" and had no intention of serving under him as Director of Prisons. I decided that I would answer his questions in a forthright army manner. He asked me several questions. First, what experience had I of prisons? I replied that I had guarded Japanese war criminals in Bangkok without one prisoner having attempted to escape. Later, when my battalion was in Malaya, I was required to witness the hanging of six of these war criminals before breakfast most mornings. I had also guarded the traitors of the Indian National Army in Bangkok jail. On my first inspection of the prison, these traitors had shouted abuse at me and spat at me from their large prison cages. I, therefore, told my senior Gurkha officer that I would inspect the prison again the next day and I expected every prisoner to be standing strictly to attention with his eyes looking upwards, and that there was to be complete silence. When I visited the prison the following day, my orders were obeyed to the letter.

I said that a number of years later during the Malayan Emergency, when I was commanding a Gurkha battalion, again I had been responsible for guarding the communist terrorists in my area of operations. Not one had escaped. How was this achieved, I was asked. I explained that I fenced the detention camp with two high fences of barbed wire with fierce guard dogs running free between the two rows of wire and there were also watch towers manned by the Home Guard.

I was then asked how I would prevent escape from prisons

in the middle of towns in the United Kingdom. I replied that all streets or roads on every side of the prison would be closed. In other words, they would be declared as "no go areas".

Finally, I was asked if I was selected as Director of Prisons, what would be my first and most important requirement? I replied that I would inspect two prisons each day and continue to do so regularly throughout the year and, therefore, would require a helicopter. Only in this way could I satisfy myself with the security of every prison, but also exercise proper man management of the prison staff and raise their low morale. In other words I would act exactly as any senior army officer would be expected to do.

I was absolutely confident that my performance had been such that I most certainly would not be selected for the post. I had great pleasure in telephoning General Cassels direct and telling him so. Once again I had thwarted the nefarious designs of the 'Whitehall Warriors'.

It was when my tenure of appointment at AFCENT was coming to a close that I received the letter from the Military Secretary that I had been appointed the next General Officer Commanding-in-Chief, Northern Command, in the United Kingdom, with the rank of lieutenant-general.

In due course this rank and appointment carried with it the honour of a knighthood. Thus Admiral of the Fleet Lord Mountbatten's prophecy made in Brunei, that a knighthood for me would 'come up with the rations' had proved to be accurate. Both General Kielmansegg and General Ducq were delighted, while Beryl and I enjoyed a happy departure from AFCENT, with many farewell parties in our honour.

The Queen and myself at the Ceremony of the opening of the Tyne Tees Tunnel

Chapter 20

GENERAL OFFICER COMMANDING-IN-CHIEF, NORTHERN COMMAND, UK, 1967-1969

As I have already recounted I was still at AFCENT Headquarters in Holland when I received the official notification that I had been appointed the next General Officer Commanding-in-Chief, Northern Command, United Kingdom, with promotion to the rank of lieutenant-general.

One of the three district commanders who would be under me as a major general was an old friend. He had joined the 1/8th Gurkha Rifles in Quetta in the late 1930s when I was adjutant. He went on to command a Gurkha battalion with distinction in Burma against the Japanese. Later he commanded a British battalion with equal distinction in Korea against the Chinese and North Koreans. This was the present Major General Horsford.

My chief of staff had arranged a programme of briefings by the heads of all the various branches, which would have lasted the best part of my first week. He was somewhat put out when I told him I would spend my first day visiting each branch of my HQ in turn, meet all the officers, NCOs, other ranks and civilians at their place of work and expect them to tell me their responsibilities, the projects on which they were engaged and their main problems. That week I would visit each of my three district headquarters, meet the District Commander – a major general – and require him to introduce me to each branch of his staff and carry out the same procedure as for my own headquarters. Having completed this I would in the following two weeks visit every regular and territorial army unit in my command. I said I wished to meet every officer, particularly the young officers, every NCO and the other ranks. I said I

239

wished to find out for myself if they were satisfied with their lot and if not what they would like me to do about it. I also wished to be included in my programme that I would like to visit a cross-section of the wives in the married quarters and that I would pick out the quarters at random.

It was my intention to assess the morale of the army in Northern Command, to encourage officers – particularly the younger ones – NCOs and other ranks to give me their frank views on what was wrong with the army and the chain of command right up to Whitehall, and what their recommendations were for all-round improvements.

I obtained the information that I was seeking and it all boiled down to low morale due to lack of confidence in Whitehall, – the army hierarchy, the Minister of Defence and politicians as a whole. Recruiting was at a low ebb and the physical and educational standard of recruits left much to be desired. I had obtained the frank view of officers at all levels, of senior and junior NCOs, of private soldiers, and also of a cross section of the wives. I decided to hold my fire until the newly appointed CGS had taken over the reins from General Cassels, the present CGS, whose tour of duty was drawing to a close.

Soon I attended my first army board meeting with the other army commanders. I spoke without pulling any punches on the failure of the recruiting campaign, the failure of the government to support the army and the low morale that existed in the army as a whole. I said that what the rank and file wanted to know was exactly what their present and future roles were, how vitally important they were to the security of the realm, to their support of the British Army of the Rhine and to being prepared for any emergency at home or overseas. I proposed that the clarion call for the army should be: 'The unexpected must be expected.' I suggested to the Chief of the General

Staff (CGS) - General Sir Jim Cassels – that he should broadcast to the army, or even the nation, just as 'Bill' Slim had done when he was CIGS. Although Jim Cassels seemed to agree with everything I had said, his response to this suggestion was very lukewarm. I then suggested that as defence appeared to be a dirty word in the view of the Labour Government, we should all resign, in protest. But I received no support for this proposal.

Cassels was reaching the end of his tenure of command and was no longer the fighting general whom I had admired. He appeared tired and uninspiring, and rumour had it that his relations with Healey were far from smooth. He certainly gave the impression that he was looking forward to retirement and that, frankly, he had had enough.

It was at about this time that I received a letter from the Military Secretary informing me that the Queen would be honouring me with a knighthood in the New Year's Honours List. I received a very nice hand-written letter from Lord Mountbatten, sent from Sandringham, in which he said: "I told you in Borneo that a knighthood would eventually 'come up with the rations' for you." A sackful of congratulatory letters reached me from the UK, NATO and the Far East, many of which contained such expressions as: 'Better late than never', 'About time too', and 'Three years too late'. What gave me the greatest pleasure was the fact that at long last Beryl, who had supported me so devotedly through thick and thin, would share the title.

Denis Healey, the Minister of Defence, was one of my first official visitors. I met him at the airfield and almost the first question he asked me was, had I any points that I would like to put to him personally. I replied that I had a number of proposals to overcome the problem of the poor state of recruiting. Healey responded at once and asked where we could talk privately on the airfield as he was on his way to Catterick to visit the 6th Infantry Brigade, which had recently arrived from Germany as part and parcel of British Army of the Rhine (BAOR). I replied that the office in the control tower would be the best place.

I started off by saying I had ten main suggestions for improving the present state of recruiting, which I called my 'Ten Commandments'. Healey said: "Good, you speak and I will jot them down." I emphasised that my Ten Commandments were based on frank talks with officers – particularly the young officers – NC0s, private soldiers and wives, of every unit under my command.

1st Commandment: Reduce the existing six-year engagement from six years to three. I reminded Healey that this proposal had previously been rejected by Whitehall.

2nd Commandment: Marriage allowance should be eligible to soldiers who married before the age of twenty-one.

3rd Commandment: Soldiers before the end of their engagement should attend a full course of resettlement.

4th Commandment: Recruiting chain of command should be decentralised from Whitehall to the four Commands.

5th Commandment: Recruiting officers were too old and not in touch with the youth and young men of the day. They should be replaced with much younger officers with active service experience.

6th Commandment: Recruiting staff should be paid commission by results.

7th Commandment: Public relations was pathetic. The soldier must be portrayed to the public as a highly-skilled professional in every arm of the army.

8th Commandment: Officers should be professionally trained to excel when interviewed on radio and television.

9th Commandment: The public should be invited to witness all arms of the service taking part in a realistic mock battle.

10th Commandment: The territorial army was sick and tired of being pruned, reorganised and treated as 'country cousins'. They had every justification to be proud of their long-established titles, achievements and military history.

Denis Healey seemed to be impressed and said he would pursue my recommendations.

In March 1968, Jim Cassels was succeeded by General Sir Geoffrey Baker. I had written a letter to him to coincide with his arrival at his office. The letter began with the usual formal welcome and congratulations, and then went on to outline the proposals that I had already given verbally to Denis Healey. Knowing that the Minister of Defence had already been briefed by me on my ideas for reform, I knew that George Baker would be bound to treat my letter seriously and with alacrity. Anyway that was my plan of campaign. I was at pains to emphasise the low state of morale that I had found on my arrival at Northern Command and the steps that I had taken to improve matters.

It was not long before George Baker paid a visit to my command, and I was able to arrange a programme which would enable him to visit all the district and brigade headquarters and individual units. He was very easy to get on with and most attentive to what was said to him. He told me that several of my Ten Commandments had been adopted. I mentioned to him that rumour had it that his Adjutant General had been seen jogging along a corridor leading to Denis Healey's office and when asked what the hurry was, blurted out, "Walker's bloody Ten Commandments". This amused George Baker, who remarked, "His figure is not exactly sylph-like".

Beryl and I were exceedingly comfortably housed at Claxton Hall where we entertained to the full, our guests being not only the usual crocodile of visitors from Whitehall and adjacent commands, but also all the VIPs within the area of my command, from the Archbishop of York downwards. But I was not happy with the large number of army and civilian staff that this and the upkeep of Claxton Hall and its extensive grounds involved. I suggested to more than one army VIP that a largish flat in York City and an entertainment allowance for entertaining visitors and guests in a good restaurant would be more appropriate. This suggestion was greeted with amazement. I was told in no uncertain terms that I had earned this privilege and on no account should the hierarchy of the army allow our existing standards to be lowered. My response was that I could think of better ways of spending the defence budget which was always being sliced to the bone by the enemy within, namely the Treasury and the Labour Government.

I decided to practise what I had preached on the all-important improvement in public relations. I enlisted the help of the Commander of 6 Brigade at Catterick, and together we simulated as realistic and spectacular a mock battle as was humanly possible. It included the combat capability of not only all the up to date infantry weapons, but also artillery, tanks, helicopters and attack aircraft. I invited all the lord lieutenants and VIPs in Northern Command and gave every facility to the media. The demonstration was widely advertised and succeeded in attracting a large crowd of spectators. Although I say it myself, it was an outstanding success and certainly impressed all the spectators. I received a large congratulatory mail from the highest to the lowest, and there is no doubt that it gave a boost to recruiting and kept the army in the public eye.

Because of my outspokenness I attracted the attention of Tyne Tees Television at Newcastle-upon-Tyne, who decided that because I spoke my mind and did not pull any punches in my speeches, I would be a good 'target' to be interviewed in my capacity as the fairly recently appointed three-star General, Commanding-in-Chief Northern Command, with headquarters at York. I was interviewed on a number of occasions with the result that Tyne Tees Television asked me if I would feature in a programme to be called 'A Day in the Life of a General'. I agreed to do this, but suddenly at the end of 1968 a letter arrived from the Military Secretary, informing me that I was on a short-list of generals being considered for the appointment of the next commander-in-chief, Allied Forces Northern Europe. He wished to know if, in the event of being selected, I would accept the appointment.

I felt pretty certain that I would be chosen, because I had a fairly shrewd idea that General Graf von Kielmansegg had asked for me by name not only to the Supreme Allied Commander Europe and through him to the Military Committee of NATO, but also to Whitehall. It was after I had assumed my new command that General Kielmansegg confirmed to me personally that this was, indeed, the case.

In February 1969, the official announcement was published in *The London Gazette* that I had been appointed Commander-in-Chief, Allied Forces Northern Europe (AFNORTH), in succession to General Sir Kenneth Darling, on 7 August 1969.

Tyne Tees Television were anxious to know if I would be prepared to feature in a documentary after assuming my new command. I agreed that all things being equal, and after having 'played myself in', I would be prepared to do so. I knew from my AFCENT days that at Headquarters AFNORTH there was an exceptionally able public relations officer, Claus Koren, who was an expert in the field of NATO defence and, of course AFNORTH defence in particular. Well before the date of my handing over command of Northern Command, England, I made discreet enquiries through Claus Koren as to whether or not the proposal to make a documentary film would be greeted with approval. He informed me that NATO as a whole would be more than enthusiastic at the prospect of obtaining such publicity. The same went for his colleagues in Whitehall. I felt well satisfied and was able to occupy myself with the preparations for handing over my present command to my successor, paying farewell visits to subordinate headquarters and units, and accepting invitations to so many private and official functions.

Chapter 21

Commander-in-Chief Allied Forces Northern Europe (AFNORTH), 1969-1972

Before I departed from England to assume my new appointment of Commander-in-Chief AFNORTH, I had interviews with Denis Healey, Sam Elworthy (CIGS) and also the First Sea Lord and the Chief of the Air Staff. Sam Elworthy said to me that he had only one directive for me and that was to ensure that Norway did not succeed in achieving its expressed desire to replace a British NATO commander-in-chief with a Norwegian admiral. He told me that this should not be too difficult because Denmark would never agree to such a proposal. It was essential that a British commander-in-chief should hold the balance, and preferably one who had been 'blooded' as a commander in World War II and on subsequent campaigns. Furthermore previous NATO experience was a desirable attribute, and in my case the key post that I had held in Headquarters Allied Forces Central Europe would stand me in great stead. I did not disclose that I had been reliably informed that General Graf von Kielmansegg had proposed my appointment to the NATO Supreme Allied Commander Europe (SACEUR). Sam Elworthy also warned me that the Norwegian Defence Minister had told him that they would prefer a British admiral rather than a British general. He was told that I had already been selected and that such a request should be made not to the British Chief of the General Staff but to SACEUR, the American General Goodpaster. This put me on my guard and alerted me to the firm stand that I would obviously have to take with the Norwegian Defence Minister.

The retired Field Marshal Sir Richard Hull, with whom I

had clashed over the run-down of the Brigade of Gurkhas, and who had rejected Lord Mountbatten's and Admiral Sir Varyl Begg's recommendation that I should be knighted for my performance as Director of Borneo Operations, expressed his disapproval at my appointment. He told a number of friends that had he been CIGS, my appointment would have been made over his dead body. This was the man who conducted the procedure for the run-down of the Brigade of Gurkhas in such a clandestine manner that the King of Nepal was not even consulted until it was too late. This was the man who, when he was CGS, and I was Director of Operations, Borneo, recalled me to London at a critical stage of the campaign and threatened me with a court-martial, without first consulting the Minister of Defence, who thoroughly deprecated such action and later offered me his abject apology. This was the man who in his capacity as Commander-in-Chief Far East Command showered me with praise when I was the brigade commander who had brought the twelve year Malayan Emergency to an end, and who wrote in my Annual Confidential Report: "He is an outstanding officer who has done extremely well in command of a brigade and is fit now to command a division." After I had retired from the army I met him at the funeral of his brother-in-law. He exuded charm and friendship which I did not reciprocate.

My wife and I flew to Oslo and were met at the airport by General Sir Kenneth Darling and his wife. They had kindly already vacated the official residence of the commander-in-chief, so Beryl and I were able to move straight in. We dined together that night and after dinner Ken Darling filled me in with his private views of the task that I would inherit. I can't recollect who it was who told me of the incident that occurred on the very first evening when he moved into this recently acquired residence for the commander-in-chief. Apparently the telephone rang and he answered the call with the words, "Darling speaking." The female voice at the other end asked what time she should come that evening. It transpired that the commander-in-chief's official residence, rented from the Norwegian Government, was formerly a high class 'house of ill repute', but was not widely known as such!

The house was far too small for having VIP house guests to stay in comfort and the accommodation for the house staff far too cramped. But it was located on the outskirts of Oslo and had a good view of the fjord. The entrance was next to a rough road devoid of all traffic and only used by pedestrians during the weekends on their way to the Olympic ski-jump and ski-slopes. Many of them would gaze at the house with interest and much chattering. I suspect this was because they were aware of its previous reputation, and not because it was the residence of the NATO commander-in-chief.

At first I was not given much time to find my feet in my headquarters because there were official lunches to attend and courtesy calls to be made.

Detailed briefs had been prepared for me by each of the staff branches. However, in my initial address to all officers on 13 August 1969, I said that my first priority would be to visit every branch in turn, meet the head of the branch, his subordinate staff officers and the clerical staff. I would want to know what their individual responsibilities were and the tasks and problems on which they were currently working. I said that in completing my tour of the whole headquarters I had found that the office of my deputy commander-in-chief, a Norwegian lieutenant general of the Royal Norwegian Air Force, was tucked away at the far end of my headquarters, amongst the staff, instead of adjacent to my office complex. Accordingly I had decided to rectify this forthwith by moving my chief of staff to the office vacated by the deputy commander-in-chief. In this way the chief of staff would be among the staff of which he was the chief or head.

As it was I already had a military assistant (MA) – a major of the British Army, a secretary of the staff – a Royal Navy lieutenant commander; an ADC – a British Army captain, a personal assistant (PA) – a civilian Norwegian lady; and a number of clerks 'to taste'.

In addition to my deputy, there were four other deputies – a German rear-admiral who was deputy chief of staff (Plans and Operations) by the name of Fritz Guggenberger, who, as a U-boat captain, had sunk the Royal Navy's aircraft carrier, the ARK ROYAL, an American Air Force two star general, a Danish two star admiral and a Norwegian Army two star general.

I was amazed at the number of 'top brass' that there were, all of whom had their own staff officers and clerical staff.

I made it clear that I did not intend to become office-bound and at a very early date would be visiting the whole of my command in Norway, Denmark and Schleswig-Holstein. In order to achieve this I issued an instruction that the relevant staff officers would be restricted to fifteen minutes to brief me verbally on his responsibilities and the tasks and problems on which he was currently involved. Such verbal briefings were to be completed in one day.

My peace and war headquarters were at Kolsas, a few miles north of Oslo. My war headquarters had been tunnelled into a solid rocky hillock about one thousand feet high and was proof against a nuclear attack. Although its site was supposed to be secret, its location was an open secret in Norway and no doubt to the Russians also, because it had been built by Norwegian civilian contractors more than ten years before my arrival. Furthermore, its precise presence was discernible by the aerials on top of this solid hillock. Not only this, but the tunnel entrances were visible from the perimeter surrounding the whole of the headquarters complex.

Before embarking on my tour of the whole command – a frontier of thirteen hundred miles from the North Cape to Hamburg – for which I had my own RAF aircraft, there were courtesy calls to be made, starting with the Norwegian Defence Minister. Sam Elworthy had warned me that he was an autocrat.

When I called on Tidemand I was more than prepared to give him as much as I got. He greeted me warmly enough but then showed his true colours by saying with a smile, but with a bullying tone in his voice, that when I arrived at Oslo he had intended to send me straight back to England because Norway would insist on an admiral. I immediately countered this by saying I had been selected and appointed not by Norway but by the NATO Supreme Allied Commander in Europe, General Andrew Goodpaster. I felt I had won the first round! Tidemand then changed his tune and said he had been told by Healey that he was sending NATO "the best fighting general in the British Army – a real professional". I told him I was flattered. Tidemand returned to the offensive by saying that Healey had also told him that I had 'rocked the boat' over the proposed run-down of the Gurkhas and that I had been right. I counter-attacked by agreeing, and added for good measure that I had succeeded in surviving because no politician or senior soldier held any fear for me. I told Tidemand that my first priority was to tour the whole of my command in order to brief myself on the 'state of play' as it existed on the ground and not be influenced by lengthy written briefs. I knew perfectly well that this encounter with Tidemand would merely be the precursor of many clashes ahead. I had taken an instant dislike to him and no doubt he to me. I had no intention of allowing him to think that he was cock of the walk and could ride roughshod over me. Norway was merely one of the countries for whose defence I would be responsible in the event of a Russian invasion. The defence of Denmark and Schleswig Holstein were also my responsibility.

Fortunately my chief of public relations was a very experienced Norwegian, by name Claus Koren, who was well known and highly respected in NATO circles. He was to be a close adviser to me, particularly in respect of the Tyne Tees Television documentary film, 'A Day in the Life of a General', which had reared its head shortly after I had assumed my appointment of Commander-in-Chief AFNORTH. More about this later. Meanwhile I had many commitments on my plate.

I had made it clear in my initial address to the whole headquarters staff that they would take my leadership as I construed my duty to be as commander-in-chief, whether it was popular or unpopular. I said the western world was suffering from a surfeit of committees, and I did not intend to follow suit. I would visit the respective commanders of Norway, Denmark and Schleswig Holstein, which came under my command, on their home ground, and not summon them to my own headquarters for consultation and periodical committee meetings. I said that the type of senior officer who was good on committees was not usually a leader who would take firm and, if necessary, unpopular decisions. A man with the qualities of leadership was not prepared to submerge his identity in the working of a committee. I rubbed this in by saying that I had been a staff officer from captain to major, to lieutenant colonel, to brigadier, and to major general. I had also been an instructor at a staff college. Too often committees devolved into the taking of minutes and the wasting of time.

Before I set out to tour the whole area of my command in my own RAF aircraft, I issued instructions that the three briefs for Norway, Denmark and Schleswig Holstein were each to be confined to an easy to handle map with the essential information annotated on it. In other words, what I required was an *aide memoire* and not a written brief. Each map would be subject to amendments in the light of the exact situation as I found it to be 'on the spot', and thereafter kept up-to-date.

Shortly after my arrival I had to sack my British house staff of four Scottish soldiers for they were obviously drop-outs from their Scottish regiment, and were lazy, untidy and drank too much. The final nail in the coffin came one night when I caught one of them red-handed in the drawing room helping himself from my whisky decanter. I asked the Gurkha regiment of which I was colonel (7th Duke of Edinburgh's Own Gurkha Rifles now the 2nd Royal Gurkha Rifles) to provide me with a smart relief team, plus a piper. Not long after I received an abrupt letter from the adjutant general at the Ministry of Defence demanding to know on whose authority I had dismissed the British house staff and substituted a Gurkha house staff. In my reply I was equally abrupt. I started off by saying, "I received your letter with some surprise and a dangerous rise in blood pressure." I then gave him the facts and stated that the British Commander-in-Chief of NATO's Northern Flank should be provided with a show-piece of a house staff and not a rabble, bearing in mind the amount of entertainment he and his wife were required to do. I said that it was his responsibility to ensure that the highest standard was maintained. I heard no more.

My wife and I were allocated an extremely nice flat in Copenhagen in the old naval fort, and we would fly to Copenhagen most weekends. The Danes were far more friendly than the Norwegians and knew how to entertain in style. Denis Healey was visiting Copenhagen shortly after I had assumed command so I asked to see him. I had breakfast with him at the British ambassador's residence. I raised with him the fact that I was being paid as a lieutenant-general and not as a 4-star general, and was, therefore, masquerading as a 4-star general. Were Norway to know this we would be playing straight into their hands for they already had a 4-star admiral, who had been Chief of the Norwegian Defence Staff for five years, and had been hankering after the NATO appointment of Commander-in-Chief AFNORTH. Healey gave me the reply which clearly showed the extent to which the Ministry of Defence was in the hands of the Treasury. He told me that the British Army was only entitled to a fixed quota of 4-star generals and that I would have to wait until the first vacancy arose. Luckily I received a handsome entertainment allowance from Supreme Headquarters Allied Forces Europe.

There was a very favourable reaction on the part of NATO Supreme Headquarters and the British Ministry of Defence to the prospect of a Tyne Tees documentary to be called 'A Day in the Life of a General', for such a film would give NATO much needed publicity. Filming was due to start in September 1969, and would take the form of me being interviewed at my peace and war headquarters and at my official residence. A short time later filming would move to Denmark to coincide with the NATO amphibious 'Exercise Green Express'.

The aims of the film were fourfold: first, to show the military preparedness of NATO, second, to highlight the nature of the Russian threat; third, to demonstrate the vital necessity for the west to realise that NATO's defence shield was securely in place to defend the free world; fourth, to reveal the potency and high level of alert of NATO's fast response force at a critical point in the Cold War.

I personally checked that every aspect of security would be one hundred per cent watertight and that no breach of security would be possible. I knew only too well that every effort would be made by certain 'ceasefire soldiers' and cowardly ministers and politicians to sabotage the film on phoney security and political grounds. This was to prove deadly accurate. This was a challenge that I relished.

My previous experience of the robust Allied Forces Central Europe had given me ample warning that I would be dealing with a bunch of ministers and politicians who were stark afraid of upsetting the Russians. Why did the former Commander-in-Chief of Allied Forces Central Europe, General Graf Kielmansegg, under whom I had served as his deputy chief of staff, recommend me privately as the ideal choice for my present appointment? He knew I would speak my mind and highlight the Russian threat and not be muzzled. I was determined to take as my text the words that Liddel Hart wrote in his book *World War Two*: "Why did not the Norwegians offer stronger resistance?" He answered his own question: "The Norwegian people paid with blood and suffering for the failure of their responsible politicians." I was not going to kowtow to any Minister of Defence, nor for that matter to my boss, the Supreme Allied Commander Europe, General Andrew Goodpaster.

The British Ministry of Defence knew my reputation for speaking my mind. When I was Director of Operations, Borneo, I stood no nonsense from the individual service chiefs in Singapore, who were my superiors in rank. By comparison my relationship with the Commander-in-Chief Far East, Admiral Sir Varyl Begg, could not have been warmer. The same applied to Lord Head, the British High Commissioner, Malaya, Tunku Abdul Rahman, Prime Minister and President-elect of Malaysia, the Sultan of Brunei, the Governor of North Borneo (Sabah), the High Commissioner Brunei, the Inspector-General of the Malayan Police, and his Inspectors of Police in North Borneo and Sarawak.

Defence Minister Tideman of Norway kicked up a fuss because he and his government had not been informed of the plans for the film. But he piped down when he was told that NATO Supreme Headquarters had already reacted favourably to the prospect of the film, and so had the British Ministry of Defence.

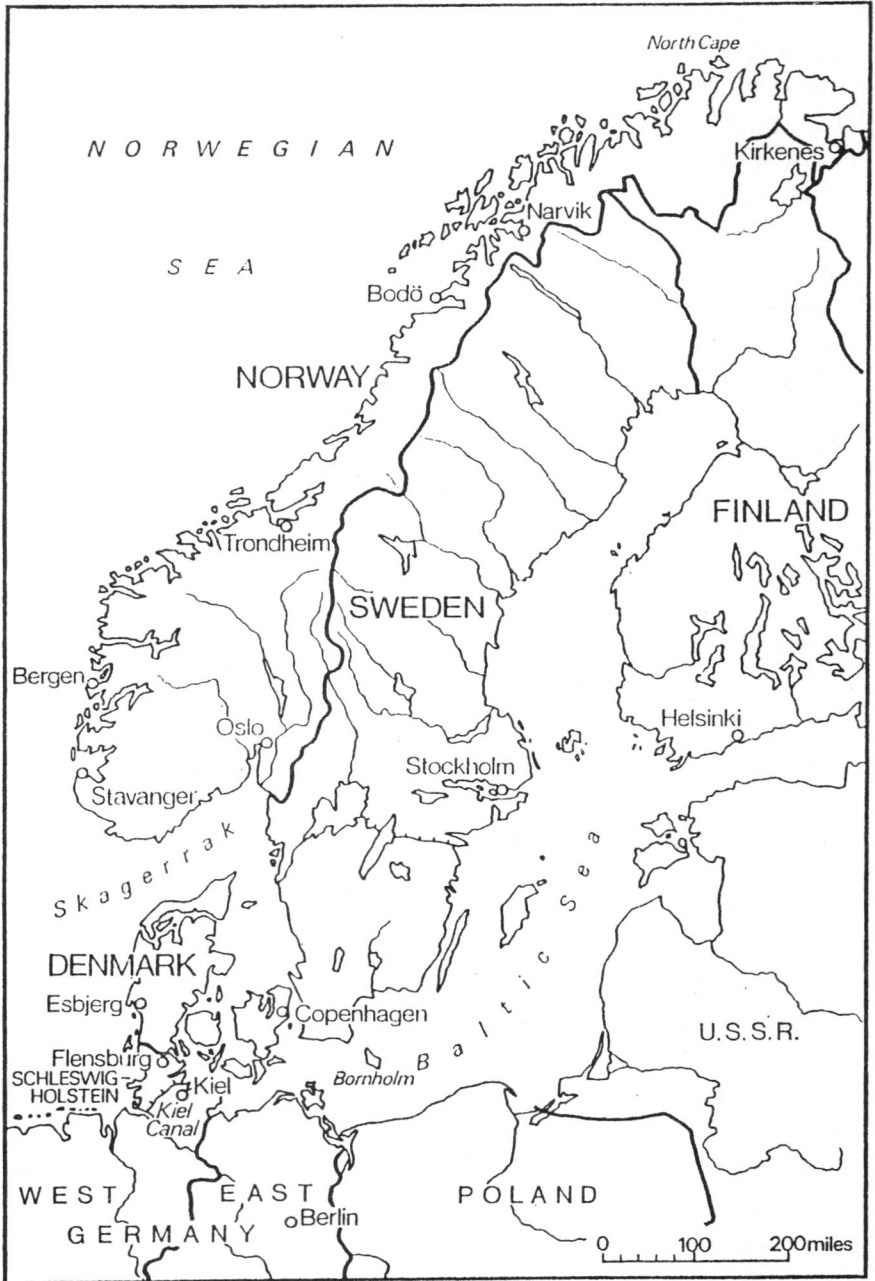

North Cape

Kirkenes

NORWEGIAN

Narvik

SEA

Bodö

NORWAY

FINLAND

Trondheim

SWEDEN

Bergen

Helsinki

Oslo

Stockholm

Stavanger

S k a g e r r a k

B a l t i c   S e a

DENMARK

Esbjerg

Copenhagen

U.S.S.R.

Flensburg

SCHLESWIG-HOLSTEIN

Kiel

Bornholm

B

Kiel Canal

WEST

EAST

POLAND

GERMANY

Berlin

0   100   200 miles

256

In mid November the film was shown to me accompanied by my deputy, senior officers in the headquarters and by Norwegian and Danish information and intelligence officials. Without exception everyone agreed that it was vivid television, a real 'knee-jerker' and there was no way in which security had been compromised. Furthermore there was nothing new in what I and others had already said. A few days later we reassembled for the formal security vetting by NATO, represented by the SHAPE (Supreme Headquarters Allied Powers Europe) Chief of Intelligence and Security – a British Major-General; the SHAPE Chief of Public Information – an American Colonel; and the British Army's Director of Public Relations – a British brigadier. These three officers were in complete agreement that there were no possible security objections and that there was no reason why the film should not be shown as it was without cuts of any description. The British Army's Director of Public Relations made one caveat, namely that there might be political objections to my criticism of NATO public relations. I knew from past experience in AFCENT that political objections invariably raised their ugly head to wreck the best of plans. Accordingly I was prepared for stormy weather ahead.

Sure enough the chief of staff at SHAPE telephoned me to say that the supreme commander could not support the views of his two security representatives who had vetted and approved the film. I asked if SACEUR himself had seen the film. The reply was that he had not yet seen it. I realised immediately that there was 'dirty work going on at the crossroads'. That very evening I received a signal from SACEUR asking me to eliminate certain statements and film shots. I immediately 'put the ferret in' and discovered that the 'nigger in the wood-pile' was none other than the British Army's Director of Public Relations – a mere brigadier – who was not in one of the combatant arms of the British Army. He had expressed doubts about the film which he had not had the guts to express to me at the security vetting at my headquarters. These doubts had been passed by the British Ministry of Defence to SHAPE.

Healey then asked to see the film, the copyright of which belonged to Tyne Tees Television. Tyne Tees agreed but only on the understanding that this was a courtesy on their part and in no way would they accept censorship. Healey showed his true colours, that of being mesmerised by the Russian threat which he considered I had portrayed too vividly. Until then I had trusted him, though I abhorred his left wing Labour Party policies. I knew him and liked him, but I had been warned that he was a socialist political opportunist. From now on I would not trust him, particularly after he had expressed a phoney security objection in the House of Commons. He then expressed his misgivings to SACEUR, who had still not seen the film, and suggested that he should do so.

The British Ministry of Defence then suggested to Tyne Tees that they should show the film to me again in the light of the objections that had been raised. After viewing the film again I pronounced loud and clear that the film made NATO and also AFNORTH look far more efficient and effective than we really were. Thus the film had achieved an outstanding coup and I was well pleased, and so should NATO have been.

The next episode in this drama was that I was told that the chief of the NATO foreign affairs department had seen the film and that he and Norway in particular condemned the film as being so politically sensitive that it could only be shown on the strict understanding that it was not shown in Norway or Denmark.

I realised that I was up against officials and two countries that were petrified by the mere shadow of the Russian bear and lacked any semblance of moral courage. At dinner one night at his residence I had a chat with my friend, Philip Crowe, the American ambassador. He was astounded at the weak-kneed reaction of those concerned so far and exhorted me to stand firm.

The film was then shown to a large audience of VIPs and officials in Brussels, including Dr. Manlio Brosio, the Secretary General of NATO, the British ambassador and acting on behalf of the NATO Council, the Supreme NATO Commander – my boss – who had still not yet taken the trouble to see the film for himself. After the film had been shown a number of NATO public relations officials announced that they were full of praise, and so much so that one of them said aloud so that all could hear, "It's a superb job – exactly what the NATO information services have been trying to do, without success, for years."

Brosio then held a meeting in his office. He complained that I had omitted to stress the political control of NATO, and had criticised NATO's information services, for which he, of course, was entirely responsible, and thus could only be adversely criticised by himself!

I then received a signal from my boss, General Goodpaster, the Supreme Allied Commander, which included a list of mandatory cuts. The cuts were so childish and so subservient to the weak-kneed NATO officials that I realised political considerations were regarded as being of more importance than alerting the public to NATO's readiness to stand firm against the Russian threat. Also because the film belonged to Tyne Tees and not to NATO, the only card that NATO could play was the phoney one of breach of security.

Then Tidemand entered the fray and decided to put a spoke in the wheels by complaining that the film had been made without sufficient consultation with Norway's government, and therefore it should not be shown.

I was then told by SACEUR to inform Tyne Tees that if

the film was to be passed for security then the mandatory cuts must be made. This put me in a humiliating position with Tyne Tees and I was not prepared to be humiliated by a bunch of 'ceasefire' soldiers and NATO officials. I thought seriously of deciding on doing a 'Carrington' i.e. resignation. But on further deep contemplation I realised that, for one thing, this would play straight into the hands of Norway by opening the door for them to press that my successor should be their Chief of Defence, Admiral Johnnessen, who, having already held that post for five years, was hovering like a falcon ready to swoop and seize the appointment. But I had a powerful friend at court – whom I shall reveal later – so I decided that I could do more good by staying at my post and achieving my aim by extensive touring of Norway, Denmark and Schleswig Holstein, and speaking in public on the Russian threat by land, sea and air.

It certainly went against the grain having to write to the chairman of the Independent Television, informing him of the mandatory security cuts that would have to be made, all of which, of course, I knew to be phoney and childish. I also had to inform Tyne Tees to bring the film back to Norway to enable me to review the film and point out where the necessary mandatory cuts would have to be made. I only hoped that Tyne Tees would realise that I was only acting against my better judgement on churlish instructions with which I was obliged to obey in my NATO capacity of Commander-in-Chief AFNORTH.

However, by now the British press had 'smelt a rat' and so had Members of Parliament. Tyne Tees had contacted the then Conservative Shadow Defence Minister, Geoffrey Rippon, MP for Hexham, who was weekending in Liechtenstein. At the same time Tyne Tees alerted *The Sunday Times* and *The Guardian* through personal contacts.

Rippon heard the Tyne Tees case and promptly asked for the film to be made swiftly available before an irrevocable ban could be imposed.

He then organised a showing at the House of Commons for 60 MPs and members of the House of Lords who had constituency links with Tyne Tees or acknowledged experience of intelligence and defence interests.

At this juncture *The Sunday Times* front-paged the issue and *The Guardian* followed with a scathing leader which began: "If NATO cannot control a film how can we trust it to fight a war?" The pre-publicity led to a flurry of activity in Brussels and Whitehall.

As his audience took their seats telegrams arrived from Healey, Lord Aylestone (Chairman of the Independent Television Authority), and Goodpaster, each giving conflicting advice. One said only Privy Councillors should see the film, another that only security-cleared MPs should see it. The audience hooted their derision calling on Rippon to show the programme. The film rolled. At the close there was applause and a unanimous view that it should be transmitted.

Problems of content were then raised by Brosio and the Norwegian Government. I realised only too well that by now the British chiefs of staff would have lost faith in my political judgement. More of this later.

After the Commons showing of the film, Rippon had pledged that, if a ban resulted, when a Conservative Government returned to power, provided he was appointed Secretary of State for Defence, he would see to it that the film was shown. As he was at that time Shadow Defence Spokesman the appointment seemed very likely. In the event he was disappointed; he became Minister of Technology. The Defence portfolio went to Lord Carrington (in later years to become Secretary General of NATO).

Nevertheless, through Rippon's good offices, Tyne Tees was able to secure a private showing of the film in the secure underground film theatre of the Ministry of Defence in Whitehall. Lord Carrington attended, with his Parliamentary secretary, Lord Balniel, with Tyne Tees present to answer any questions. There was none. Poker-faced, Carrington and Balniel refused any comment, rose and left silently after the viewing.

The following letter, prompted by an MP friendly to the Tyne Tees cause, was passed to them:

Minister of State for Defence
Whitehall, London SW1

D/MIN/EB/859

Dear Geoffrey

The Defence Secretary has asked me to reply on his behalf to your letter of 14th January, about the Tyne Tees TV film 'A day in the life of a General'.

Lord Carrington and I have now seen the film. As a result we are satisfied that the decision whether it should be released for public showing remains a matter for the NATO authorities and that the British Government should comply with whatever they decide. We have consulted them and have ascertained that they see no reason to depart from their earlier decision.

Yours ever,
Robin Lord Balniel
Geoffrey Stewart-Smith Esq. MP.

It was about two years later that Tyne Tees received an unexpected invitation at Christmas to attend the seasonal shindig for special media guests at the Ministry of Defence. As it drew to a close the motive for the invitation became clear.

262

They were asked to meet the permanent secretary of the Ministry of Defence to receive an unofficial and belated apology over brandy for the way Tyne Tees had been treated over the film.

Sir James Dunnett put his fingertips together for the moment of truth:

"You see, Walter was a damn fine fighting soldier, but he was a bloody awful diplomat ..." More about this later.

Although Tyne Tees and I and my staff had taken every safeguard to ensure the total cleanliness of the production in security terms, the film was nevertheless banned on phoney security grounds. What was the real reason behind this?

The ostensible security reasons evidently cloaked a political imperative: the first SALT (Strategic Arms Limitation Talks) were on the horizon between the USA and the Soviet Union. The then Secretary General of NATO (Italian Signor Brosio) took the view that the robust nature of the film could jeopardise those talks.

This conviction evidently pressured the NATO military command and the British Labour Government to bow to the *force majeure* of the international political situation as interpreted by Signor Brosio.

Apparently General Goodpaster had complained that the vexed question of the Tyne Tees film had given him more work and anxiety than any other problem since he had taken over the reins of SACEUR. In fact, after I had retired from the British Army in 1972, I was invited to take part in a Defence symposium in Washington. Several senior American officers, who had previously been on General Goodpaster's staff, came up to me and said they had entirely disagreed with General Goodpaster's immature attitude and would like me to know how much they entirely agreed with the film, and would like to congratulate me on the unshakable stance I had taken and the moral courage I had shown throughout.

To revert to NATO and my key position as Commander-in-Chief AFNORTH. I received a directive from Goodpaster which stated that his three Commanders-in-Chief (AFNORTH, AFCENT and AFSOUTH) and all the subordinate officers holding senior appointments, were to seek advice from their superiors before making public statements which had a bearing on NATO policy. I sent back a blunt, stinging reply which was tantamount to saying that I was a four-star Commander-in-Chief and had no intention of being shackled as if I was an immature child.

As 1969 was drawing to a close I was invited to give a lecture at the Royal United Service Institution (RUSI), London, on 'Problems of the Defence of NATO's Northern Flank'. The lecture was not due until 28 March 1970, which gave me ample time to circulate it through NATO's tremulous bureaucracy from whom I expected the usual objections to the fact that I had revealed too much of the true state of affairs and should play down the threat. I was not to be disappointed.

Naturally I informed my boss, the Supreme Commander, also the British CGS, the governments of Norway, Denmark, Germany and the British and American Ambassadors in Oslo, that I had been invited to give this lecture. The Supreme Commander, General Goodpaster, told me he was so pleased that it would give me the opportunity to improve the existing public ignorance of NATO and its role. I thought to myself that he, for one, would not have the guts to prevent my script from being watered down by those cringing member nations of NATO. I thought to myself that I would be unable to tell the truth until I retired, when there would be plenty of opportunities for me to speak my mind in public and to write letters to the press. I sent personal copies of my script to Goodpaster, Brosio, and purely out of courtesy, a copy also to Tidemand for his permanent under secretary at his Defence Ministry, who not only studied the script, but agreed with it.

However, the lily-livered Tidemand poked his head above the parapet and, ever fearful of the Russian shadow, raised his usual objections. Brosio, being of the same ilk, even wanted to have the lecture cancelled. This impertinence was frustrated by the fact that the lecture had already been advertised by the RUSI, which was entirely a British institution over which NATO had no jurisdiction whatever.

I had been told by a friend that the British chiefs of staff – the 'old men of Vichy' – had lost faith in my political judgement. I told him that the feeling was mutual.

The British CGS stipulated that the script would have to be cleared by the British Ministry of Defence, and that I should be briefed in Whitehall. If he thought that any briefing would have the slightest effect on me, he had another think coming. Little did he or NATO know how strongly my views were being supported by Philip Crowe, the US ambassador in Norway, and also by all the American ambassadors in Scandinavia. But there was also strong support coming from a certain source of far greater importance than any NATO VIP, Minister of Defence or the defence ministers of the individual countries in AFNORTH. This will become clear when reading the events shortly before my departure at the end of my assignment as CINCNORTH.

My Secretary of the Staff – a Royal Navy lieutenant commander – met me at the RUSI and before going into the lecture hall told me this: "There are a number of MOD 'spies' – officers and civil servants – attending your lecture so I have drawn this seating plan for you, which shows where they are sitting." I was determined that my audience should know from the very beginning that I would be speaking on behalf of NATO, rather than expressing my own views as Commander-in-Chief, Allied Forces Northern Europe. Therefore I made this clear in my opening remarks, so that my audience would know straight away that I had been gagged. By the time I had finished my lecture, only a dimwit would not have realised that my lecture had been 'sanitized' from beginning to end.

During the question period the importance of training NATO forces was raised. I replied that, off the record, during the space of one year up to two thousand Allied servicemen had taken part in exercises. When the audience dispersed, the Soviet defence attaché collared the Norwegian defence attache and accused his government of hiding the truth on the grounds that Norway had invariably stated that Allied troops only came to Norway for NATO exercises and acclimatization, whereas the Commander-in-Chief AFNORTH had now clearly stated that there were always two thousand NATO troops in Norway.

This came to the notice of the cantankerous Tideman, who was smartly told that I had been deliberately misquoted and that he himself had fallen headlong into the Russian trap. Relations between us were now about as cordial as those between Cassius Clay (the former world champion boxer) and the US Army Draft Board.

Tideman's days as Minister of Defence were now over and he was succeeded by a Mr. Gunnen Hellson, an ex-school master. When Tideman took his successor to a NATO Council meeting in Venice, he told General Goodpaster that I did not agree with his proposed new command structure for Norway. He said that Norway could no longer tolerate me as Commander-in-Chief. Goodpaster replied that he did not agree with Tideman's sentiments, nor with his proposed new command structure. I was told that Tideman left the meeting in such a huff that he forgot to take his hat with him. He must have looked extremely foolish when, a few weeks later, the Norwegian Defence Committee agreed that the command control structure should be that which I had proposed.

I was now able to escape from the 'hothouse' of NATO for a break of a few weeks. In my capacity as Colonel of the 7th Duke of Edinburgh's Own Gurkha Rifles, who were stationed in Hong Kong, I received permission from all concerned to pay an official visit to the regiment. From there I was invited to visit Malaysia in my capacity as a Knight of Malaysia. I was greeted and treated as an honoured guest and made to feel at home. The Commissioner of Police, Singapore, also invited me as his guest to visit Singapore after completing my visit to Malaysia. This was another welcome break amongst old friends, a number of whom had served with me in Borneo, when I was Director of Operations during Indonesian Confrontation. I was also invited to visit Brunei in my capacity of a Knight of Brunei. While I was there the Sultan – father of the present Sultan – invited me to return as his defence adviser when I retired from the army. It was certainly a welcome change to be amongst old friends who appreciated what I had been able to achieve for them.

My old friend, General Sam Manekshaw, who was then Commander-in-Chief of the Indian Army, had sent me a signal before I left Oslo on this tour, to say that I was not allowed to trespass in India's air space without visiting him in New Delhi! I had to obtain official permission from London and NATO because of the strained relations between England and India on account of India's rapport with Russia, particularly in defence co-operation. At first permission was refused and when I informed Sam Manekshaw of this he sent a signal to me which amounted to, 'Leave it to me to sort out'. Apparently he succeeded in convincing the 'powers that be' that this was purely and simply a private invitation from one friend to another. Furthermore, he now happened to be colonel of my and my grandfather's regiment, the 8th Gurkha Rifles, and would like to greet me on his and the regiment's behalf.

We had a most friendly meeting and spoke with complete frankness and mutual trust. He had very firm views on the role of politicians with respect to the Indian Army. His rule was that the politicians had their responsibilities to perform and the soldiers had theirs and the two should never mix. He went on to say that the discipline, efficiency and reputation of the new Indian Army depended entirely upon its being totally divorced from politics. I was naturally intrigued when he said to me, "I do everything possible to avoid having any personal contact with politicians and will not meet them socially." I said, "Lucky man, I do my best to follow suit, but in NATO more kudos is accorded to politically minded generals than to military competent ones."

Our meeting took place not long before the Indian Army invaded South Pakistan, now Bangladesh. Sam Manekshaw exuded confidence and was every inch a fighting general, so much so that there was no doubt in my mind what the outcome of such a conflict would be. Later he was promoted to Field Marshal.

As colonel of my former regiment, the 8th Goorkha (Indian spelling) Rifles, he had organised in my honour a reception and luncheon attended by past and present officers and their wives. They were obviously so pleased to meet me that anyone would have thought that I was colonel of the regiment, by the way they treated me. I was made to feel one of the family, just as I was in 1968, when I was guest of the regiment in Shillong, Assam. I have seldom been the centre of such a friendly and happy gathering. What struck me most was the attitude towards me by the wives, all of whom spoke perfect English, and made me feel that I was a member of the family who at long last had come home to be among them. During the luncheon, just as in 1968, I was strikingly impressed that all the regimental traditions and customs were so proudly and lovingly preserved. It was

268

with sadness that I said goodbye to my hosts with the feeling that I was still a member of, and indeed belonged to the regiment. I returned to Oslo feeling completely uplifted.

I spent a considerable amount of my time visiting and revisiting all the strategically important sectors in Norway, Denmark and Schleswig Holstein. Wherever I went I gave a speech to as wide an audience as possible and ensured that the press were present in force. I spoke my mind and did not pull any punches. To drive the military lessons home and to silence the doubters about Russian intentions, I would quote extracts from the belligerent speeches made by Russia's military leaders. I quoted them so often that I knew them by heart, and would step aside from the lectern and pronounce slowly and in measured terms, without any reference to my script, exactly what the Russian military chiefs had said. For example, General Savechin had said: "The role of the Soviet Army was to stand by, ready to shake the tree when the rotten fruit is ripe to fall." What about the aims of the Soviet Fleet? I would quote the Russian Chief of Naval Staff who said: "In the past, our ships and naval units have operated principally near our coasts. Now we intend to be prepared for broad offensive policies against the sea and land forces of the imperialists in any part of the world's oceans and adjacent territories." I usually ended these quotations by reminding my audience that it was Kruschev who said the Soviets would 'lead us to our grave with one arm round our shoulder'.

It was in November that the next crisis occurred. In an off-the-cuff discussion with the newspaper, *De Telegraft*, I had said, "Those who dismiss warnings of the Russian threat as alarmist don't know what they are talking about. I want to emphasise that for my task the early arrival of NATO reinforcements to Norway would be essential, for Norway could not possibly be expected to stand alone against the might of a

Russian invasion. Therefore I must stress the importance of NATO reinforcements to Norway. This country would be hopelessly lost unless reinforcements arrived in time."

This quotation was taken out of its context and twisted to give another meaning. In talking about the Norwegian and Danish policy to exclude Allied military bases on their soil, I was quoted as saying, "They don't know what they are talking about. Just take Norway. Now in war-time this country is hopelessly lost."

This misquote occurred not long before the official visit of the Soviet Prime Minister, Mr. Kosygin, to Norway. A few days before this visit the Norwegian left wing newspaper, *Dagbladet*, published the *De Telegraft* article under the headlines, 'Kolsas Chief Attacks Norwegian Defence Policy. Norway Would Be Hopelessly Lost in War.' This, quite naturally, caused an uproar.

The press was divided. I was either denounced as 'The Sword Rattling General' and 'The Talkative General', or supported with headlines such as, 'General Walker's Unpleasant Truths', and 'Do Not Disturb the Ostrich General'. Welcome support came from a Norwegian military magazine, '*Offisier-bladet*'. A leading article stated: "After the incident with General Walker it is natural to raise the question whether a military commander – within certain security limits – must have the same right and duty to make his view and evaluations known in line with other professional leaders of our society. That this might not suit our politicians and others very well is no argument. Or are generals only experts and advisers to the responsible politicians? In such case, who is to inform the common man in our democratic society how the military professionals look upon the situation."

Equally strong support came from King Olaf of Norway himself. I had invited him and his recently appointed Minister of Defence – Gunner Hellson – to a defence study that I was to hold in my War Headquarters underground bunker. I met the King at the entrance to the bunker where he dismounted from his motor car and we walked together through the long tunnel to the amphitheatre where all the officers were assembled, and where the study period was to take place. During our walk the King was extremely pleasant and supportive. After the morning session he apologised to me that he would be unable to accept my invitation to lunch because he had to receive the credentials of a newly arrived ambassador. While walking back down the tunnel to his car it became obvious to me that he had thoroughly enjoyed the morning session, and said that he had learned a great deal, and was looking forward to the afternoon session. Again I met him on his arrival at the entrance to the tunnel, and we discussed some of the high points of what had transpired at the morning session. Nothing seemed to have escaped his attention, and he asked me to highlight certain points in my afternoon address.

As the King took his seat he turned round and could not see his Minister of Defence. He asked me where he was. I replied that he had told me he had an important brief to prepare for King Olaf. The King was obviously extremely annoyed and whispered to me: "The stupid idiot, he is new to his job and would have learned far more of real importance here than writing a brief for me."

At the end of the day's session we walked together again and he was most complimentary about the study period. I mentioned to the King that I attached great importance to Norway's home guard, and was full of admiration for the courage and expertise of his Resistance fighters against the Germans. I said that on all my tours of his country I always made a point of visiting the graves and memorials of those Resistance fighters who had sacrificed their lives for their country. The King expressed his pleasure and thanked me. Just as he was about to climb into his car, he drew me aside and said, "I am so glad that at long last there is someone who has the courage to stand up to the bully. Good luck to you and keep up the good work." It was nice to know that there was someone of his calibre who appreciated what I was saying in public, and which had his full support. So much for all those ministers, those politicians and military chiefs who had been so vehemently critical of me and wanted my head on a platter. As far as I was concerned they could now put the King's sentiment in their pipe and smoke it.

A few days later I received an official sealed plain envelope in which was an unsigned message which read, "As matters now stand you have emerged from the scrap with considerable dignity and sympathy." To this day I do not know who sent it, but I could have a good guess.

Having given praise to Norway's Resistance fighters, I must also highlight the gallant role performed by Denmark's Resistance fighters. The Danish Resistance and their families voluntarily risked capture, torture and execution by helping British forces. More than 100 RAF air crew were able to return to Britain as a result of the efforts of Danish civilians. A rapidly growing clandestine press was developed in answer to German censorship, and the contributions made by the Danish Secret Service were highly esteemed by Great Britain. A secret poll in early 1943 showed that 70 per cent of the population supported the Resistance.

By the end of the war more than 100 Danish Resistance fighters had been executed, 400 had been murdered and more than 500 civilians killed by German terror tactics. Some 5,871 Danes were deported to German concentration camps.

Both Norway's and Denmark's Resistance attacks were a proper and praiseworthy response to Churchill's request to set Europe ablaze. Their members of the Resistance were primarily concerned with proving the error of their respective government's belief that an occupied country could be useful to the Allies.

I knew that at the NATO Council meeting in Brussels in December, the new and recently appointed Norwegian Defence Minister and his Chief of Defence had lodged a strong attack against me to General Goodpaster, and to the British Minister of Defence, Lord Carrington, and to the British Chief of the Defence Staff. I was not unduly perturbed and, in fact, was by now impervious to the clandestine efforts to dismiss me. I held too many cards and now had the support of General Goodpaster, the Supreme Commander. I think this change on Goodpaster's part came as a result of the performance I put up during the concluding conference after an Exercise known as SHAPEX. The three NATO Commanders-in-Chief – AFNORTH (myself), AFCENT (a German general), and AFSOUTH (an American admiral), were asked by Goodpaster to give our verbal appreciation of the lessons learned and our recommendations. I had prepared a careful and hard-hitting Appreciation of the situation which I knew by heart, so that I only had to glance at a few headings. Apparently I spoke with such conviction that Goodpaster's deputy – a British four-star general – came up to me during the lunch interval to say that my performance had been most convincing and impressive and that everyone was saying so, including Goodpaster, who was delighted.

Apart from this I had been invited to give a number of lectures to various institutes, including in England, and had been far more controversial than I had ever been in Norway and Denmark. None of these lectures had drawn forth adverse criticism, but rather praise for revealing the true state of affairs which the politicians were hiding from the public.

At the end of my lectures I always rubbed the lessons home by pronouncing several hard hitting quotations. These were:

1. It was a Norwegian poet who said: "Peace is the most ruthless creature in the world. One must fight for it all the time."

2. It was General de Gaulle who said: "Treaties are like roses and young girls. They last while they last."

3. But it was a Russian Marshal who said: "The rule of the Red Army is to stand by ready to shake the tree when the rotten fruit is ripe to fall."

4. And it is General Walker who warned: "The price of liberty is eternal vigilance."

These quotations invariably proved to strike home, judging by the loud applause.

As my time for handing over to my successor in February 1972, drew closer, my days were devoted to farewell visits, inspections and dinners. All my former critics, even enemies, went out of their way to bury the hatchet and to emphasise that any previous difficulties and difference of opinion had been due to misunderstandings! I was presented with extremely nice farewell gifts and so was my wife.

Throughout my whole time as Commander-in-Chief AFNORTH, my wife, Beryl, had captured the hearts of both friends and foes alike. As Tom Pocock wrote in his Appreciation of her, "Beauty of looks and beauty of spirit, combined in Beryl, the one reflecting the other." She was always beautifully dressed and much admired and had the knack of making friends wherever she went. She made our house in Oslo and our flat in Copenhagen a haven of peace where I was able to relax and enjoy her wonderful companionship. Her dinner parties – often for twenty-five – were the talk of the elite of both Norway and Denmark. She was a marvellous hostess and exuded charm and friendship. She could read me like a book and knew exactly how to cope when the pressure was on. The greater the pressure on me the more understanding, calm and placid she became, so that my mind was able to switch off from my problems to one of peace and relaxation. She was a wonderful wife and an equally wonderful mother and grandmother.

Shortly before leaving Oslo and officially vacating my appointment, I was invited to attend the King's Guard Church Parade on 16 December 1971. Unfortunately I was due to visit for the last time the very north of Norway, as close as permissible to the border with Russia, on that date. So unfortunately I was unable to accept the invitation. When I returned to my headquarters, my personal assistant, a Norwegian lady, handed me a type-written memorandum, in which she said she had spoken to the adjutant of the King's Guards and explained the reason why I could not alter the date of my visit to north Norway. She said the adjutant made the following comment: "What I say is not as an officer but as a private person. It is nice to know that the General dares to speak out. There are also others here who support him. We are therefore very sorry that, in the light of recent events, he will be unable to attend."

Later, shortly before my departure from Oslo, I received two messages from the palace, the first on a coloured foolscap size special telegram form bearing the Norwegian national flag and the royal arms, with the following typed message: "SIR WALTER WALKER. I THANK YOU AND GIVE YOU HEREBY MY FULL SYMPATHY AND SUPPORT."

The second message was in an ornate folder of the same size as the former. On the outside cover was the royal arms surmounting two intertwined oak leaves in gold, and the four borders of the cover bounded by oak leaves on a gold

background. Inside was the following typed message:
"SIR WALTER WALKER, I THANK YOU FOR YOUR CLEAR TALK AND I AM CONVINCED THAT IT IS SAID BECAUSE YOU FEEL RESPONSIBLE FOR THE FREEDOM OF NORWAY AND OUR SECURITY IN FUTURE."

It was comforting to receive 'in writing' such messages of support and vindication from the royal palace, and obviously from His Majesty the King himself. He knew what it was to have his country invaded and occupied while he was forced to take refuge in England for the whole duration of World War II.

POLITICALLY RELIABLE GENERALS VERSUS MILITARILY COMPETENT ONES

I was strongly criticised by the Norwegian Parliament (Storting), because I was alleged to have said that Norway's defence in the north could not contain a Russian attack. This was interpreted and regarded by some as unwarranted meddling in Norway's bases policy.

As for political judgement, there may come a time when a Commander-in-Chief must either speak his mind or take the easy way out.

As I was the commander who would have had the responsibility in war of defending the whole of the northern flank from the Russian border in the north to Hamburg in the south, on land, sea and in the air, on which could depend the very future of Western Europe itself, and even mankind, I had come to the conclusion that I would certainly not have sufficient forces and means to accomplish my mission, should a serious situation occur.

Was I then to keep quiet, bowing to the principle that soldiers are prevented by formal boundaries from speaking their minds? I decided that if I kept quiet, I would, in point of fact, have been giving my blessing to Norway's and Denmark's poor defence capacity and outdated defence policies.

Politicians may have a monopoly when it comes to making public statements on vital defence strategy. But, wearing my NATO hat, I decided that it was no longer any good jollying people along, or ruffling their feathers. They had to be jolted out of their apathy and told the brutal truth, and in the process, therefore, I decided that political etiquette would have to take a back seat.

Had I run with the herd as, I fear, most other commanders would have done, I would no doubt have been regarded as a politically reliable and loyal general. It always looks loyal to be running with the herd but true loyalty consists in moral courage not in conformity. When there is conflict between the choice of military competence and political reliability then I know where to place my money.

The public criticism of me in the Norwegian Parliament – mainly confined to left wing quarters – showed up the super-sensitivity and bad conscience of those concerned. I seemed to have hit an extra tender spot. Memories are short, for it was precisely such a miscalculation in 1940 that led to such a catastrophic situation.

War is a tough and dirty business but it is pat ball compared to politics. We must learn our lessons from what went wrong at the beginning of the last war, not from what went right at the end of it, and Vikings must be Vikings.

Unhappily, it was not only the politicians of Norway and Denmark who gambled with the security of their countries. Others were just as guilty, and what happened? The soil of so many countries became richly watered with the blood of young men, whom we could ill afford to lose – so many lives of infinite promise cut short in their prime.   /

One had certainly been hitting one's head against a brick wall, and I often thought how the Commander of the Soviet Northern Fleet must have held his sides with laughter to learn that a Norwegian politician had described his fleet as 'A fragile basis' on which to draw conclusions.

It was some recompense to receive, almost on the eve of vacating my appointment as Commander-in-Chief, Allied Forces Northern Europe, this somewhat belated official recognition from one of the highest NATO sources:-

"I cannot over-emphasise the importance of putting the picture of our defence situation before the public in clear and candid terms. I think that what you have done in this regard throughout your service as Commander-in-Chief, Allied Forces Northern Europe, difficult as it has been at times, has a value that will last far beyond your time here."

I have seldom crossed swords with those whose professional ability and leadership qualities I have respected and whom I have trusted.

In the latter years of my army career, my real fear as a professional soldier had always been of a desk job, particularly in the MOD, with, at that time, 1962-72, its unpleasant bitchiness, its prima donnas, ceasefire soldiers, old men of Vichy, old-fashioned fusspots, its 3rd XI material – all devoid of humanity and out of touch with the true feelings of proper soldiers at the sharp end.

As Secretary of State for War, Profumo said in 1962: "Working at the War Office is like sleeping with an elephant. Either you are over-lain or whatever you do takes two years to produce." A joke going round the army was: The new British missile was to be called 'Civil Servant' – it didn't work and it could not be fired.

At that time the services were breeding too many sleek and trusted fat cats of the Establishment, too many sanctimonious creeps, for my liking. They worshipped technology, encouraged slick talking, hunted with the hounds and ran with the hare.

Too few of the Service inmates of the MOD put up any resistance; they seemed to have forgotten how to fight. A proper soldier does not go about whimpering because he happens to have been born into a generation of clay-pigeons; he fights all the harder.

A politician (if I may soil my pen with that ten letter word) has no credibility to lose. His footwork is without compare. I learned long ago that politics is about power, not principles, and therefore the word integrity is not to be found in the politician's dictionary. Too often have the politicians been allowed to get away with savaging the services so as to be able to preserve their sacred political cows. Had they but served their armed forces with half the zeal they served themselves!

The trouble was that the type of senior officer who was good on committees was not always a leader who would take a firm and tough line, whereas a real leader is not prepared to submerge his identity in the working of a committee. He will speak his mind without fear or favour, without looking over his shoulder and certainly without any regard for his own future prospects and advancement. There were precious few of these in circulation. I had known a number of commanders whose ineptitude certainly was no worse than what was customarily thought acceptable and even praiseworthy in a general officer.

In my latter years, 1962-1972, the Ministry of Defence was breeding too many schoolmaster types who comforted themselves with the reflection that the majority of their top prefects were nice, quiet, studious boys of the sixth form. Those who did have the moral courage to speak their minds and question the system were admonished with headmasterly reproofs.

I had never allowed myself to become a *fidus achates* (devoted follower, henchman) of the Establishment. Rather had I gone to the other extreme of expressing my views with undiplomatic candour, in the certain knowledge that only in this way would the 'old men of Vichy' and the 'old-fashioned fusspots' be stirred into action. Unlike the politicians I was not hypersensitive to criticism.

My views were merely a reflection of my inner disdain and contempt for the political and military hierarchy in Whitehall during my last ten years service in the army, 1962-1972, from brigadier to 4-star general.

Commander-in-Chief
Allied Forces Northern Europe 1969-72

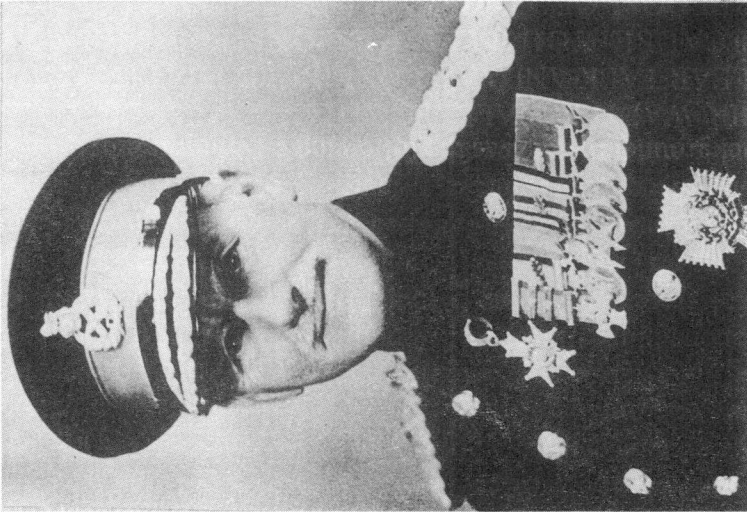

C in C in full dress

Talking with Lt. Gen. Blixenkrone-Moller, C-in-C of the
Danish Army, Frederiksborg Castle 1971

Sitting next to the Queen of Denmark at the ball in
Frederiksborg Castle 1971

Celebert besøk på Værnes

Sjefen for NATO's Nordkommando på Kolsås, den britiske general Sir Walter Walker, var i går på meget kort rutinebesøk på Værnes flystasjon. Det var første gang general Walker besøkte Værnes, etter at han tiltrådte sin nåværende stilling siste høst. På Værnes ble han møtt av stasjonssjefen, oberstløytnant Gudbrand Strømmen, og ble ellers ledsaget av stasjonssjefen på Ørlandet, oberst Nils W. Arweskoug. Besøket varte en times tid, før general fortsatte videre til Trondheim og Gråkallen med sitt spesialhelikopter.

Bildet viser general Walter Walker, i midten, i samtale med stasjonssjef oberstløytnant Gudbrand Strømmen og oberst Nils Arweskoug.

Visiting Units in Norway when C-in-C, AFNORTH

Saying farewell to C-in-C Allied Forces Southern Europe, 1971

284

Queen of Denmark visits my HQ, Oslo, 1971

Sitting beside King of Norway at my annual study period in
my underground War HQ, 1971

My farewell visit to General Westmoreland, Chief of
America's Defence Forces, Washington, 1972

Supreme Headquarters Allied Powers Europe with Supreme C-in-C American General Goodpaster during my farewell visit, February, 1972

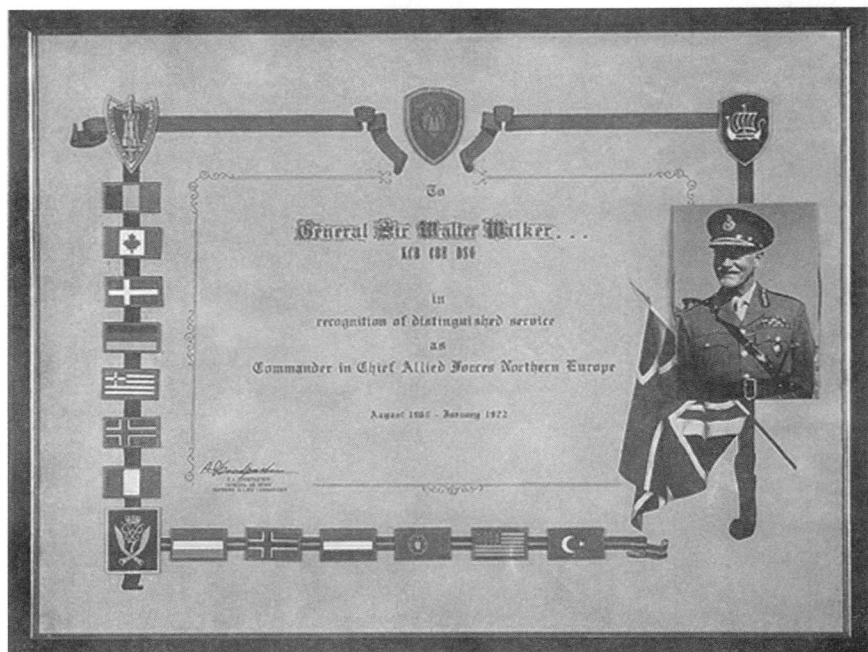

Citation presented to me by General Goodpaster, Supreme
Allied Commander Europe at our final farewell meeting

Chapter 22

Before my retirement I, together with Peter Myers, who was by then a brigadier, were the guests of the 4/8 Goorkhas (Indian spelling) in India. I flew to Calcutta, where I was welcomed by the Chief of Staff to Lieutenant General Sam Manekshaw, MC, General Officer Commanding Eastern Command and now Colonel of the 8th Goorkhas. He was an old friend, having taken over from me in 1947 the appointment of General Staff Officer, First Grade, Military Operations Directorate, General Headquarters, New Delhi. This was the beginning of the Indianisation of the Indian Army.

At Calcutta Peter Myers and I stayed at Government House for the night. I had a comfortable night with the air conditioning working well, but Peter did not sleep a wink as the air conditioning in his bedroom was not functioning. He decided to go out in the grounds to cool off. As he reached the large entrance hall he found it crammed with prostate bodies, who must have come in from the streets of the city!

I received a very warm and friendly letter of welcome from Sam Manekshaw in which he said my old battalion, the 4/8th Gurkhas, would be thrilled at having me with them. He added: "In another way I almost feel sorry for you and do hope you will be in drinking trim!"

I had asked to visit my grandmother's grave and tombstone on my way through Gauhati, the roadhead to Shillong. I had had it renovated and cleaned many years ago when the lst/8th Gurkhas were stationed in Shillong in 1937. This request caused consternation for, after a long search, it

289

was found that the cemetery at Gauhati had been built over. I received profuse apologies from Sam Manekshaw. Luckily in 1937, I had arranged for a professional photograph to be taken of the exceptionally nice white tombstone of a marble cross mounted on a plinth, which my grandfather had had erected. The carved inscription read: "Sacred To The Memory of Maria Elizabeth, The Beloved Wife of Colonel T. N. Walker, BSC, Commandant 44th Gurkhas. Born 1st July 1836, died 13th April 1879, of Cholera, in Gauhati."

Peter and I flew from Calcutta to Gauhati, the railhead to Shillong, and thence by road to the 4/8th barracks at Happy Valley, Shillong. We were most warmly welcomed outside the officers' mess by the commanding officer, Lieutenant Colonel Depinder Singh, later a general, and escorted into the officers' mess, where we were introduced to all the officers and wives. After an excellent lunch we rested until the evening when we attended a very well staged variety show and, as usual plied with drink. Next we were entertained to dinner at the Junior commissioned officers' (Gurkha officers) mess hosted by the Subedar Major, just like the old days.

The next day, 13 May, was VC Day, in celebration of Havildar Lachhiman Gurung's outstanding gallantry at the Battle of Taungdaw, more than 20 years earlier, when he was awarded the V.C.

In the morning I had a conducted tour of the battalion, including the Goorkha family quarters. Everything was in impeccable order. They had not only achieved the 8th Gurkhas pre-war high standards, but exceeded them. The *pièce de resistance* was meeting so many Gurkha pensioners, including the Gurkha officer who had been my Subedar Major when I was commanding 4/8 GR during World War II.

We were invited by Lieutenant Colonel and Mrs. Depinder Singh to have lunch at their residence. This was quite exceptional, with everything done in English style. The activities that evening were preceded by a faultless march past with Havildar Lachhiman Gurung, VC, by my side, which certainly brought a lump to my throat. We then sat down to watch the expertly organised sports, followed by a delicious English-type tea beautifully served by the officers' wives in their glistening saris.

Then came the Beating of Retreat by the brass band and the pipes and drums, once again a brilliant performance. Later that evening we were entertained by the General commanding the communication zone area, where we met many non-Goorkha officers serving in the area. This was followed by a formal dinner at the 4/8th officers' mess at which all the British traditions were strictly observed. This was followed by English style ballroom dancing. It was so nice to experience at first hand that all the old regimental traditions had been so proudly preserved.

The next morning we exchanged presents including a beautiful sari for my wife, said our warm good-byes and then departed by road for Gauhati. From there we flew to Calcutta through stormy weather. The general who received us at the airport remarked that he was thankful that he was not "up there being tossed about so violently". Peter and I again stayed the night at Government House. That evening we had a most enjoyable and friendly dinner with Lieutenant General Sam Manekshaw. Little did I realise that I would be meeting him some years later when he had become Chief of the Indian Army, and later promoted to Field Marshal.

The next day, 15 May, I spent one hour at St. John's Church (the old Calcutta Cathedral) where Beryl and I had been married on 9 November 1938. Next on my programme was to pay a courtesy call on the Deputy High Commissioner for the UK, who was surprised at the VIP treatment I had received. That evening I flew from Calcutta back to London, and thence home to my wife at our official residence. Thus ended a momentous visit which firmly cemented a long lasting friendship between the former British officers and the present Indian officers of the 4/8th Goorkha Rifles.

1972 ONWARDS

Not until after I had retired in 1972 was my biography *Fighting General* published by Collins in 1973. I myself was the author of two books – *The Bear at the Back Door* published in 1978, and *The Next Domino* published in 1980, and republished as a paperback by Corgi in 1982. In the foreword, Lord Amery wrote: "His two devastatingly factual books are a strategic study of the then Soviet global threat. We shall ignore their warning and their message at our peril."

A former British high commissioner of Pakistan, India and Australia – Lord Saint Bride – wrote this to me about my second book: *The Next Domino* is a cogent and illuminating work on which I would like to congratulate you very warmly indeed. It is a major contribution to the task of enlightening our compatriots about the true extent of the Soviet threat. What I find so dishonest about such campaigns as CND is that it is the process of catching up by the West which they regard as immoral, and not the overwhelming Soviet build-up, of up-to-date nuclear and other weapons, which has occasioned it."

I was persuaded to enter the newsletter field. I published a monthly newsletter in 1976 which I called *International Summary*. But I ceased publication after one year because I was a one-man band with only a half-day secretary and the burden overwhelmed me. I had a heavy speaking programme plus all the invitations to visit and speak abroad.

There were several episodes in the last nine years of my army career which I shall never forgive.

First was when the CIGS threatened me with a court-martial in 1963 – without having first consulted the Secretary of State for Defence – because I had fought for my Gurkhas against the Army Board's intention to cut their strength by no less than 10,000, and in such a clandestine manner that His Majesty the King of Nepal had not first been consulted, until it was too late.

Second was the rejection by the CGS of the combined recommendation of the Chief of Defence (Admiral of the Fleet Lord Louis Mountbatten) and the Commander-in-Chief Far East (Admiral Sir Varyl Begg) that I receive the accolade of the KCB in recognition of my achievements as Director of Borneo Operations. I was then recommended for the award of the CMG. Again this was rejected. Instead I received a second bar to my DSO. This led to a flood of letters from officers under my command expressing their utter disgust and their contempt for the army hierarchy in Whitehall. As far as I was concerned, the two rejections were being used by the CGS as a weapon against me for having fought for my Gurkhas.

Third was the shabby and disgraceful treatment accorded to me by the CGS and the Army Board when they completely ignored my existence on my return to England in 1965, from my successes in Borneo as Director of Operations against Indonesian confrontation.

Fourth was the abortive attempt by the Army Board to pension me off when my tour of duty as Deputy Chief of Staff HQ AFCENT came to an end in 1967, without the knowledge either of the Army Minister or the Secretary of State for Defence.

Fifth was the failed attempt of the political mandarins in Norway, Denmark, the UK, and the Secretary-General of NATO to terminate my appointment as Commander-in-Chief, AFNORTH, 1969-1972, and to castigate my political judgement, so mesmerised with fear were they of upsetting the Russians. The King of Norway and others were not so cowardly.

Sixth was the false inference by the CGS, supported by several retired field marshals who should have known better, that in 1974 I was raising a 'Private Army'.

Therefore it came as a pleasant surprise when I read in my favourite newspaper – *The Daily Telegraph* – on 23rd October 1981, the following article by Peter Simple in his column 'Way of the World':

Urgent Note

If there is one man in this country who can be called the victim of a 'conspiracy of silence' (an essential part of which is, of course, the denial that there is any such conspiracy) it is General Sir Walter Walker, whose distinguished career in the British Army culminated in his service as Commander-in-Chief, Allied Forces NATO, Northern Europe, from 1969 to 1972.

His outspokenness about the dire threat to the West from the Soviet Empire in that most important area did not exactly endear him to those who, for various reasons which can only be guessed at, did not care to listen to his warnings.

Since his retirement from the army, General Walker has continued to warn us with increasing urgency. From 1974 onwards he issued a series of newsletters in which he dealt not only with the military threat from the Soviet Empire but also with the growing threat of subversion within this country. Even the most wilfully blind and complacent can hardly deny, in 1981, that his warnings have proved correct in almost every detail.

He also published a book *The Bear at the Back Door*, which contained, among other things, a detailed analysis of Soviet military intentions in the North Atlantic. In his latest book, *The Next Domino* published last year, he turned his attention to the vital role of South Africa and dealt with the global 'grand strategy' of the Soviet Empire: to outflank Europe at sea from the south as well as the north and ultimately to isolate the United States of America.

This very important book, needless to say, has so far been virtually ignored in this country. However, I now learn that it is shortly coming out in paperback form, published by Transworld Books among whose subsidiaries are Corgi Books, Bantam Books and Carousel Books, in a substantial edition.

So there is hope that this strange conspiracy of silence (or is it really strange?) may be, if not completely destroyed, (that would be too much to hope for) at least impaired and made less capable of harming the vital interests of the West, that is to say, ourselves.

The admirable persistence of this remarkable man in the face of discouragement may be rewarded at last. More important, as he would be the first to say himself, his urgent warnings of our mounting danger may at last get through to brains, which have been numbed too long.

Peter Simple

I was about to write my third book which was to be called *Red Alert*, when cruel fate struck me in 1985, in the form of two botched hip operations performed by an RAF surgeon followed by an army surgeon. This devastating blow resulted in seven further major operations by the best surgeon at the Hip Centre, Wrightington Hospital, Wigan, Mr. Kevin Hardinge. I was admitted seventy times to hospital, examined by thirty consultants and rendered disabled, a house-bound recluse for eleven years. I received many pain-killing injections, every pain-killing drug under the sun, treatment by healers of every description, hypnotherapy and acupuncture – all to no avail at the time of drafting this chapter. I had to buy special equipment to enable me to function, including a specially adapted car, which had to be driven for me; special reclining chairs; an adjustable bed with special monkey pole hoist to enable me to get in an out; a special shower cubicle and many other pieces of equipment. A very kind donor provided me with an electric stair-lift.

Before 1985, in my retirement, I had travelled the western world as the guest of the countries concerned. I travelled widely in each country, lecturing on the precarious world situation and the threats ahead. The countries which invited me to visit and give lectures were Greece (once), Switzerland (once), Luxembourg (once), Hong Kong (four visits), Singapore (twice), Taiwan (twice), Canada (once), Norway (once), South Africa (six times), Pakistan (four times), Brunei (once), India (twice), Malaysia (once), United States of America (twice), and others.

I had invitations ahead to visit so many countries, when in 1985, I was struck down by this terrible, excruciatingly painful disablement. By now (1996) this was more than eleven years ago, but although I had then reached the age of 84, I was still fighting against this appalling pain, unable to walk without the aid of a four-wheel zimmer frame.

I successfully sued the Ministry of Defence for medical neglect. After a four year fight against the Treasury solicitor, I won my case out of court with full payment for damages and legal expenses. In all I received £130,000, half of which I had already had to spend. The details of this disablement are described in the last chapter, 'The Final Battle'.

What else did I do shortly after I retired? I was so shocked by the then appalling state of this country, what with the power of the militant trade unions (even the grave diggers were on strike!), that I wrote a number of hard hitting letters to the right wing press.

As a result of the publication of my letter in *The Daily Telegraph* of 4 July 1974, with the heading 'Lack of Leadership in Britain', I received a flood of letters for several weeks, each one enclosing money, and urging me to give a lead. I reproduce this letter:

"Sir – Why is this country in such a mess? We are even called the sick man of Europe, pitied by friend and foe alike; no longer admired, envied and looked up to as we used to be. What on earth has gone wrong?

The answer is complete lack of inspiring and trusted leadership, not only at the top in government, but also in almost every walk of life, be it industry, the professions, the home, schools, universities, or the media.

What is lacking is dynamic, invigorating, uplifting leadership. A true leader who inspires trust and confidence; who puts love of country and its proud heritage before all else – patriotism if you like; who puts country before career; the national interest before party politics; who has the moral courage to expose and root out those who try to rot us from within and hold us to ransom by anarchy, blackmail and brute force.

The Communist Trojan horse is in our midst with its fellow-travellers wriggling their maggoty way inside its belly. Only firm and dynamic leadership can deal with this; it requires high moral courage and moral courage is to physical as four to one.

A real leader puts service before self, fully aware that he is the servant of the state and as such must enter into full joint consultation at all times right down to grass-roots level; be it the worker on the factory floor – yes, in Ulster too – the miner at the coal face, or the private soldier in the ranks.

Once a man has been brought into his leader's confidence and is convinced of the sound reasoning and justification for the decision reached, however unpleasant that decision may be, he will carry it out in the spirit in which it is meant. A man who cannot inspire this sort of leadership is no leader.

What the country expects, above all else, is a simple explanation in words of one syllable that everyone can understand of the essential issues that are the root causes of our discontents. What do we get instead? Mostly a flow of official jargon and gibberish, evasive answers which few people can comprehend. The stock-in-trade of today's politician is on the one hand deviousness and concealment of the truth, and on the other lofty, stodgy superiority and a condescending manner.

The patience of some of us is beginning to wear thin and our political leaders would now be well advised to take heed of the words of Abraham Lincoln: 'You can fool all the people some of the time, but you cannot fool all the people all of the time.'

This country yearns for a leader capable of explaining the facts to the people and rousing them to determination and to valour as Churchill did during the war. It is inconceivable that we should not be able to produce such a man – before it is too late."

With the encouragement of Admiral of the Fleet Sir Varyl Begg, Marshal of the Royal Air Force Sir John Slessor, a number of British generals, ex-MPs, the popular goon comedian, Michael Bentine, and above all the shipping magnate, Lord Cayzer, I launched an England-wide organisation – which I called 'Civil Assistance' – and which future events were to show was not a good choice of titles. A better title would have been 'Service to the Community'.

Lord Cayzer donated £10,000 for three years running. At my first business lunch with Lord Cayzer's board, I was invited to speak first and was followed by a retired admiral who was an MP and working in the Conservative Central Office. Naturally the admiral was concerned to put up a good performance lest I should put up a better one, and thereby reduce Lord Cayzer's contribution to the Conservative Party!

The admiral failed so lamentably that Lord Rotherwick, a member of the Cayzer Board, said to me, "It was so nice to see a British general sink a Royal Navy battleship with rifle fire."

Before I closed down Civil Assistance, I had organised committees the whole length and breadth of England, without the aid of one single civil servant and in spite of 4-star generals such as 'Creepy Carver', trade unionists and pathetic BBC journalists, inferring that I was trying to raise a 'private army'.

Even Field Marshal Templer was taken in. At a certain event he asked Major General 'Bala' Bredin, DSO and bars, MC and bars, what he was doing now that he was retired. General Bredin replied that he was working for Cancer Relief and also for Walter Walker's organisation. Templer said, "You must be mad." Bala Bredin replied: "You are always gnashing your teeth about the b....y politicians, but doing nothing about it. Walter has had the guts to take up the cudgel." Templer walked away.

General Sir Peter Hunt, when he was Chief of the General Staff, came up to me at a reunion and asked me how my organisation was progressing. When I told him that I had committees set up in practically every county, he said: "Good for you, Walter."

Both Admiral of the Fleet Lord Hill Norton and General Sir Farrar Hockley in turn attempted to raise an organisation not all that dissimilar to mine, but never got it properly off the ground. Tom Pocock, my biographer, wrote to me and said: "This at least vindicates you."

By now I was a public figure and was urged by a number

of Tory MPs and certain public figures to stand as a Member of Parliament. But I had such a low opinion of MPs and their behaviour in the House of Commons, which I called 'The Monkey House', that I decided to go my own way.

I suppose because of my outspokenness in my letters to *The Times* and *The Daily Telegraph* about the IRA, and the enemy within England, I was suddenly visited by Special Branch. I was asked to move my study from a downstairs room in our adjoining cottage to an upstairs room and not to sit facing or with my back to the window. Then I was asked not to travel to and from London on the same day each week. On one Sunday I was the sole occupant of a first class compartment of a train from Sherborne to London, when I noticed two unkempt youngish men walking backwards and forwards past my compartment. After about half an hour the door of the compartment was opened and in came these two ruffians. I was reading a Sunday broadsheet newspaper at the time and had placed on the small shelf under the window a pair of scissors with which to cut out any articles which were of particular interest to me. I was holding the newspaper up in front of my face and by looking underneath the newspaper was able to see two pairs of grubby footwear facing me. I lowered the newspaper and slammed my hand onto the scissors. This obviously shook the two ruffians for they looked distinctly startled. I immediately looked upwards to the communication cord whereupon one of the men said: "We only came to ask how you were, Sir" and immediately hustled out of the compartment. As the train was pulling into Waterloo Station I put my head out of the corridor window to check if they had jumped off the train as it was pulling into the station. But there was no sign of them so I waited until all the passengers had moved to the exit gate. They must have jumped off the train as it approached the platform.

On another occasion my wife and I attended my elder

sister's wedding in Sussex. She was a widow and had a nice country house quite near the church. I was driving a metallic grey Mercedes and as I was approaching the parking area, I was stopped by a man in a dark suit and asked if I would follow him. He then stopped my car and asked me to keep it there while my wife and I attended the wedding service. We were shown to our seats in the front row. Our two sons had been asked to give up their seats and move to another pew. When they asked the man why, they were told that he wished to keep me in view throughout the service. One of my sons asked if he was armed, and was told 'yes'. After the Service we were asked to follow the car parked next to ours, and found ourselves parked in a special place against a wall of my sister's house. During the reception my wife had occasion to go to my sister's bedroom when she found the door locked. It was opened by a well-dressed man who asked my wife to identify herself. Having done so, she entered the bedroom and asked why the door was locked. She was led to a window and saw our car parked underneath. She was told that he would be watching our car throughout the reception. On our return journey to Somerset we were followed by a car which gave two hoots on reaching the Somerset border and turned back.

I had given a television interview about the IRA and also written the following letter to *The Daily Telegraph*, which caused a stir in some quarters:

"Sir – If one of our main cities came to be gutted and demolished and some of our towns and villages devastated on a scale that we have not experienced since the Second World War, would the public stand idly by at such an appalling outrage and permit the political pundits to parrot their persistent platitude, namely that a political solution was the only proper response?

I think not. Therefore is not the time long overdue when

we should stop indulging in double standards and forthwith seize the horror in Northern Ireland by the throat?

Our troops there are engaged in nothing less than a savage and ruthless war of terrorism waged by cold-blooded, brutal, murderous thugs, whose elimination should have been top priority from the very outset. And *The Daily Telegraph* reported me as saying as much almost two years ago.

In this type of warfare there is no place for appeasement, conciliation, a low profile or similar soft options. Some of us have had bitter experience of this in the past elsewhere, and the outcome has always been the same – the velvet glove thrown back in one's face.

We must realise, and make the outside world realise, that our indomitable soldiers are having to fight, for the most part, irreconcilable Communist-backed murder gangs of hardened criminals, and it is about time that we regarded and treated them as such. In this respect our efforts to counter hostile propaganda have been pathetically inadequate.

The army must regain the initiative, be relieved of static duties by non-combatant manpower, act and not react to events, and "get stuck in". Northern Ireland should now be declared a proper operational area, or even war zone, in which would-be murderers caught carrying or using arms would be subject to summary trial and execution."

The IRA never could believe their luck years ago when we could have taken them out, lock, stock and barrel.

About one year after I had retired, Admiral of the Fleet Earl Mountbatten spoke to me immediately after leaving the royal box at the Albert Hall, where we had been watching the annual reunion of the Burma Star Association. Lord Louis Mountbatten urged me to be the next and immediate Chairman of the Burma Star Association, in succession to a certain general, who had lost his grip. I agreed on one condition, namely that my appointment would receive the unanimous approval of the Council of the Burma Star Association. Earl Mountbatten responded by saying that he was the president and as such the council would fall in with his wishes. Nevertheless I stuck to my guns, which was just as well because the council's decision as conveyed to Earl Mountbatten was that I was far too controversial a character to be the next Chairman of the Association. Earl Mountbatten was not amused, and then asked me if I would become the president of all the branches in South-West England. I agreed and my wife, Beryl and I spent every weekend attending the annual reunion of each branch in turn, giving the after dinner speech and joining in the dancing. This was terminated when I became so desperately disabled, but I agreed to become the President of the Salisbury Branch only.

Because the severity of my chronic disability has forced me to become a house-bound recluse for the past eleven years I am an avid reader not merely of the daily newspapers but, more important, I receive a number of well informed private intelligence publications world-wide, which keep me abreast of the real situation at home and overseas. I see no reason for optimism, far from it. There are storm clouds ahead wherever one casts one's eyes.

RUSSIA

In February 1995, *The Daily Telegraph* defence editor, John Keegan, published an article under the heading, 'Russia's Army – a bear with blunted claws'. This was his opinion, not only as a result of the Russian army performing so poorly in the battle to seize Chechnya, but also because they do not have the money to fund the military budget; their officer morale is abysmal, while the calibre and training of their under-strength units is so low. But here I must emphasise a word or two of caution. For how long will the Soviet officer corps tolerate this state of affairs, particularly while their country controls the world's second largest nuclear arsenal? Furthermore, are the KGB professionals intent on convincing the world that the armed forces are a shambles, using Sun Tzu's aphorism: "When strong, appear weak".

Russia's new SU-33 Flanker Fighter is one of the most powerful and agile fighters in the world. Russia is still launching submarines and although Mr Yeltsin declared at the Paris Summit on 27 May, 1997, that all nuclear weapons targeted on NATO countries would be removed, Alexander Lebed, Mr Yeltsin's nationalistic opponent, immediately denounced the agreement as 'an act of surrender', which he would rescind if he came to power. Russia now has the latest and most powerful aircraft carrier, the 60,000 ton Admiral Kuznetsov, with the SU-33 fighters. Anything could happen were Vladamir Zhirinovsky, a fanatical extremist nationalist, the most powerful man in Moscow after Boris Yeltsin and his party, to be suddenly swept to victory in a Russian election or *coup d'état*. This man is highly dangerous. He is a fanatic like Hitler. 72% of those serving in Russia's strategic military forces in control of the country's nuclear arsenal voted for Zhirinovsky. These Russian servicemen, in a number of elite units, overwhelmingly back this extremist neo-fascist nationalist.

An eminent American defence analyst wrote to me on 1 January 1996, and said: "I must congratulate you on being so wise in your analysis that Zhironovsky would win so many votes in Russia's recent election. You are the only person I know of who got that right. I got it plum wrong!"

CHINA

The next flash-point is China. As a military force, Communist China, with a population of 1.2 billion, inspires growing alarm. She intends to control the sea lanes and the skies. Her navy is already growing up. Intercontinental ballistic missiles, with a range of 5,000 miles, can reach anywhere in Europe and the west coast of the USA. We will have a monster in our midst – a hungry giant.

What is of great concern is Beijing's relentless pursuit of military expansion over the past several years, a period marked by the end of the Cold War and the lack of a powerful, menacing adversary in the region. When immense military power is in the hands of irrational political figures on top of an unstable dictatorial regime without democratic safeguards, one should be concerned about the possibility that this 'time bomb' could go off at any time, anywhere and without warning. Hardly the recipe for a tranquil international order. The red dragon is alive and well.

ISLAMIC FUNDAMENTALISTS

I am very concerned about a sinister threat not only to this country but to the western world at large. This is the threat from Islamic Fundamentalist extremism, which is now worldwide. Islamic fanatics in the Middle East are now being exported as they intensify their campaign to wage terrorism worldwide, including the furthest corners of the world. They have no interest in their own survival and are determined to sacrifice their own lives for the cause of Islamic Fundamentalism, employing the vicious technique of the Islamic suicide bomber.

We must never forget that in the early 1980s the American embassy in Beirut and the military compounds of French and American soldiers, undertaking peace-keeping tasks in Lebanon, were destroyed by suicide truck bombs, killing 350 people.

I give this warning: the post-Cold War world is a dangerous place in which it is unwise to throw away our shield. And yet our politicians have already reduced our armed forces beyond the dangerous point. They have very short memories and no sense of history, and in most cases have never heard a shot fired on the battlefield.

European governments, especially that of France, are worried that if fundamentalist ideas gain a foothold among immigrants, it could do serious damage to the country's social fabric and its tradition of secularism. The spread of this threat across the Mediterranean now threatens Europe with social and security problems, such as terrorism and the proliferation of weapons of mass destruction.

European alarm is sharpened by the realisation that the conflict is on the continent's doorstep. Many of the zealots have relatives living in European cities, above all in France. The longer this threat continues, the greater is the danger of terrorists extending their activities abroad.

DEFENCE CUTS

We shall live to regret the emasculation of British and Gurkha regiments, for we are living in mortal danger. Few are aware of this – perhaps fortunately. The black market in nuclear and biological materials is now a very serious threat. If they fall into the wrong hands we may not survive. Then there is the ever-growing threat of world-wide Islamic Fundamentalism, which I have already highlighted.

The reductions under 'Options for Change and Front Line First', which cut the British Army by 25 per cent, were far too hasty. By mid-1995 the army was stretched beyond breaking point. Why did the field marshals, who never retire, allow these savage suicidal cuts to be implemented without fighting them

306

tooth and nail? They should have resigned in protest. The Conservatives should be warned: do not depend on the 'Service vote'. Their old fear of major cutbacks and redundancy under a Labour government have gone. The Tories have already cut our defence to the minimum.

Our men in the services are now once again going through far too many vicissitudes. I remember one of them after the First World War – 'the war to end all wars' – when we blithely stripped down our defences; then we rightly blamed politicians for not restoring them fast enough when Mussolini and Hitler struck their almost mortal blow, followed by Japan. This country stood alone until Japan struck at Pearl Harbour, which brought America into the war.

It is an axiom that 'if you wish for lasting peace, then prepare for war'. We in Britain should remember 1938's appeasement and the price we paid for not being prepared.

With British regiments now finding it so difficult to attract recruits, it is obvious that it was a monumental mistake to have decided to reduce the Brigade of Gurkhas from 6,500 to 2,500. The powers that be are not only short-sighted but grossly incompetent.

Her Majesty's ministers and service chiefs have not been notable for putting their careers on the line and it is about time they did.

The future is so murky that it is sheer folly to reduce our armed forces in today's world, especially since we are bound to have to bring them back sooner than those myopic bureaucrats believe.

There are now fifteen or more Third World countries possessing nuclear weapons, not to mention a chemical warfare capability. With despotic, aggressive, unstable or terrorist states having few scruples about using them, and disregarding the norms of civilised behaviour, it is imperative that we and our allies possess an effective ballistic missile deterrent, a chemical and biological warfare capability, and strong conventional forces. But with the Treasury representing the driving force behind all defence policy, the outlook is bleak indeed.

There are 73 flashpoints around the world with 26 places where fighting is going on. And there are 15 countries known or suspected to have nuclear weapons. The snag is that the Treasury cannot read and have been allowed to become a law unto themselves.

FORMER YUGOSLAVIA

The fighting in the former Yugoslavia tested the United Nations and NATO to the limit. I had discussed with former members of S.O.E. (Special Operations) who operated in Yugoslavia after the German invasion in World War II, Britain's decision to send in British troops in a peacekeeping role, with orders to attack only if attacked. With one accord they condemned the decision as military and political madness. They pointed out that the Germans and their satellite troops from Croatia never managed to destroy the partisans although they deployed several divisions. The warring factions, whether Muslim, Croatian or Serb, will fight each other and anyone else who interferes.

EUROPEAN UNION (EU)

The European Union is coming under heavy fire, and quite rightly too. It is no use the sheep passing resolutions in favour of vegetarianism if the wolf holds a different opinion.

By 1995 it became only too apparent that people in this country were fed up to the back teeth with the EU. They were appalled at the avalanche of directives from Brussels, the move toward a single currency, the imminent transfer of Britain's gold reserves to a central bank in Germany, the destruction of our monarchy, and the emasculation of parliament.

In World War II, and in other campaigns in which I have taken part, I thought I was fighting for freedom, but was I?

With membership of the European Union, our freedom is gradually being eroded until we will eventually have no sovereignty left. British law will count for nothing and we will simply be puppets dancing to the expensive Brussels tune. Further, we have in some cases lost our freedom of action, and some of our freedom of speech.

This is not the sort of country I fought for, nor is it the kind of country for which far too many of our young men gave their life's blood.

For those of us who fought in Burma against the barbaric Japanese soldiers, the epitaph on the Kohima War Memorial will for ever be etched deep in our minds:

> "When You Go Home
> Tell Them of Us and Say
> For Your Tomorrow
> We Gave Our Today."

· To me it is obvious that there should be a referendum before any inter-governmental conference. It should ask the British people whether they wanted to retain our present nationhood and constitution or become a vassal state with the EU.

A stop has to be put to the subterfuge and half-truths being used to cover up Britain's loss of sovereignty. The British people have to retain the right to govern themselves.

The fact is that Britain bankrupted itself in the Second World War defending constitutional government against dictatorship. The British have every reason to remain proud of this achievement. No political party or politician could have 'saved' Britain after the War. Exhaustion means just that – exhaustion. The British people have been saved from financial ruin since 1980 by one single factor – North Sea oil. The politicians have nothing to do with it, and neither does the European Union.

I cannot help feeling sometimes that our European friends are apt to forget that if it had not been for the resolute line this country took against Hitler 57 years ago, there would be no free Europe to be discussing these matters. It would do no harm to remind the younger generation in particular among our friends in Europe, that in 1940 we and we alone stood up against Nazi Germany, when the whole of the rest of Western Europe was conquered and subservient to them.

A European federation could quickly end up being dominated by Germany. Germany had not hitherto dominated the rest of the European Union. But if the EU pushed ahead with a single currency, that is what might happen, because the Germans will not accept monetary union without making steps towards political union.

As Prime Minister, Mr. Major so tactfully said in his speech at the Conservative Party Conference in October 1995, "Unoccupied, undefeated, the war left Britain with a very different perspective from the rest of Europe."

I am a strong supporter of a Europe of nations which firmly rejects federalism and centralised bureaucracy and restores responsibility entirely to individual nations.

In my view a single European people within a single European state would be disastrous.

A former Speaker of the House of Commons (1976-83), Viscount Tonypandy, lifted his voice in April 1995 to warn of the grave threat that exists to the greatest parliament and the incomparable British heritage. He warned that "the question of our national sovereignty towers above all", and went on to state: "Our Westminster Parliament is in dire danger of being denuded of its responsibilities, and of being supplanted by a European assembly controlled by a hotchpotch of European politicians and bureaucrats who have no love for this country ... No political party in Britain has a mandate from the electorate to surrender our national sovereignty to foreign hands. The current slide towards a single European currency threatens both our economic and our political independence, and thus our sovereignty. Subterfuge and half-truths have been used to persuade the nation that neither our sovereignty nor our relationship with the Commonwealth is endangered ... It is not too late for us to save our sovereignty."

MORALS

By 1995, this country had become inflicted with the prominence of the foul and disgusting sexual orientation of so-called Gay Rights groups of homosexuals and lesbians. Physical homosexuality is sodomy and those who practise such filthy acts are sodomites, and should be called as such. These sexual perverts are guilty of unnatural behaviour. By perverts I mean people who use the main sewer of the human body as a playground. There is no place for these people in our armed forces. It is imperative that the iron law of war must remain fundamentally different from the softer world in which civilians live. Homosexuals in our armed forces arouse the violent hostility of their comrades in arms, and undermine authority.

In this respect alone the armed forces of the Crown must be set apart from those in civil employment. The situation becomes intolerable when that person has been given some authority over the object of his or her attentions.

We need to point out, especially for the benefit of many of our bishops, how evil the consequences if it is permitted in the armed forces. It is time we all stood firm.

TELEVISION AND RADIO

Television and Radio are constantly under fire. I find I can no longer derive any enjoyment from so many television programmes because the guidelines issued to controllers of programmes on what is unacceptable are now disregarded with impunity. Obscenities are so frequently used that they are regarded as acceptable parlance; children of all ages and classes use obscene language in public, gratuitous violence and sex appear to be the common place behaviour. Will degrading sexual behaviour also be regarded as normal?

What alarms me for the future of this country is the rising output of smut, vulgarity and lewd programmes in current television programmes. I am sure there would be wide popular approval if it were made a criminal offence to defy official guidance, punishable with a very heavy fine.

I see in the press that those who feel as I do are referred to as 'silver-spoon goodie goodies'. There seems to be no limit to the filth and depravity to which television will subject this nation.

It is timely that the BBC's charter is subject to review in 1997. This should provide an excellent opportunity for parliament to scrutinise its activities with the utmost care and be quite ruthless in doing so.

After a BBC film crew were caught allegedly planting a drug syringe and other rubbish in a respectable area of an Italian city in June 1995, the popular saying should be amended: lies, damned lies and television.

It is patently obvious that those programmes which feature a wretched politician being interviewed by one of television's 'Smart Alecs' in front of an audience are stage managed. A certain number of seats in the studio are reserved in the names of chosen individuals. The occupants of those seats are directed to them. These individuals represent, or are members of, particular bodies or pressure groups. A higher proportion of them are called upon to speak than those in the rest of the audience. Presumably the 'television hack' has a chart, or knows where these 'chosen disciples' are sitting. Such is the impartiality of these wretched programmes. Individuals in the audience are referred to as 'That Man' and 'That Woman' instead of 'That Gentleman' and 'That Lady'. Do they not know the meaning of courtesy? Unfortunately the media wield enormous influence over the majority of the lives of the unsuspecting population of our country. Where honesty and openness are concerned they care not one jot.

The media, particularly television, have acquired greater influence over the administration of the country than the elected parliament. There is only time, or space, for less than ten per cent of what is said in parliament to reach the public. The rest is buried in the unread pages of Hansard, the media having selected what is most controversial or discreditable.

Fifty years ago there was no television, and less than half the population read any newspaper. Now politics is carried into every home. Both BBC and ITV are accused of political bias, but in fact most of what appears on our screens is just relentlessly 'anti-Establishment'.

Television consistently undermines respect for any institution, service, or individual who exercises authority or has responsibility. Commentators trivialise the judiciary, royalty, Church of England, police, civil service, Foreign Office – even the English cricket XI.

The overall situation has now been reached when one has to listen on radio, as well as watch on television, politically

313

motivated and insolent commentators who are so grossly inflated with their own self-importance that they behave as if they were Counsel for the Prosecution. Their manners are such that they constantly interrupt or intervene with such remarks as, "time is short", or "in a few seconds give your reply to...", or "there I must cut you short". Politicians have no option but to go on television and radio and take what is coming to them. But for the rest, they would be well advised to give these non-persons a wide berth.

Why does the BBC consider it necessary to give the viewers a resumé of a speech they have been listening to? Is it because it considers the viewers incapable of understanding what has been said or is it an ego trip by the presenters? Surely the object of the broadcast is to hear the speeches from the floor of the hall and platform, not the opinion of persons selected by the presenters in the hope of stirring up controversy.

On whose authority did BBC Radio 4 fail to broadcast the traditional ceremony of Trooping the Colour in 1995? The decision was an affront to many listeners and the reason given was beyond one's comprehension bearing in mind that the subject in question is a national tradition. Had the BBC completely forgotten or had it no consideration for the numerous blind and visually impaired listeners, ex-members of the forces (no doubt many who have taken part in the ceremony), non-television owners and others who simply want to listen to a descriptive broadcast and the military music?

THE PRESS

The press is also in the firing line. British politicians have grown bitter about certain sectors of the media wolf pack. Too often are they the victim of a campaign of nuance and innuendo. Time and time again the nation is rocked by disclosures of incompetence, or worse. The arms-to-Iraq is a case in point. Far from being 'rocked', the nation was bored to tears with the whole media-hyped business. The majority of people in this country could not care less if we sell arms to Iran, Iraq or Timbuktu. If we do not, someone else will. And is it not time we all grew up and recognised that all governments have their secrets which will at times involve duplicity?

In this country there has always been a double standard in attitudes towards the arms trade. It is customary to look askance at individuals who engage in it, while applauding the contribution that arms sales make to our national coffers.

War is a dirty 'game', but it's pat-ball compared to politics. There are certainly some notoriously raucous newspapers which are inflicted with the cancer of bent and twisted journalism.

Some of the leader writers seem to assume the mantle of moulders and manipulators of opinion. They are bent on wielding power over public opinion; power without responsibility. The intention of these mischief makers seems to be to make our minds up for us. Whereas the experienced and intelligent members of the public want factual news of what is going on in health, education, economy, European Union, NATO, Middle East, Russia, China, USA, Armed Forces and Trade Unions.

My Disillusionment with the Conservative Government (1995)

My letter published by *The Daily Telegraph* more than 20 years ago (page 10 of this Chapter) could not be more applicable than it is today.

Gen. Sir Walter Walker at East Lambrook with his gun dog and dachsund, 1972

Gen. Sir Walter Walker at home at Charlton All Saints, 1978

Charlton House, Charlton All Saints

My medals and Decorations, which I presented to my
Regiment after I had been crippled in 1985

Chapter 23

MY OVERSEAS VISITS

I have already mentioned the countries which had invited me to pay a visit as their official guest.

SOUTH AFRICA

I was invited to South Africa in 1977, 1978, 1980, 1981, 1982 and 1983.

In September 1976, a former Member of Parliament asked me if I would be willing to pay a visit to Rhodesia to assess the military situation, to familiarise myself with the country, its problems and its peoples and to meet a number of old friends who had settled in Rhodesia and who had expressed a desire to extend their hospitality to me.

I considered it prudent to seek counsel's advice, because although it was then four years since I had retired from the British Army, I had to be careful that I would not be transgressing any rules or regulations.

In his six page Advice, counsel pointed out a number of factors, four of which influenced me in deciding to refuse the invitation.

In the numerous lectures that I had been giving in England since my retirement from the Army in 1972, I had been highlighting the strategic importance of the Persian Gulf, and the sea Cape route round South Africa, and the mineral wealth of Africa. Hence the six visits I paid to South Africa as their guest, when I gave a number of speeches, radio and television interviews.

In October 1977, my wife and I were invited to visit South

Africa as honoured guests and were given VIP treatment from the day we flew first class from Heathrow.

I had more than one meeting with everyone of importance from the Prime Minister downwards on the civil side, and on the military side from the Chief of Defence to his army, navy and air force Chiefs, and from them to their subordinates. The same went for the police.

I returned to South Africa in May 1978. On both visits my programmes were so comprehensive and the travelling facilities by road and air made so readily available that I met more key personalities and saw more of Rhodesia, South-West Africa and South Africa, and their peoples, than many visitors could hope to achieve in a lifetime. Also, in my case, I was treated as a privileged guest and, therefore, no secrets were withheld from me, no doors closed, no security restrictions imposed – military or otherwise – and, above all, no strings were attached to either visit.

At Combined Defence Headquarters in Pretoria, I faced a panel of senior army, navy and air force officers and civilian staff and was questioned on the tactics and techniques for border, rural and urban anti-terrorist and anti-guerilla operations.

On both visits to South Africa, I spent some time in Namibia (then South-West Africa). I toured the operational area astride the then Angolan border, watched the South African soldiers in action and saw the prisoners of war, the enemy wounded and the captured Soviet weapons. I was most impressed by the battle-worthiness and the weaponry of the Army. Both were up to NATO standard.

On both my visits to Namibia I had long meetings with the Administrator General, Judge Steyn, who arranged for me to visit the whole of the administrative and production side of his territory as well as the military side. When we first met he said: "General, the Battle of Kohima was the turning point of the war against the Japanese in Burma, as you, yourself know only too well." This showed how well informed he was. Later he was appointed his country's ambassador in London.

My wife and I were attending a cocktail party at the Wanderer's Club, Johannesburg, during our visit in October 1977, when I was introduced to Air Vice Marshal Harold Hawkins, the Accredited Diplomatic Representative of Rhodesia (now Zimbabwe) in South Africa. He drew me aside and suddenly asked if I would be willing to fly to Rhodesia as the guest of Lieutenant General Peter Walls, the Commander Combined Operations, who would brief me, accompany me on a tour of one of the operational areas, after which I would meet Mr. Ian Smith, the then prime minister. Harold Hawkins said that if I did not wish to accept the invitation then Peter Walls was prepared to fly to Pretoria to meet me. (Peter Walls and I had been operating in adjacent areas during the Malayan Emergency).

In explaining my predicament to Harold Hawkins I said I was perfectly willing to visit Rhodesia, but on the strict understanding that my visit would be purely as a civilian under an assumed name, that it would receive no publicity whatsoever and that my passport would not be stamped with a Rhodesian entry permit.

A few days later my wife and I were guests at a large dinner party given by Harold Hawkins and his wife. At this dinner party was Ken Flower, the head of Rhodesia's Central Intelligence Organization. After dinner Ken Flower explained to me that: my departure from Pretoria would be handled by South Africa's special branch and by the airport security staff; on arrival at the airport at Victoria Falls I would be met by his representative and an army officer in plain clothes; there would be no passport formalities; and finally, I would travel under the assumed name of Mr. Wilkins. There would be similar arrangements for my return journey.

321

Everything went according to plan. Lieutenant General Walls took me completely into his confidence, gave me a personal, private and privileged briefing behind locked doors and then arranged a working lunch with his combined staff in Salisbury. I then flew with him and his army and air force commanders to Umtali, on the Mozambique border, where I was given another briefing by the local brigade commander and his combined civil and military staff. That night we all sat down to a full, frank, working dinner and the next day visited, by helicopter, infantry and artillery positions some distance away overlooking the border with Mozambique.

I had a meeting with Prime Minister Ian Smith, with Mr. P. K. van der Byl, his Minister for Foreign Affairs, with all the service chiefs, the police, intelligence and special branch, and met a number of retired British Army officers and others who had settled in Rhodesia after the Second World War.

The only awkward moments came during my visits to the troops on the ground when I asked questions which a civilian would not have had the military knowledge to ask. Furthermore, a number of warrant officers and sergeants were wearing World War II medal ribbons and I asked them which British regiment they had served with. There was a stunned silence. I said to one warrant officer, "It is obvious to me by your salute and military bearing that you served in the Brigade of Guards!" It was quickly decided to reveal my true identity to the military, also because otherwise it would not have been possible to brief me fully and make me privy to sensitive and classified information.

I decided that the best way of revealing the fact that obviously I had been to Rhodesia would be to write a letter to *The Daily Telegraph* of London giving my personal assessment of the situation and marking the letter as coming from Pretoria. I gave the letter to Harold Hawkins, whose secretary dictated it on the telephone to someone else's secretary in London, and the next day the letter was hand delivered to the offices of *The Daily Telegraph*. The letter was promptly published on 24th October 1977.

On my return to England I was invited to address a meeting, which I did in one of the conference rooms of the House of Commons. The outcome of this was that I was prevailed upon to write a book.

Having agreed to write a book, it was arranged that I should pay another visit to Zimbabwe, South West Africa (Namibia) and South Africa to enable me to check on certain facts and fill in one or two gaps in my knowledge. It was also agreed that I would be permitted to go everywhere and anywhere to meet anyone of my choice and that no secrets would be withheld from me.

For the reasons that I have already explained, my visit to Zimbabwe was again to be under the assumed name of Mr. Wilkins. Personally, I would have relished standing trial for treason. If a trade union leader like Jack Jones could go to Cuba, then Walter Walker could go to Zimbabwe. Similar parallels could be drawn, such as the KGB murderer, Shelepin, being invited to London as the guest of the British trade unions. Or the trade union leader, Clive Jenkins, claiming that as a political institution, the KGB was no different from the House of Lords. Or Mr. Alex Kitson, of the British Labour Party's National Executive Committee, suggesting how pleasant it was to be in the Soviet Union where there is no unemployment and a continual growth of living standards. It would be a red-letter day if such people would go to Russia and stay there.

When visiting the operational areas in Zimbabwe, the classified maps were uncovered for me so that I could see the deployment of their SAS and the Selous Scouts. On more than one occasion I was asked to autograph in secret operations rooms a document pinned on the inside of the door. The document turned out to be a copy of a letter written by me to *The Times*, London, published on 19th June 1977. My letter read as follows:-

"RHODESIAN RAID INTO MOZAMBIQUE
From General Sir Walter Walker.   8 June 1977
    Sir, It ill becomes any of us in this country to adopt a holier-than-thou attitude to the recent Rhodesian raid into Mozambique. It is no longer a secret that during the three year Indonesian confrontation against Malaysian Borneo I, as Director of Operation, was authorised by the then Labour Government to conduct cross-border operations several miles deep into Indonesian Borneo. Indeed, a *cordon sanitaire* was eventually established and virtually all contacts with our enemy took place on his side of the border.
    Offensive action is the only solution to guerrilla or terrorist operations. A policy of containment is the passport to defeat.
        Yours faithfully
        WALTER WALKER"

I found Prime Minister Ian Smith warm and friendly and completely relaxed. He has a very incisive mind and must have an ice-cool brain to have achieved what he had against tremendous odds and against both outside and inside pressures. Here was a man with leadership, dogged determination and iron nerve. He seemed to thrive under pressure and will go down in history as a shrewd and clever negotiator without equal – a world statesman.

For a long time, the West had been led to expect the political extinction of Mr. Ian Smith, whereas he had proved himself to be one of the great survivors of politics and had remained firmly in the driving seat. He had every reason to be proud of the exemplary leadership and ingenuity of the commanders of the armed forces and police at all levels, and the pronounced fighting qualities and morale of those under them. There was no doubt that this high respect was reciprocated.

I paid a second visit to Rhodesia (Zimbabwe) during April and May 1978.

I was told in Rhodesia that Dr. Owen had been more reasonable at his April meeting with Mr. Ian Smith than he had been at their first meeting. On the first occasion I was told by someone who was present that Dr. Owen "was brash and had given an appalling display of ill manners, rudeness, arrogance, impertinence and impudence. The temptation to seize him by the throat had been hard to resist".

Also severely criticised by civilians and military alike was the first appearance of Field Marshal Lord Carver wearing uniform. I was told that this went down extremely badly and was regarded as a tactless display by a British Field Marshal arriving to negotiate with people who had to be reminded that they were outranked in status and seniority. One general put it to me like this: "By his attitude and fantastic proposals for our army, anyone would think that he was dealing with a bunch of colonial hangovers suffering from heatstroke. He did not seem to realise that we were all trained at Sandhurst and the British Army Staff College, Camberley".

Despite the 15 year old United Nations arms embargo against South Africa, it had been able to build up an impressive military capability. It was far bigger than any of the publicly-available estimates made by military watchdogs, such as the London-based International Institute for Strategic Studies (IISS).

The number of combat aircraft in the South African Air Force was nearly double the figures given by the IISS. Also there were more than twice as many helicopters and three times as many tanks. South Africa had 300 self-propelled guns and 400 medium and light artillery pieces. No figures were given by the IISS.

According to the official statistics of the US Arms Control and Disarmament Agency, South Africa received £250 million worth of military equipment between 1965 and 1974. The actual figure was nearly three times as great. Between 1963 and 1975 the value of war material imported by South Africa came to nearly £600 million.

In other words, the UN embargo resolutions, numbers 181 and 182 passed in 1963, because of South Africa's apartheid policy were, in fact, completely ineffective.

I was fortunate enough to attend Exercise Quicksilver held near Kimberley. This was the largest army and air force exercise to be held since 1973. I was by myself, conducted personally by the chief umpire, and was not inhibited from seeing anything or asking any questions.

The exercise was modern conventional mobile warfare and I can give no higher praise when I say that in many respects the standard was higher than was to be found in NATO. The soldiers looked like soldiers, not long-haired shaggy sheepdogs. The South African is a fighter – tough, fit, as hard as nails, well disciplined, with a high morale and a tremendous pride in his unit. He knows he is fighting for the very survival of his country and that arrayed against him are not only the Soviets and the Third World, but the West also. If the country were to be put on a war footing with all white males under fifty years of age being called up, the mobilisation strength would be of the order of 400,000-500,000.

Soldiering to every citizen was now a serious business and military attributes like convoy discipline, dispersal, concealment and camouflage were second nature. Furthermore the South Africans were as proficient at conventional warfare as they were at counter-insurgency operations. Their deep pre-emptive assault into Angola by parachute and armoured columns was proof enough of this, for the resistance they met was fierce and they were attacking entrenched strongholds, and suffered only five killed in the process.

All these facts and opinions were based on my personal experience from six visits to South Africa in 1977, 1978, 1980, 1981, 1982 and 1983. Further visits were planned but had to be ruled out because of my chronic disability.

Since then, of course, Nelson Mandela has become the symbol of post-apartheid South Africa, but old tensions remain. While the vast majority of South Africans have embraced democracy, the real danger to peace and progress lies more in the bloody antagonism between Khose and Zulu, the ANC and Inkatha.

Meanwhile South Africa is still enjoying something of a honeymoon following its first democratic elections in 1994. Nevertheless the whites run the airlines, the buses, the trains, the hotels, the game parks and the safari lodges.

INDIA 1969

On 3rd May 1969, I was detailed to represent the British armed forces at the funeral of the President of India, Dr. Zakir Husain, who died on the 3rd May, after a heart attack. I accompanied His Royal Highness the Duke of Kent, who represented Her Majesty the Queen, and also by the representative of the British government, a Minister by the name of Mr. George Thompson.

We flew from London by special aircraft and arrived in India at midday on 5th May. The funeral took place later that evening and we returned to London the following day.

The Duke of Kent and I wore army ceremonial dress at the funeral.

327

The British High Commissioner in New Delhi reported to London that the British representation was admirably matched to the importance of the occasion and received very favourable notice in India.

CANADA 1975

In August 1975 – three years after I had retired from the British Army – I was asked by the Major General Brigade of Gurkhas if I would be willing to take out to Canada three military bands and a small staff of British officers, to raise funds for the Gurkha Welfare Appeal. Canada, like a number of other countries, had been quick to come to the aid of our Appeal and had launched their own Gurkha Welfare Appeal. In March 1975, the Appeal had obtained Canadian Government charitable status and the target in Canada was $500,000.

I readily agreed to undertake this task which was one so close to my heart. Indeed, I had been closely involved in it when I, myself, was Major General Brigade of Gurkhas from 1961 to 1965.

I was told that Canada had its own Patron for the Appeal in Ottawa, who was the popular and well known General Spry. It was he who would be sponsoring our visit and suggest the tour programme.

I took out by air in one aircraft three bands and my small staff. The bands were:

1. The Pipes and Drums and the Regimental Band of Scotland's Senior Highland Regiment – The Black Watch (the Royal Highland Regiment).

2. The Band of the Brigade of Gurkhas.

3. The Bugles of the 2nd Battalion of the 2nd King Edward VII's Own Gurkhas (The Sirmoor Rifles).

On arrival at Ottawa these three bands would be joined by the Band of the Royal Fiji Military Forces.

328

We had a strenuous tour programme visiting all the major cities at which the combined bands gave a stirring and loudly applauded performance. We were invited to lunches and dinners in our honour, and it was my task to meet the VIPs and heads of businesses, and to make speeches, while my staff distributed leaflets and obtained generous donations from individuals and business firms.

Towards the end of our tour I was invited to be the guest of honour and to open the Central Canada Exhibition at Ottawa.

Although the exhibition was basically an agricultural fair, it was augmented by grandstand attractions, such as a Military Tattoo, and by internationally famous personalities and entertainers of the highest calibre.

Then there were commercial exhibits, spectacular riding events, and so on, attracting more than 600,000 patrons in a period of eleven days.

As the guest of honour, I was asked to give the key speech at a grand dinner on the evening of the opening of the exhibition by me.

It was on the subject of the military tattoo that I decided to speak first. I had been told that the last military tattoo to be held in Ottawa was at the exhibition during Canada's Centenary Year in 1967. I thought that this would be the best way of firing the enthusiasm, patriotism, generosity and the attention of my large audience.

The specific points which I drew to the attention of my audience were:

"Few spectacles can hold the spectator's attention and match the sheer grace and dignity, the military precision and incredible impact than a tattoo. Men, impeccably dressed, marching and wheeling in unison to the skirl of the pipes, the beat of the Drums, the music of the Bands and the notes of the bugles.

329

It is a combination of a concert, a pageant, a parade. In this particular case, it is more than this – it is a tribute to the British Commonwealth, in the light of the bands which were taking part.

As the tattoo in the previous week in Toronto showed, it elicits a tremendous feeling of comradeship, cooperation, chivalry, and pride in our heritage.

Military bands, and their civilian counterparts, were a part of our tradition which, I trust, will never be lost.

Quite apart from their worth and their weight in gold as a crowd and tourist attraction, there was their appeal as a morale booster.

And, speaking entirely for my own country in its present difficulties, we desperately need to revive the spirit of patriotism, national pride, loyalty and unity. We need more tattoos and similar pageantry to stir the nation into a get-up-and-go attitude."

This brought forth loud applause.

I then went on to talk about the Gurkha soldier – known affectionately as Johnny Gurkha – who had fought alongside British and Commonwealth soldiers for 160 years, contributing 200,000 soldiers in World War I, close on quarter of a million in World War II, keeping the peace ever since, and in the whole process losing many thousands of lives, the good health of many more, and leaving almost destitute so many widows and children.

In this day and age, I asked, why had it been necessary to launch an appeal world-wide for the 450,000 Gurkha ex-servicemen and their families, who lived in near poverty in their mountain villages on the southern slopes of the Himalayas, in the shadow of the highest mountain in the world – Mount Everest?

The answer was simply this. Because there were no welfare benefits or social services in those inaccessible mountains; because of the dreadful natural disasters that occurred in the severe monsoon conditions at such a height; because those who were forever making cuts in military manpower had now made 60 per cent of our Gurkha force redundant.

And so, I said, in these phoney days of *Détente*, when defence is a dirty word – and with apologies to Rudyard Kipling: "It's Johnny this, an' Johnny that, an' 'Chuck him out, the brute!' But it's 'Saviour of our country' when the guns begin to shoot."

Canada, I reminded my audience, like a number of other countries, was quick to come to our aid and had launched their own Gurkha Welfare Appeal.

In March that year, the Appeal obtained Canadian Government charitable status and the present target in Canada was $500,000.

It was hoped that the bulk of this money would be subscribed by individuals and business firms, who would now be able to offset their donations against tax.

I stated that the Patron for the Appeal in Ottawa was General Spry, who was well known to most of them, and to whom the Gurkhas owed so much.

I ended with these words:

"The inflexible loyalty of the Gurkha soldier to the British Crown had been such that little wonder was it that he had been portrayed in these words:-

"Bravest of the brave, most generous of the generous.

Never had a country more faithful friends than you."

This brought forth thunderous applause, and I received a standing ovation of great warmth.

There was no doubt that my speech had done the trick, for cheques were being written, wallets being opened and donation forms signed.

·

PAKISTAN 1979

During my month's visit to Pakistan as a privileged guest in December 1979, I travelled extensively and met a large cross-section of people holding positions of high responsibility. The exchange of views was frank and uninhibited. In addition to official engagements, I also had the opportunity to talk to individuals at all levels during purely informal social occasions.

I had the additional advantage of knowing the country and people well for I had served there in the old Indian Army on and off for fourteen years and I understood their language, their religion, customs and traditions. I value the friendships that I made in those days and the new ones I made during my visit.

I returned to England with old ties strengthened, but perturbed by the sound of the alarm bells ringing throughout Asia, from the Gulf to Peking.

I was convinced that the situation, and that in the Gulf as a whole, posed a crisis for the West – as well as for Australia, New Zealand, Japan and the ASEAN nations (Association of South-East Asian Nations).

What concerned me and my hosts was the fact that America and western governments in Europe had not yet woken up to this potentially mortal danger.

The hostile attitude of the outside world towards Pakistan continued to revolve around the execution of deposed Prime Minister Zulfikar Ali Bhutto, who lost his appeal to the Supreme Court against the death sentence for charges including murder.

The world's media and, indeed, the former president of Pakistan, Chaudhary, had voiced serious portents if Bhutto was executed. In the event the tensions did not explode into the predicted massive violence. General Zia-ul-Haq maintained that he had proved by this one action of his that the rule of law exists for everybody – high and low. He stated categorically that he could not allow Mr. Bhutto, who had appointed him Army Chief of Staff over seven other more senior officers, to get away with murder just because he happened to be a former prime minister.

Furthermore, according to General Zia, the country by now had become aware that Bhutto had prostituted all the institutions in the country, including the legislature, judiciary, police, administration and bureaucracy. But he had been unable to shake the army, which remained the only solid and united institution that Pakistan possessed. General Zia was determined that the army would have the constitutional power to act in an emergency to save any given situation.

General Shahid Hamid, the Minister of Information and Broadcasting, had stated to me in his letter of May 1979, inviting me to Pakistan, that it was the sincere desire of the military government in power, under the President and Chief Martial Law Administrator, General Zia, to hold a general election in November 1979 in an impartial, peaceful and orderly manner, and that within the country every effort was being made to create conditions conducive to that end.

Power was to be transferred to civilian government, providing it would bring about a party or a group of parties capable of governing the country for a specified period of time. This was the proviso and in the opinion of General Zia this stipulation was not met. Hence the elections were not held.

According to the Director General of Pakistan's Institute of Strategic Studies – Brigadier Noor Husain – the political and military traumatic experience of 1971 – the war in East and West Pakistan – was the product of a conspiracy in which Mr. Bhutto and a few megalomaniac politicians of the country were involved with Mrs. Gandhi, Prime Minister of India. It not only shook the entire Pakistan nation, but also made it sit up and ask many questions to fit the jigsawpuzzle together. Brigadier Noor Husain informed me that with full freedom to the insiders, writers, scholars, credible and balanced journalists, many books, articles and research papers had appeared during the last two years inside and outside the country, giving an objective, unbiased and analytical account of what happened in 1971, and in 1965 – the war in Kashmir and West Pakistan – and even earlier.

Brigadier Noor said there was little doubt that the separation of East Pakistan, now Bangladesh, was connived at by Mr. Bhutto and a small gang of politicians with the dual purpose of firstly eliminating the overall majority party from the political scene of Pakistan, through a confrontation with the armed forces, and secondly, in the process bringing the military regime down and into disrepute by accusing it of exaggerated atrocities.

The brigadier, who was commanding a brigade in Bangladesh at the time, stated that, having satisfied themselves that Pakistan army units – operating in East Pakistan under adverse terrain, climatic and logistic conditions for over a period of eight months, and against Indian infiltrators and saboteurs, constantly cutting communications, mining roads and bridges and laying ambushes – had reached the end of their stamina and endurance, the Indian Army was launched in a multi-dimensional thrust in overwhelming strength in numbers, fire power and air superiority, and at a time of the year when the North Himalayan passes had been closed.

Noor said that the strong revulsion left in the minds of Pakistan's senior officers was that while a ceasefire of the 1971 war could have been arranged by the UN resolution, Mr. Bhutto, the leader of the Pakistani delegation to the UN, tore up the ceasefire resolution, walked out, feigned illness and did not attend the debate, because he was determined to destroy the image of the Pakistan Army throuh surrender – which indeed, came about.

It was obvious that the strong impression they all wished that I would take back with me was this. While wishing to live in peace and goodwill with its neighbours, this nation was resolved, as in the past, to defend its sovereignty and freedom and determined to extract a heavy price from any aggressors – irrespective of their size. Pakistan had had a fair share of teething troubles but let no one doubt, they emphasised, the patience, resolve, fortitude and determination of its God-fearing, simple, resilient, brave, frugal, hardy and above all martial people, to survive and live as one nation.

The bitter hatred that the armed forces had for Bhutto knew no bounds.

I had an hour's audience with the President, General Zia, whom I found to be highly intelligent, a good listener, very friendly and not at all the ogre that he had been painted by the mass media.

General Zia renewed public flogging for a wide range of offences. Amongst the first 200 victims were corrupt officials, black marketeers, hoarders and vice racketeers. General Zia said his government had four priorities: maintenance of peaceful conditions; keeping prices at a reasonable level; ending bribery; and the availability of quick and inexpensive justice for the people.

In my opinion a little medicine like this, but of a milder kind, is what is required in Britain to put an end to vandalism and street and other violence. Such crimes should carry a public stigma, the culprits being made publicly ashamed of what they had done by being put in stocks.

Three days after the massive Soviet armed intervention in Afghanistan on 27th December 1979, the American Government publicly reaffirmed its binding commitment to Pakistan under a 1959 defence agreement.

The strategically situated country of Pakistan, which not only borders Afghanistan but also Iran, and fronts on to the Arabian Sea, was the country most directly involved, after Afghanistan itself, in the Russians' arrival on the Khyber Pass.

With the neighbouring provinces of Iran also in turmoil and susceptible to provocation to rise against the Teheran regime, the American fear was that Pakistan and Iran might eventually disintegrate and the Russians would then reach the Indian Ocean.

Relations between Pakistan and the United States had been very shaky since the beginning of the Carter Administration, primarily due to the controversy over Pakistan's nuclear development programme.

The paradoxical result of the invasion of Afghanistan was that it had turned President Zia into an ally, to be supported as a bastion of the free world.

In June 1979, President Zia had categorically denied that Pakistan was making the nuclear bomb.

However, the BBC programme Panorama 'Project 706 – The Islamic Bomb' was very detailed, and unfolded a story in which for the first time details of Libyan involvement in Pakistan's so-called 'Islamic Bomb' were exposed.

Although General Zia had denied any intention to build a nuclear bomb, nevertheless BBC reporter, Philip Tibenham, revealed that he had unearthed the evidence of a massive Pakistan purchasing effort for the bomb's programme, organised from the Pakistani embassy in Paris. Panorama showed that the French had known since 1975 that Pakistan intended to build a bomb, yet still permitted the purchasing operation to be run from their capital. Among those interviewed were engineering firms in Italy, France and elsewhere, who supplied equipment of various kinds and who were only too pleased to take Pakistan's money and ask no questions. The film was not so much a criticism of Pakistan itself, but of Western nations who made the equipment available and would have made it possible for Pakistan to be ready to test its first nuclear bomb by the end of 1981.

PAKISTAN 1981

The government of Pakistan invited me to be their State guest for a week from 22 to 27 August, 1981. I was received at Islamabad Airport by the Director General External Publicity and the Protocol Officer to the Chairman Joint Chiefs of Staff Committee. I was then conducted to the VIP lounge for television photographs. Next we proceeded to the State Guest House where I was accommodated during my stay at Islamabad. There I was handed a letter in a sealed envelope from the President of Pakistan, General Mohammed Zia-ul-Haq, in which he included the following about my book *The Next Domino*, published in 1980, and later published as a paper-back by Corgi. At the same time the President extended an invitation to my wife to enjoy his country's hospitality at a future date. "Your book, *The Next Domino*, is a masterpiece. It will come to be regarded in my country as a strategic classic. It is brilliantly written and the case you make throughout the book is expertly and logically argued and has already proved to be prophetic.

"Your background knowledge of my country and the course of events in Afghanistan is amazingly accurate. You have performed a great service to my country and earned our profound gratitude and the highest respect.

"You will always be a most welcome and, I hope, frequent guest of my country. We hold you in the highest esteem and regard you as an exceptionally valued and firm friend.

"I cannot tell you how pleased I am that you have decided to write a third book which is to include an up-to-date assessment of events in my country and in Afghanistan.

"While you are engaged in writing your third book, I would be delighted if your wife would accept our hospitality in order to complete her convalescence."

This could not have been a nicer and more friendly greeting to his country by the President himself.

I had no engagement on the day of my arrival until 8p.m. that evening when I was the guest at a big dinner hosted by the Information Minister at the Banquet Hall, Ministry of Foreign Affairs. I was given a most friendly reception and had a thoroughly enjoyable evening among so many newly found friends. Obviously I had to 'sing for my supper', but it was by talking to individuals before and after dinner that I gleaned so much useful information, imparted to me 'off the cuff'.

The next morning I had a long meeting with the Secretary General to the Ministry of Foreign Affairs, who never hesitated to answer my probing questions. During the remainder of the day I was given a conducted tour of Islamabad and Rawalpindi; visited the vital installations and the dominating features essential to the defence of the two cities.

That evening I called on the President, for a private and personal talk which lasted one hour. He was most friendly, courteous, outspoken and did not flinch from giving me a straight answer to some highly embarrassing questions. We exchanged views on the prevailing international situation including developments in his country. We were all alone for one hour with a guard outside the door. Punctually at 9.30 p.m. the doors were opened and in trooped his guests for dinner. The guests included many of his ministers and high-ranking civil and military officials. Zia made a flattering speech after dinner which was loudly applauded.

The President came with me to the steps of his residence to bid me a personal farewell which, so I was told, was an exceptional courtesy. On return to the State Guest House my conducting officer handed me a hand-sewn Pakistan rug as a gift from the President.

The following day I was briefed by Brigadier Noor Husain, Director General Institute of Strategic Studies, who proved to be a mine of information and was obviously close to the President, his ministers and the service chiefs. He and his wife were aristocrats and it became obvious that he would have been chief of the armed forces had he not been wounded and captured as a brigade commander in the Indo-Pakistan War. We became firm friends and our friendship blossomed for a number of years into the future.

I then had an hour's meeting with the Director General Inter Services Intelligence who was open to any questions and had obviously been briefed by General Zia to withhold nothing from me.

I then had a one hour meeting at Rawalpindi with the Chairman of the Joint Chiefs of Staff Committee, followed by an official lunch which he hosted in my honour. There I met all the senior officers of his headquarters and was presented with a gift. I was listened to most attentively and plied with questions both at my private meeting and also throughout lunch. The atmosphere was extremely friendly and the fact that I had taken my military law exam in Rawalpindi in 1936, and served on the North-West Frontier for more than three years forty years ago, 1938-41, produced a flood of questions. Altogether it was a most enjoyable morning, and I was made to feel as if I was one of them, and certainly a very welcome and honoured guest.

That afternoon I was interviewed by Pakistan television, and then departed in the President's motor car for Peshawer, accompanied by Brigadier Noor and an armed conducting officer. When we reached the Attock Bridge I was escorted through tribal territory by the armed Frontier Constabulary. We then reached Peshawer where we spent the night.

The next morning I had a meeting with the Corps

Commander of the North West Frontier Province, a most impressive man. My next meeting was with the general officer commanding the 7th Division. This caused immense interest because it was with the 7th (Indian) Division – the 'Golden Arrow' Division – that I served with in Burma in World War II against the Japanese, and subsequently became Chairman of the 7th Indian Division (1939-45) Dinner/Luncheon Club, London.

I then proceeded by road, with a Frontier Constabulary armed escort through the famous Khyber Pass. We stopped at an Afghan Refugee Camp where I was addressed by the tribal elder of the Afghan refugees, to which I replied, giving due praise to their country's gallant resistance to the Russian's devastating invasion of their country. I received thunderous applause when I said that no country, including my own, had yet succeeded in occupying their country, and that likewise the Russians had bitten off more than they could chew.

We then continued our journey by road, now with an escort of the famous Khyber Pass Rifles, and reached the Pakistan-Afghan border itself. There I inspected a Khyber Rifles guard of honour and then, with a strong armed escort, climbed the ridge along the legendary Durand Line from where I viewed the Afghan frontier and outposts. I was able to pick out individual heavily armed Afghan soldiers.

It was now time to retrace our steps to the Landi Kotal railway station, which was the rail head of the Khyber railway – one of the seventh wonders of the world – built by my uncle, Colonel Sir Cussack Walton, who had been seconded from the British Army's Royal Engineers. He also built many of India's railway bridges. I had lunch at the Khyber Rifles' officers mess, hosted by the Inspector General Frontier Corps. After lunch I was treated to a display of traditional Khattack dances by soldiers of the Khyber Rifles, and then presented with an exceptionally fine Khattack dagger.

We then made the three-hour return journey by road to Peshawer, where, on arrival I called on the Governor of the North West Frontier Province, and received a private briefing. By now it was late evening, and I was more than ready for a soak in a warm bath followed by a cold shower, and a late evening meal at the Khyber Hotel.

The following day I returned to Islamabad by road in the President's car, visiting en route a remarkable feat of engineering, the Tarbela Dam. That evening I was invited to a private dinner by the Minister of Information and his wife at their residence. The next morning, 27 August 1981, I flew from Rawalpindi and arrived at Heathrow in the early evening.

PAKISTAN 1982

I was once again a state guest of Pakistan, and arrived at Islamabad on 15 August 1982. This time I had a suite at the Hotel Intercontinental. That day I had a long meeting with the Foreign Minister, General Sahibzeda Yoqul Khan, a highly intelligent and most impressive man. He was a diplomat-cum-soldier with unrivalled world-wide experience. He spoke perfect English without a trace of an accent and was a 'gentleman' to his finger tips. I learned a great deal not only about Pakistan and India, but also about Pakistan's relations with, and views on, the major and minor countries in the world.

I spent the whole of the next morning at the Joint Services Headquarters with long meetings and briefings by the Chairman of the Joint Staff Committee, and then moved to General Headquarters for meetings with the Vice Chief of the Army Staff and the Secretary General Ministry of Defence. Without warning I was asked by General Mohammed Iqual Khan, Chairman of the Joint Staff Committee to address the students of the newly formed Joint Services Staff College for half an hour before lunch. I relished this for I enjoyed speaking off the cuff, having been promised that my views would be non-attributable.

That evening I had a private dinner with Brigadier and Begum Noor Husain, who had asked a number of influential guests, and I was able to be filled in with sensitive issues affecting politics, personalities, defence and other matters.

The following day I had more meetings with Ministers and top officials before flying to Peshawer by special aircraft, where once again I spent the night in great comfort at the Intercontinental Hotel. Before dinner that night I had a most informative meeting at Government House with the Governor of the North West Frontier Province, and we continued the meeting at breakfast early the next morning. After visiting an Afghan refugee camp and sight seeing of Peshawer, which was immaculate with its parks, and its overall cleanliness, I returned by special aircraft to Islamabad. That evening, once again, I had a long, friendly and informative meeting with the President, followed by a formal dinner.

The following day I flew by special aircraft to Lahore, the capital of the Punjab, which I knew well from my pre-World War II days. I was accommodated in style and great comfort in the State Guest House. I had a heavy programme in front of me. First I called on the Governor of the Punjab at his imposing residence with its extensive and beautifully kept grounds. We had a long talk sitting in the shade, during which he was a mine of information. I then had a meeting with the Vice Chancellor of Punjab University, who gave me his private and personal opinion on internal and external affairs. My next port of call was the Administrative Staff College where I was asked to meet the students in their lecture hall and subject myself to their questions. I found them to be highly intelligent and eager to extend their knowledge of the 'state of play' beyond the boundaries of Pakistan.

The remainder of the day was spent on a sight seeing tour of Lahore when I was able to compare the tremendous progress that had been made since my last visit many years ago.

The following day I flew by the President's aircraft from Lahore to Karachi and spent the remainder of the day on a detailed reconnaissance of the city. It was fifty years ago that I had been stationed in Karachi as a second lieutenant, and been involved in inter-communal riots.

The next day I had a heavy programme starting with an early morning meeting with the chancellor of Karachi University, followed by an extremely interesting visit to the Institute of International Relations. There I was asked if I would have an informal meeting with the students who bombarded me with searching questions. I gave them straight answers which they seemed to appreciate, for I was able to draw on all my meetings with the highest in their country plus my own world-wide background knowledge.

My next engagement was to pay an official call on the Governor of Sind. Like all the governors he was a distinguished retired general. He was a charming and most impressive man, and opened his inner thoughts to me.

That evening I had an informal dinner with the military chiefs of the three armed services in Karachi when they really let their hair down – so did I.

The following day I flew home early in the morning from Karachi, arriving back in London in the mid-afternoon, where, as usual, I was met by my wonderful wife, Beryl. I was able to tell Beryl that the President would be sending an invitation to both of us to visit Pakistan as his personal state guests in 1984.

My wife and I were invited by the President of Pakistan to be his personal guests from 1 to 11 April, 1984. This was my fourth visit since 1979, and my wife's first return since 1946.

The welcome, hospitality and courtesy throughout our visit were to prove quite overwhelming. We were greeted as real friends and made to feel absolutely at home. Indeed, we regarded Pakistan as our second home.

We had been fetched from our home in England by an embassy driver and were treated by the PIA staff at Heathrow as VIPs. We travelled in great comfort to Islamabad with one stop at Paris. Two of our fellow passengers were the delightful Imir of Hunza Gilgit (Pakistan) and Begum Imir Ehazarfar Ali. They very kindly invited us to visit them at Hunza at the end of our official programme, an invitation that, unfortunately, we were unable to accept.

We were met at Islamabad airport by the Protocol Officer and by a representative of the Ministry of Foreign Affairs.

On being handed a copy of our tentative programme, I was somewhat concerned to see that I was due to address that very afternoon the Institute of Strategic Studies, the subject being 'Terrorism as a new form of Warfare'.

This was the very subject that I had already informed the Minister of Information, Embassy of Pakistan, London, would not be suitable for a Pakistani audience.

It is true that it was one of the two subjects that I had suggested to the minister in the first instance in late February. But having researched the subject and written the lecture, I decided it would be unwise, diplomatically and politically, to address an open meeting in Pakistan on such a controversial subject.

Therefore, I was expecting to speak on 'The Global Focus

– 1984', and had asked the minister to inform all concerned that the appropriate map must be available, namely the map in my book *The Next Domino*, entitled 'The Global Grab'.

Accordingly I asked my protocol officer to arrange for me to meet Brigadier Noor Husain at 1100 hours that very morning as a matter of urgency. Brigadier Noor was unable to see me until mid-day, when I explained the predicament. The brigadier explained that the subject of the lecture had already been advertised in the press and it would now be too late to change it. He enquired if it might be possible for me to tone down my lecture. I replied that this could not possibly be done in the two hours available.

Furthermore, I was tired and suffering from jet lag. After all, I was nearly 72 years of age and not 27! I said that I would be speaking as an ex-NATO Commander-in-Chief, and a former Head of Intelligence Allied Forces Central Europe, and could not 'tailor' my speech to suit my audience.

Brigadier Noor informed me that an old acquaintance of mine, but no longer a friend, Major General Shahid Hamid, had accepted his invitation to be the chairman for my address.

Before giving my address, General Shahid, Brigadier Noor and I met in the latter's office. When Brigadier Noor told General Shahid that it was the custom for the chairman to introduce the speaker, General Shahid said that he would rather not do so but confine his role to chairing the question period.

A friendly argument ensued between the two of them and in the end Brigadier Noor gave way. Caught unawares, he had to confine himself to merely reading out to the audience the official biographical notes on me.

This was the first error. What he should have said was that:

a. I would be speaking as an ex-NATO Commander-in-Chief, and also as a former Head of Intelligence.

b. I was not a politician, but an ex-military man and a recognised author and strategist.

c. My facts might be unpalatable but they were based on sources and evidence available to me and to my American and other NATO colleagues.

d. I would answer questions posed as such but would not comment on statements.

e. Nor would I become involved in any political arguments.

Having given my talk, the first member of the audience to catch the chairman's eye resorted immediately to a hostile tirade against me. I was even called 'the worst terrorist of all' for having committed acts of terrorism against Pathan tribesmen on the North-West Frontier in 1939 and thereafter!

I had no idea who the speaker was because the chairman failed to ask him to state his name and employment. The same omission occurred in the case of all subsequent speakers.

As a guest speaker I was not prepared to comment on hostile statements nor sink to the gutter, so I remained silent.

There then followed a series of similar hostile statements of a political nature. Accordingly I declined to comment. I was astonished that the chairman should have remained passive instead of exercising proper control. In my view his chairmanship was singularly inept.

At one stage of the proceedings individuals in the audience even argued with and harangued each other!

Eventually the chairman brought the proceedings to a close. By this time, inwardly, I was seething with anger, but throughout had refrained from opening my mouth. I did not listen to the chairman's closing remarks, for my thoughts were directed elsewhere. But I seem to remember that he made a veiled criticism about the framing and structure of my speech. This was most improper.

As I left the rostrum, several ex-army members of the

Institute came up to me and said how much they had learned and how impressed they were by my precise facts and figures. Brigadier Noor also stated that he thought my address had been thoroughly worthwhile.

I kept my private thoughts to myself.

The next day, and the day following, the newspaper *The Daily Muslim* had a 'field day' in their attack on me. The Russian Embassy must have been laughing all the way to Moscow. Two Russians were sitting in the front row during my talk and must have been delighted to see that they had so many dedicated allies in the audience.

The West and visitors to Pakistan were unaware that this newspaper toed a pro-Moscow line and was often in conflict with the Government of Pakistan.

Not only should the chairman have asked each questioner to state his name and whom he represented, but a note should also have been passed to me saying, for example: "anti-government", etc. etc.

Why was this newspaper pushed under the doors of so many hotels in Islamabad, Rawalpindi and Peshawar? Were the hotels receiving cut-price copies, financed by the Russian embassy? This was not the way to win the propaganda war against the Soviet Union, nor to win support of tourists, visitors and the free world.

Perhaps my critics, and *The Moslem* newspaper in particular would sit up and take notice now that the uncivilised and barbaric Libyan outrage in the centre of London, on 18 April, 1984, had confirmed my forebodings and done so in only a matter of days after my lecture.

To be forewarned is to be forearmed.

I had to ask why there should have been this unfortunate breakdown in communications between London and Islamabad, which obliged me to give a lecture which I had stated specifically was not suitable for an open audience in Pakistan.

The next day I had a very interesting and friendly meeting with the Director Intelligence Bureau. When I asked him outright if there was any truth in the report published in the London *Sunday Times* of 18 March 1984, entitled: 'Indians helped plot to assassinate Zia, says Pakistan', he replied: "You should put that question to the President himself."

I then had a most instructive meeting with the Secretary of the States of the Frontier Regions who gave me a most comprehensive briefing on the refugee problem.

This was followed by a meeting with the Minister for Information and a most enjoyable luncheon hosted by him. He had foregathered many officials and their wives, which enabled my wife and myself to meet a cross section of such friendly and interesting people.

The minister, for whom I had the highest regard, did not evade my questions when I asked him about the newspaper article mentioned above.

As the Foreign Minister was out of the country, I saw instead the Additional Secretary, who could not have given me a more warm and friendly welcome. He was keen to know if my programme was suitable. At that stage, of course, the programme had only just begun – with the one 'hiccup' at the Institute for Strategic Studies.

I told the Additional Secretary that I was anxious to receive Pakistan's up-to-date assessment of the true situation in Afghanistan as I had no less than six conflicting reports. I said that I had extracted the appropriate pages from my lecture 'The Global Focus' and that they had been passed to his Department for examination and comment. He promised to take the necessary action.

Later a protocol officer informed me that the written comments would reach me at Karachi before my departure for the UK. This did not materialise and I never did receive the report.

That evening I addressed the National Defence College, my subject being 'Global Focus'. It was a pleasure to address such an attentive audience and to be asked sensible and intelligent questions.

Afterwards the commandant informed me that the students had asked for a copy of my address, so I gave him my one and only spare copy to be photocopied. I asked the protocol officer to ensure that it was returned to me before my departure from Karachi on 11 April. It did not arrive and I never did receive it!

On the third day, the President invited us to a dinner in our honour. This was an extremely kind and courteous act, bearing in mind that the President had been out of his country for a number of days and had not returned until late in the evening the day before. The President was, as always, the warm friendly host, radiating impeccable 'old world' charm, courtesy and manners.

I had previously sent to the President's military secretary a brief by me and a folder concerning a film – *Green Shadows* – which the producers would like to film, in part, in Pakistan. The President immediately gave the project his blessing and then and there called to his side the Secretary for Information, and asked him to give the matter his personal attention. I gave the Secretary for Information my copy of the folder and, true to his word, he had two copies photocopied and sent to me in Karachi to reach me on my arrival there.

The President asked me if I was satisfied with my programme and mentioned that I could extend it by several days if I so desired. Both the President and the Foreign Minister made light of the explosive articles published by *The Daily Muslim* newspaper.

At Peshawar on the fourth day, my meeting with the Governor North West Frontier Provinces, was cancelled because he was unwell. Instead I had an interesting and informative meeting with a General who was Minister for Communications and Works. He could not have been more friendly and helpful and took great pains to answer my questions.

My call on the Inspector General Frontier Corps at Balahisar Fort was a most pleasant experience. I was received with great warmth and made to feel a most welcome visitor.

That evening my wife and I were taken to the old bazaar and we walked through the streets and alley ways without fear or hindrance. This was something that one can no longer do, even in the West End of London, for fear of being mugged or robbed.

I found Mr. Rusdan Shah Mohmand, Commissioner Afghan Refugees, to be a most engaging personality and a highly intelligent and well read man. Our visit to the Afghan refugee camp at Jalozai was most instructive. This was my third visit to a refugee camp and the first time that so many young men were present. This was due to the time of the year. A week or so later these same men would have been engaged in operations against the hated Russian invaders.

On the sixth day, we were flown to Lahore and were accommodated in great comfort in the State Guest House.

Unfortunately we were not told until 0745 hours the next day that the Governor of the Punjab would be pleased to receive us at 0900 hours! We only just succeeded in arriving on time.

The Governor was his usual charming self and received us with great warmth in his beautiful garden. We talked as we sat and we walked round the grounds admiring the flowers, the birds and the animals.

In spite of the fact that the new corps commander had

350

only recently assumed command, he and his officers and their ladies invited us to a thoroughly enjoyable luncheon.

Radio Pakistan suddenly appeared out of the blue, unannounced, at 1800 hours at the State Guest House. Having checked their credentials and then consulted by telephone with the Controller of the State Guest House, I agreed to give an interview. Later I received a tape of the full interview.

On the eighth day we flew to Quetta. On arrival at Quetta airfield at 1245, the protocol officer informed me that the programme had been changed and, instead of addressing the Staff College at 1230 hours the following day, I was now required to give my address at 1330 hours – in less than one hour's time.

By now it was 1250 and I had yet to collect our luggage, proceed to the Circuit House, unpack, change my clothes and then drive to the Staff College. We arrived only about 5-10 minutes late.

I started off my talk by saying that less than an hour ago I was still in an aircraft about to land at Quetta airfield, and firmly under the impression that I would be giving my address the next day. This, I said, was a good example of an important principle of war, namely: "The unexpected must be expected".

The question period could have gone on for some time as the students warmed to the subject, but by then it was already 1500 hours and none of us had had any lunch!

We had a most enjoyable lunch in the officers' mess with some wives present. After lunch the commandant presented me with a Staff College Shield and my wife with a handsome necklace. In return I presented the Staff College with my 4-star general's ceremonial gold and red sash. I can think of no better resting place for it, having been both a student and an instructor at the staff college – old boy made good!

We then visited the most impressive studio with its banks

of visual and recording instruments – a veritable television centre. I doubt if there are many staff colleges, if any, in the world which can match this highly advanced technology.

By now I was well overdue at the School of Infantry and Tactics. There the commandant gave me a briefing and I met and took refreshments with officers of the directing staff.

Meanwhile my wife successfully found the two houses which we occupied, both when I was a student and as an instructor, and also the hutted accommodation which she occupied when I was away at the war in Burma. She also saw the hospital where our twin sons were born.

That night we dined at the residence of the corps commander where we met a large number of officers and their ladies. It was a most happy, friendly and enjoyable occasion.

The next day we visited our pre-war bathing and picnic place, Hanna Lake, which sadly, was no longer in the mint condition that it was at the time of my last visit several years before. We were taken on a conducted tour of the tulip farm and the fruit development farm. These are remarkable achievements, and the future development of the province must hold great promise thanks to the pioneering work of the Secretary of Agriculture, a retired brigadier, and his dedicated and highly professional and qualified staff.

The brigadier then took us to the Hazar Ganji Reserved Forest where we marvelled at his accomplishment and revelled in the panorama and the breath-taking views. There we had a sumptuous lunch on site in the most attractive chalet. The brigadier proved to be a most entertaining and interesting host and a brilliant raconteur. We could have stayed on for hours listening to the clear answers he gave to our many questions.

That night we dined with the Governor of Baluchistan and his wife, despite the fact that the Governor had only recently assumed office and his wife did not arrive until a matter of a few hours before the dinner. Such is the hospitality of Pakistan.

And so our return to our second home had come to an end. Many happy memories flowed back to us and it was an eye-opener to see how much Quetta had developed in the intervening period.

On arrival at Karachi on our tenth day, I called on the newly-appointed corps commander.

My wife and I then met him again at a splendid luncheon which he hosted in our honour and which was attended by his officers and wives and other guests. Two bands were in attendance and after lunch we went outside and listened to them playing some old favourites.

We returned to our generously appointed suite at the Sheraton Hotel in the late afternoon, by which time I was already overdue for a television interview. I just had time for a wash and brush-up before the interviewer got down to work.

That night my wife and I called on an then dined with yet another recently installed Governor of Sind, and his other guests. The governor was kindness itself and said he only wished we could have stayed on for a few more days to enjoy the many places of interest in the Province.

Speaking personally, I thoroughly enjoyed and appreciated the conversation between the Governor and myself.

And so we ended our visit to Pakistan – a visit never to be forgotten. I can only repeat what I wrote at the beginning of this account. My wife and I owe a real debt of gratitude to the President and to all those who entertained and looked after us so magnificently.

I learned a lot about the importance of the strategic and pivotal position of Pakistan in the arc of crisis that now extends from the Pacific to the Caribbean Basin.

TAIWAN (REPUBLIC OF CHINA – ROC)

I was invited to visit Taiwan twice, in 1981 and again in 1982. I had always regarded Taiwan as being of significant strategic and economic importance. It must be particularly galling to Communist China to watch non-communist Taiwan flourishing with its economic boom and with its exports continuing to make greater and greater inroads into the huge consumer markets of the West. A large proportion of the trade between Taiwan and China currently goes through Hong Kong to avoid the difficult issue of trade between the two countries, which is not officially permitted. And that is the rub. What happens now that Hong Kong has become a part of China again?

Taiwan and the Taiwan Strait are a vital 'choke point', which Communist China is determined to control. China has never said they would not use force in pursuing their ultimate objective of 'liberating' Taiwan. They may very well resort to military action if other means of bringing Taiwan back into "the fold of the motherland" have failed, either by seduction, coercion or subversion.

Meanwhile China is intent on sowing discord among the people in Taiwan and to alienate the government from public support. At the time of my visits – now nearly fifteen years ago – China was doing its best to lull the Taiwanese people into a false sense of security, thus lowering their guard against the threat. Through the medium of the many speeches I made and the interviews with everyone of importance, from the Prime Minister downwards, and the publicity I received in the press and on television and radio, I am certain that I achieved my aim of putting across the truth, and the vital importance of strong armed forces at a high degree of readiness. I said: "If a hawk can take a chicken easily, it will."

This 'Gibraltar of the East', 100 miles off the east China coast, commands the strategic waterways linking the Indian

354

and Pacific Oceans. With strong standing forces of 500,000 and a reserve of more than three million men ready and trained for instant mobilisation, Taiwan is determined to remain an 'unsinkable aircraft carrier'. It has air bases, good harbours and 'fortresses' dedicated to the security of its homeland. It is of such strategic importance to both the Communist and the non-Communist worlds that it is far too valuable to pass into Communist hands.

During my two visits I had long interviews not only with the Prime Minister but also with all his ministers. I spent many hours with the chiefs of the army, navy, marines, air force, police, psychological warfare, intelligence and armaments industry. Also I spent some time with units and formations of all the armed forces and saw them in action on manoeuvre. I lectured to all their staff colleges and was particularly impressed by the work of the Fushing Kang Political Warfare College. It was impressed upon me by all quarters that the Chinese nationalists have never perceived the recovery of the mainland as being a military proposition. What was envisaged was a contest for the hearts and minds of the people of Communist China. They envisaged that at the end of the day it was the people who would have to make the choice, whether they would eventually discard the communist system and embrace the system of a democratic government and a free economy.

I was flown to Quemoy Island (known as Kinmen by ROC). There I spent a whole day with the Commander-in-Chief, Kinman Defence Command. I inspected the camouflaged dug-in defence positions, the bunkers, the gun emplacements, the strong points, and toured the underground defences. The latter was quite astonishing. It resembled a garrison with its own roads, buildings and a magnificent very large and fully equipped hospital. The whole complex was nuclear proof with its own garrison.

I witnessed a mock attack on the island and saw the deployment of the defence forces both from the defence and the attack angle. I was most impressed by the aggressive professionalism of the defending forces. It would take many Chinese Communist divisions to succeed in denting the defences. They tried once before and failed miserably. Taiwan would be a hard nut to crack and the casualties in doing so would be horrendous. I was the first British general to visit Kinman since World War II.

I was also flown to Kachsung Island (South Taiwan Island), where I was briefed by the General who was Commandant of the Taiwan Marine Corps. I watched amazingly impressive demonstrations of Marine Corps skills. I inspected the Military Academy followed by a visit to the Armed Forces Preparatory School. Altogether these visits to both the islands left a deep impression on me.

I received many gifts wherever I went and amongst them was a Taiwanese 'Rolex' wrist watch presented to me by the Minister of Defence. At the head of the dial are four silver stars indicating a 4-star general. I took it to a Rolex dealer in Bond Street, London, who said it was the best replica of the real thing that he had ever seen. Fifteen years later, so far, it has neither gained nor lost one minute, nor has it required any repair.

Knowing the countries of the Far East so well, I thought to myself what would be the fate of the Malacca Strait if Taiwan should fall into the hands of the Communists. At the time of my visits to Taiwan there were three million Chinese in Malaysia and Singapore, and another three million in Indonesia. The majority of these sided with Free China (Taiwan). If Free Taiwan were to disappear, they would have no choice but to listen to the Communist Chinese. This would endanger the free world.

In October 1982, shortly after I left Taiwan on my second visit, a 25-year-old Chinese Communist pilot, flew a MIG-19 from the Chinese mainland to a South Korean airforce base to seek freedom. From there he safely arrived in Taiwan.

Also shortly after my departure, the Nobel Prize winner and the world-wide renowned Russian freedom fighter, Aleksander Solzhenitsyn, arrived in Taiwan for an 11-day visit of the island. Apparently he gave an extremely inspiring and up-to-date speech entitled "To Free China".

What is the state of play today? Taiwan is well within the range of Communist China's strategic missiles. Within a distance of 400 to 800 kilometres there are 33 Chinese military airfields, capable of launching approximately 2,500 fighters which could reach Taiwan in minutes. Furthermore, nearly 100 of the Chinese Communists' more than 1,400 ocean-going military vessels are submarines, which illustrate even more clearly her capacity as a threat on the high seas.

There are also 628 boats moored at harbours as a military reserve force, while more than 80 vessels are in planning or construction stage. Add to that the world's largest land and air forces, and this constitutes a military force which must be taken seriously. What is cause for doubt, though, is this: Does Communist China need to have such powerful military might? Which country in the Asia-Pacific region has the capacity and military might to threaten China?

It would be an unforgivable mistake if the world's democratic nations viewed Communist China solely from the perspective of rapid economic development. If we simply view the Asia-Pacific region as a huge market and overlook questions of strategy related to Communist power, then sooner or later we must answer the following questions: How will Asian nations on the road to democracy protect their territorial integrity and sovereignty? How can their people live under principles of self-determination?

As I was writing this in August 1995, China, determined to bring what it describes as its 'rebel province' to heel, had begun test-firing missiles into the East China Sea less than 100 miles from Taiwan.

Communist planes and frigates entered the testing area. They conducted sea and air exercises, including missile tests and artillery firing. At its closest, the target area is about 80 miles from the north-east coast of Taiwan. But the exercise did not constitute a direct threat to the island.

Taiwanese leaders condemned the move, but there were no reports of public concern, and the local stock market gained four percent in a sign that investors had other things on their minds.

However, the economy was regarded as vulnerable to sudden closures of sea and air lanes of the kind imposed by the latest missile tests.

It was the second time Beijing had conducted war games near Taiwan in less than a month, and was seen as a heavy-handed, potentially dangerous reaction to the diplomacy of Lee Teng-hui, the Taiwanese president.

In June 1995, Mr. Lee made a landmark 'private visit' to America. This undermined China's campaign to isolate the Taiwanese leader diplomatically, and plunged Sino-American relations to their lowest point since troops crushed pro-democracy demonstrations in Beijing six years ago.

High level contacts ceased between the two powers, which downgraded representation in each other's capital to *chargé d'affaires* level. The arrest in June on charges of espionage of Harry Wu, the American Chinese human rights activist, soured relations further, and September's meeting in Brunei between Warren Christopher, US Secretary of State, and Qian Qichen, his Chinese counterpart, did little to reverse the tide.

A new attempt was made when Peter Tarnoff, US Undersecretary of State held talks with Chinese officials in Beijing. These diplomatic efforts had little immediate impact on China's policy towards Taiwan, which had assumed a belligerence that could get out of hand.

Political miscalculation, a grab for power by senior Chinese military leaders or – now that missiles were flying around the East China Sea – even an unexpected technical problem, could produce a crisis in the Taiwan Straits.

With billions of pounds of trade and investment flowing between the 'two Chinas', Beijing had too much to lose to attack Taiwan. Rather, China's mission was to frighten the island into accepting that it could have no significant international stature other than in the context of re-unification on Beijing's terms.

In this context, President Lee's reluctance to accept a 'Hong Kong style' future and seek wider living space for Taiwan had made him China's chief target. The current show of force was designed to intimidate the ruling Nationalist party into dropping him in favour of a pro-unification leader.

The Chinese leaders on both sides of the Straits will have to exercise restraint if they are to avoid a conflagration that could cripple East Asia's economic miracle.

BRUNEI 1984

My wife and I were invited by His Majesty the Sultan of Brunei to attend the first National Day Celebrations in Brunei on 23 February 1984. This followed the resumption on 1 January 1984 of the status of a fully independent and sovereign state. Sadly, my wife was unwell and unable to accompany me.

Brunei began its independence with many advantages which most emerging nations could only dream about. Blessed with revenue from huge oil and natural gas resources, it did not have to grapple with questions of economic survival – a common obstacle which newly-independent states had to overcome.

At the time of my visit it was estimated that the wealth of oil and gas would last at least until the turn of the century. The per capita income was the highest in the region if not in the world, and was the envy of all. There was free education, medical and health benefits and no personal income tax.

With a surplus then estimated at about four to five billion dollars a year, the government of Brunei had been able to finance all its many development projects.

During the twenty-five year "gestation" period before full independence, the Sultanate had had its own constitution since 1959, leaving only defence and external affairs in the hands of the British. This had helped to evolve a well-established civil service.

The parameters of the new state were made clear in a proclamation address by the Sultan before thousands of citizens at the town padang.

He proclaimed that Brunei "shall be forever a sovereign, democratic and independent Malay-Muslim monarchy based on the teachings of Islam and the principles of liberty, trust and justice".

It was clear that the sultanate, which had been in existence since the beginning of the 15th Century, would not adopt western-style democracy in the running of the state.

Instead, it would continue to rely on the traditional institutions associated with the monarchy and the teachings of Islam in the administration of the country.

The announcement of members of the Cabinet by the Sultan, who had been described as a working monarch made it clear that he would continue to hold sway over the sultanate as in the days when it was a British protectorate.

The statement stressed that the posts of Prime Minister and Deputy Prime Minister would always be in the hands of the ruler of the state. In addition, the finance and homes affairs ministries were also under his charge.

The dominance of members of the royal family, the Sultan's father, the Seri Begawan Sultan, was Defence Minister, while one of the Sultan's brothers was Foreign Minister and the other Culture, Youth and Sports Minister, disappointed some people who had expected greater changes after independence.

But some felt that the adoption of a cabinet-style government was a good start even though power rested mainly in the palace. "It will have to evolve downwards slowly", they added.

Even in his announcement, the Sultan conceded that changes to the Cabinet would have to be made from time to time in the light of experience gained.

It would take some time before there was semblance of the sharing of power between the ruler and his people but many Bruneians did not appear to be impatient.

"The system has served us well for centuries. We should not change for the sake of change or to please others," said a senior official.

There were many Bruneians like him who felt that the stress should be on bringing about rapid progress to the country and the people rather than experimenting with political changes.

The real test of the leadership in Brunei was whether it could create a new Bruneian society which was progressive and affluent yet firmly imbued with the true Islamic spirit.

The role of the religious sector would obviously be enhanced but there was little danger of it dominating the policy-making process as equal emphasis was given to the acquisition and development of skills.

As a prominent Bruneian put it, "Islam science and technology must march side by side towards a brighter future".

His Majesty, while acknowledging that the government was seriously looking at diversifying its economic base, was also aware of the existing constraints, be it manpower or the attitude of the people who generally preferred white-collar jobs, especially in government service. "These things take time," His Majesty said.

Among the social challenges was the question of getting optimum results from the education system.

The people of Brunei His Majesty said, enjoyed the benefits of free education, medical and health services.

Welfare benefits were also extended to the aged and to the unfortunate, such as orphans, widows and those suffering from tuberculosis.

The general well-being of the population in the interior, His Majesty said, had been enhanced generally especially in the field of education and health care.

The government's policy of encouraging and sponsoring Bruneians for higher studies, His Majesty added, had resulted in an impressive ratio of graduates in the population, one of the highest in the world.

Currently there were about 2,000 students overseas, and the total number of graduates exceeded 600. His Majesty the Sultan promised to continue with this open policy of promoting education and hoped that Bruneians would respond positively to it.

Basically His Majesty the Sultan was a family man. At that time his main hobby was polo. He also played squash and badminton. I was told by his company commander that when he was a cadet at the Royal Military Academy, Sandhurst, he was a keen boxer and had been a model cadet when, suddenly, he was recalled to Brunei by his father to succeed him as Sultan and head of state.

The Prince of Wales, on behalf of Queen Elizabeth, was representing Britain at Brunei's first National Day celebrations. His presence indicated the importance Britain attached to its long-standing links with Brunei.

I had two free days before the National Day, which enabled me to fly by helicopter to see the Shell oilfields at Seria and visit my former Regiment the 1/6th Queen Elizabeth's Own Gurkha Rifles, which I had commanded from 1951-54, during the Malayan Emergency.

I was also able to meet members of the British community who were serving the Sultan in 1962-1965, when I was Director of Borneo Operations during Indonesian Confrontation.

On 23 February 1984, the British High Commissioner held a buffet lunch to enable the Prince of Wales to meet the senior members of the British community, including the British Commanding Officer of the Sultan's own Gurkha Reserve Unit (GRU).

That evening at 1930, His Majesty the Sultan held a royal banquet in the Banqueting Hall of his new staggeringly enormous Palace. There were more than one thousand guests seated and waited on by trained staff imported from Singapore. As I was a Knight of Brunei, I was seated in the very large Throne Room. The Sultan made an impressive speech in faultless English.

On my left was the daughter of Sheik Adnan Khashoggi, the billionaire Arab entrepreneur. She asked me who I was and when I told her, and also went on to explain that it had been my responsibility to quell the Brunei Revolt in 1962, before President Sukarno of Indonesia started Confrontation against Sarawak and North Borneo, she expressed great interest. Indeed, she plied me with so many questions that I found myself having to give her a run-down of the operations that I conducted as Director of Borneo Operations. After dinner she insisted on introducing me to her father and telling him who I was.

Sheik Adnan Khashoggi arrived in Brunei aboard one of his private jets. But it was his ocean-going yacht that was stealing the attention. The 300 foot Nabila, named after Mr. Khashoggi's daughter, arrived a few days before its owner. The vessel was said to have "everything under the sun". There was a helipad, fully-equipped operating theatre, cinema, discotheque, gymnasium, sauna, swimming pool and a suite of offices. A crew of over 50 manned the boat, built in Italy about five years before.

Mr. Khashoggi immediately invited me to be his principal guest at a VIP dinner on board his yacht the following evening. At 0730 the next morning, 24 February, I was a VIP spectator at the Ceremonial Military Parade held at the grand Stadium, in celebration of the first National Day of 'Negara Brunei Darussalam', following the resumption on 1 January 1984, of the status of a fully independent and sovereign State. His Majesty the Sultan together with the Prince of Wales took the salute at this most colourful and impressive parade.

Among the participants in the parade were the first and second battalions of the Royal Brunei Armed Forces, its armoured Recee squadrons, its air defence battery, and the Royal Brunei Police force and its mobile squad.

The air force was represented by a squadron of Bell and Sikorsky helicopters and Siai Marchetti aircraft.

Apart from giving a colourful performance the parade also gave an opportunity for the sultanate to show off its sophisticated defence equipment, which included missile gunboats complete with Exocet missiles, Rapier air defence missiles and Scorpion light tanks.

After the parade, I had an audience with the President of Pakistan, General Zia-ul-Haq, who greeted me like an old friend. He asked me to give him a run-down on the Brunei Revolt of

1961, and my stewardship of Director of Borneo Operations 1962-1965.

After this I met those British officers who were serving with the Sultan's Gurkha Reserve Unit (GRU). I had persuaded the Sultan's father, the Seri Begawan Sultan, when he was Ruler of the State during my three years in Brunei, that, in the light of the Brunei Revolt, and in order to safeguard the security of his State from the threat from without and from within, he should build up an entirely neutral, loyal, and trustworthy force of Gurkha soldiers. This reserve force would be entirely independent of his own armed forces. The Sultan agreed one hundred percent with my proposals and thanked me profusely.

I am told that the strength of the Gurkha Reserve Unit is today (October 1995) between three thousand five hundred and four thousand, organised into three regiments, each of five companies.

On the evening of 24 February, I dined aboard Sheik Adnan Khashoggi's yacht, Nabila. I was put at the top table with his wife and daughter and his personal close friends. There were a number of other guests seated at separate tables. We were dined, wined and entertained most lavishly and I thoroughly enjoyed the evening. Khashoggi expressed a wish to publish my next book – *Red Alert*. But when subsequently it became obvious to me that he and his cronies wished to vet the manuscript with a view to inserting their own political opinions, I declined the offer of publication.

Before leaving Brunei on 26 February, I had an audience with the Sultan's father, His Highness the Serio Begawan Sultan, who had abdicated the throne in favour of his eldest son. He was now Minister of Defence and although we had the usual cordial conversation, it was not difficult to discern that his health was failing him. He died late in 1986. Before taking my leave he presented me with yet another gift and also a beautiful length of gold threaded material for my wife.

Later in 1984, I received an invitation from His Highness the Seri Begawan Sultan of Brunei, Sir Omar Ali Saifuddin, Minister of Defence (the father of the ruling Sultan) to attend the opening of the Churchill Memorial in Brunei. Sir Omar was a keen and very great admirer of Sir Winston Churchill. There were twelve guests who were flown out from England, including the then Mrs. Christopher Soames, Churchill's daughter. The British Government was represented by a Minister and a Foreign Office official. Also present were two former British Residents of Brunei. My successor as Director of Operations, General Sir George Lee was also present.

It was a great and enjoyable occasion, and after the ceremony we were given a conducted tour of the magnificent Churchill museum with all its Churchill exhibits.

This proved to be the last time I would have the opportunity to have an audience with Sir Omar, although we corresponded regularly, for he died at the age of seventy-one on the 7th September 1986. He had been Sultan of Brunei from 1950 to 1967, when he abdicated in favour of his eldest son.

Even after his abdication he wielded strong political power in a State where the monarchy is supreme and the state legislature can only advise the ruler. By abdicating he felt more able to negotiate and iron out details of state, including independence.

Chapter 24

The Final Battle

It was in early 1985 that subsequent events were to prove that I had been rendered chronically disabled and would be inflicted with excruciating pain for the rest of my life. I have mentioned briefly in Chapter 22 the two disgracefully botched hip replacement operations to the same hip.

The extent of the initial damage inflicted on me by these two botched hip operations can best be exposed by summarising the steps that my surgeon, Mr. Kevin Hardinge, was forced to take before he could possibly contemplate resorting to a third total hip replacement operation.

At his very first examination of me, Kevin Hardinge immediately identified from the X-rays, which I had brought with me, that I had suffered a spiral fracture of the femur, which had been perpetrated at the time of the second hip replacement operation nine months before, and had remained undetected. This meant that during those nine months I had been limping on a fractured femur, and had also been subjected to all manner of strenuous exercises by several physiotherapists. Kevin Hardinge told me that any form of surgery was now impossible until the fracture had healed. I was immediately confined to bed for three months, lying on my back with my leg strapped in a calliper. It was incomprehensible, and scandalous that during those nine months a number of Consultants and doctors had failed completely to identify this fracture.

After three months I returned to the care of Kevin Hardinge. He asked me why on earth I had gone to RAF and army surgeons when there were so many civilian hip surgeons whose practical experience had reached three or four thousand

367

hip replacements. I told him that when I retired from the army, I had received a letter from the army side of the Ministry of Defence asking me to patronise military service hospitals. I had checked with a retired officer, who had recently had a successful hip replacement at the RAF Wroughton Hospital, and he had sung its praises.

It was now June 1986, when I decided to consult the most renowned medical negligence solicitors in England. They confirmed that they would act on my behalf in legal action against the Ministry of Defence for medical neglect.

I was still suffering from stabbing pains and electric like shocks, and severe spasms. Because my overall recovery was being hampered by the increased degeneration in my other hip, Kevin Hardinge, in October 1986, carried out a total hip replacement on that hip which was completely successful.

Because the intense pain continued, I underwent a series of electromyographical investigations and a number of scans, which resulted in three separate operations having to be performed before it was possible for me to undergo a third total hip replacement operation.

These investigations showed that the pain was coming from the sciatic nerve and in December 1986, Mr. Hardinge decided to open up the hip. During the operation he discovered a wire and knot 5 inches long, lodged behind my sciatic nerve. He skilfully removed the wire and knot, which I have to this very day in a glass jar.

I remained in intense pain and after more tests Mr. Hardinge, in March 1987, again opened up my hip, and during the operation he found and removed a piece of cement 5cm long by 1.5cm which had leaked from the fractured femur.

Five months later, after yet more tests and scans, Mr. Hardinge again operated on me and severed the tendon in my groin.

Three months later, in November 1987, the pain was still as intense as ever, and tests and scans revealed a piece of loose bone. Mr. Hardinge had to open my hip once again, and succeeded in removing the piece of bone, measuring 2 inches by 1.25 inches, which had broken off at the time the femur was fractured, and was jammed against the neck of the prosthesis. It was a tricky operation and a masterpiece of surgery.

For the next ten months I underwent pain relief injections and various tests which showed that the bottom of the prosthesis was loose, which meant that Mr. Hardinge would have to perform a third total hip replacement operation. This was now September 1988, and the operation proved to be extremely difficult and hazardous, and took six hours to complete. It knocked me for six.

There was no improvement in my condition and I continued to be racked with such pain that Robert Jones, Professor of Orthopaedics at the Institute of Orthopaedics at Oswestry, recommended that I should undergo an upper partial or total femoral replacement, or even amputation, and that this should be done by his colleague, another consultant orthopaedic surgeon. After intense tests and scans, this Consultant declined to operate because, in his view, the chance of my being relieved of my existing pain by such an operation was nil. He wrote the following opinion:

"The important question is whether removal of all of the proximal femoral bone would be likely to relieve General Walker's pain and improve his quality of life. My answer to this is a qualified 'no'. In my view the chance of him being relieved of his present pain by such an operation is nil. Furthermore, removal of all his proximal femur bone leaves amputation as the only possible salvage procedure should further surgery fail, either because of persistent pain, or infection, or both. In essence, therefore, I have counselled him against further surgery. Similar views, I know, have been expressed to him in the past."

This consultant went on to say:

"My overall impression of Sir Walter is of a man whose life has pivoted around his distressing and intractable symptoms in the right leg. All aspects of his life style have been affected and I see no prospect of his symptoms easing with the passage of time."

This expert medical opinion was passed to my medical solicitor. Further medical opinions were also submitted to him by my own doctor and by other consultants.

My own doctor expressed his view as follows:

"I have been involved in General Walker's care for very nearly five years. After five years of innumerable consultations, hospital admissions and operations, the situation is unchanged and I fear that for General Walker there is no escape from a life of irreconcilable pain.

The opinion of one of the other main consultants was:

"Unfortunately, I think that the persistence of the symptoms and signs after so long, and the fact that the further procedures have made not the slightest difference to his symptoms, makes me sure that the general's symptoms will continue indefinitely. I believe that the only hope for relief is with the use of pain killing and other drugs, but it may be that the dosage and combination will never be found."

Having had acupuncture, numerous pain killing injections and one drug after another, I resorted to hypnotherapists and healers of high repute. The latter two gave me partial relief but for limited periods. I am hoping that my present healer will succeed where others have failed. But it will take time.

My litigation to sue the Ministry of Defence for medical neglect was completely successful in that I achieved a favourable out-of-court settlement with substantial damages and costs.

Therefore, the court case which was due to take place in April 1990, was cancelled.

When John Woodhouse – my SAS Commander in Borneo – heard that the case was likely to be heard in court, he arranged for me to be given suitable SAS transport to the court from King Edward VII Hospital for Officers, London, also an SAS medical orderly, and an SAS NCO Escort for the duration of the court case, which was expected to last ten days.

In the event, and only a few days before the case was due to be heard, the Treasury Solicitor surrendered and decided to settle the case out of court. I had won my case. It was extremely ironical that this final great battle had to be fought against my own countrymen – or, at least, a few of them and unworthy ones at that.

My QC was kind enough to write:

"The fact that we achieved an out-of-court settlement was due to your own determination to fight on despite your serious disability and the grave illness of your wife. You are a remarkable man."

Although I had won my final battle, this was nothing compared to the battle for my restoration back to full health. Indeed, as I write this, I shall have been in persistent and agonizing pain for more than eleven years and had several collapses, black-outs, thromboses, falls and fractured ribs. But I shall continue to fight the good fight to my dying day. I am now approaching my 85th birthday, November 1997.

> "Fight on, Fight on",
> Sir Walter said
> "I'm wounded a little, but
> I'm not dead.
> I'll lay me down and bleed awhile
> and then I'll rise and fight again."

"I understand he's decided to settle out of court."

Christmas card from my son, Anthony, which my solicitors
had enlarged and hung in their office

Chronology of my life and career

GENERAL SIR WALTER WALKER, KCB, CBE, DSO** PMN, PSNB

Date of Birth: 11th November 1912.
Place: Cuttack, Orissa, India.
Schools: St. Petroc's Preparatory School, Bude, Cornwall 1919-1923.
Norwood Preparatory School, Exeter, Devon, 1923-1926.
Blundell's Public School, Tiverton, Devon, 1926-1931.
Commissioned: 1933, 2nd Lieutenant, Indian Army.
Married: 9th November, 1938.
Children: Twin Sons, 30th September, 1942, and one daughter, 23rd February, 1947.
Wife Deceased: 24th June 1990.

APPOINTMENTS

1. Royal Military College, Sandhurst 1931-32.

2. Commissioned into Grandfather's Regiment 1st Battalion 8th Gurkha Rifles, India. Attached for 1 year.1933-34 to 2nd Battalion Sherwood Foresters 1933.

3. Company Commander 1/8th Gurkha Rifles 1934-37. Quetta Earthquake 1935.

4. Regimental Adjutant 1/8th Gurkha Rifles. 1937-40 North West Frontier. Mentioned in Dispatches.

5. Staff Captain Headquarters Razmak Brigade 1940-41. North West Frontier. 2nd Mention in Dispatches.

6. Student Staff College, Quetta 1941.

7. General Staff Officer, Grade 3 Headquarters 1 Burma Corps, on staff of General (later Field Marshal) Slim 1942. World War II - Retreat from Burma.

8. Instructor Staff College, Quetta 1942-43.

9. Battalion Second-in-Command, 4/8th Gurkha Rifles 1944. Burma World War II

10. Battalion Commander 4/8th Gurkha Rifles 1944-45. Burma, World War II. 3rd Mention in Dispatches. DS0.

11. General Staff Officer, Grade 1, Headquarters 7 Indian Division 1945-46. Burma Thailand, World War II.

12. General Staff Officer, Grade 1, Military Operations, General Headquarters, New Delhi 1946-47.

13. Battalion Commander for second time, 4/8th Gurkha Rifles 1947.

14. General Staff Officer, Grade 1, Headquarters Malaya District 1947.

15. Commander "Ferret Force" 1948. Outbreak Malayan Emergency.

16. Commander Far East Jungle Warfare School and Training Centre 1948-49. Malayan Emergency. 4th Mention in Dispatches OBE.

17. Attended Joint Services Staff College, England 1950.

18. Battalion Commander for 3rd time, 6th Queen Elizabeth's Own Gurkha Rifles 1951-54.

19. Accelerated promotion to Brevet Lieutenant Colonel 1952.

20. General Staff Office, Grade 1, Headquarters Eastern Command, England 1954-57.

21. Selected to attend British Atomic Trials, Maralinga, South Australia 1956.

22. Brigadier Commanding 99 Gurkha Infantry Brigade Group, Far East 1957-59. Malayan Emergency. CBE.

23. Attended Imperial Defence College, London 1960.

24. General Officer Commanding 17 Gurkha Infantry Division, and Major General Brigade of Gurkhas, followed by Director of Operations, Borneo 1962-65. Brunei Rebellion. Borneo Campaign. CB 2nd Bar to DSO. Knighted by Sultan of Brunei, Paduka Stia Negara, Brunei 1st Class (PSNB) 1964. Knighted by Paramount Ruler of Malaysia, Panglima Mangku Nega, Malaysia (PMN) 1965.

25. Appointed Colonel of 7th Duke of Edinburgh's Own Gurkha Rifles 1964-75. Borneo Campaign.

26. Deputy Chief of Staff in charge of Plans, Operations and Intelligence, Headquarters Allied Forces Central Europe (AFCENT), France and later Holland 1966.

27. Special Appointment of Chief of Staff for move of HQ AFCENT from France to Holland 1966.

28. General Officer Commanding-in-Chief Headquarters, Northern Command, England 1967-69. KCB.

29. Promoted to Lieutenant-General 1967.

30. Commander-in-Chief Allied Forces, Northern Europe 1969-1972.

31. Promoted to Full General 1969.

32. Retired from British Army, at age of 59 16 May, 1972.

Promotions

1. Commissioned 2nd Lieutenant	2 February, 1933
2. Lieutenant	2 May, 1935
3. Captain	2 February, 1941
4. Substantive Major	15 August, 1948
5. Temporary Lieutenant Colonel	1944 - 1952
6. Brevet Lieutenant Colonel	1 July, 1952
7. Lieutenant Colonel	9 June, 1953
8. Colonel	9 January, 1956
9. Temporary Brigadier	9 November, 1957
10. Local Major-General	23 January, 1960
11. Substantive Brigadier	9 June, 1960
12. Substantive Major-General	1 February, 1961
13. Substantive Lieutenant.-General	3 October, 1967
14. Substantive 4-Star General	1969
Retired from the British Army aged 59.	16 May, 1972

Medals, Awards and Decorations

1. KCB   1965

2. CBE   1959

3-5. DSO**   1946 (Co. 4/8GR Burma)
                 2 - 1953 (Co. 1/6GR Malaya)
                 3 - 1965 (D. of Ops. Borneo)

6. PMN   1965 Panglima Mangku Negara, Malaysia
                 (Tan Sri)

7. PSNB   1964 Paduka Stia Negara Brunei (Dato)

8. Indian Service Medal with Clasp. NWFP Twice MiD*
    1939-42

9. 1939-45 Star

10. Burma Star

11. War Medal 1939-45. MiD* Burma 1945

12. Indian General Service Medal 1939-45

13. General Service Medal with Clasp. Malaya and Brunei.
    MiD* 1949 and 1952

14. General Service Medal with Clasp. Borneo

    5 MiD's* - NWFP 1940 and 1942; Burma 1945; Malaya
    1949 and 1952

    Previously awarded OBE Malaya 1949; CB Borneo 1963

    Promoted Brevet Lt. Col. 1952. Co. 1/6GR

*MiD - Mentioned in Dispatches

Index

A

Alexander: General 62, 63
Allen: Charles 115, 116, 117, 215
Amery: Lord Julian 134, 292
Anderson: Brigadier 'Tottie' 126
Armstrong: Lt Gen Geoffrey 70

B

Balniel: Robin Lord 262
Baxter: 2nd Lt John 22,23
Baxter: Colonel 23
Begg: Admiral Sir Varyl 159, 160, 163, 166, 172, 181, 191, 192, 193, 194, 196, 197, 202, 248, 255, 293, 298
Bhutto: Zulfiker Ali 332, 333, 334, 335
Bird: The Reverend 13, 14
Bramall: Field Marshal Lord 4, 223
Brunei: The Sultan of 174, 175, 255, 267, 359, 360, 362, 363, 365, 366

C

Carrington: Lord 261, 262, 273

Carver: Field Marshal Lord Michael 3, 4, 5, 299, 325
Cassels: General Sir James 180, 234, 235, 236, 241, 243
Cayzer: Lord 298, 299
Coleman: Lt Gen Sir Charles 128
Collins: Sir William 1, 2, 3
Connaught: The Duke of 18, 19
Cowley: Maj Gen John 125
Crowe: Philip 259, 265

D

Darling: Gen Sir Kenneth 245, 248, 249
de Gaulle: General Charles 232, 274
de la Billiere: Sir Peter 212, 213
Dickens: Captain Peter 197, 198, 201, 202, 203, 204
Ducq: Lt Gen Jean 229, 230, 231, 236
Dunnett: Sir James 263

E

Eden: Sir Anthony 113
Elworthy: Sam 247 251

Evans: Maj Gen Geoffrey
65, 71, 72, 73, 74, 75, 78,
79, 80, 82, 83

F

Farrar Hockley: General 299
Festing: Field Marshal Sir
Francis 125, 128
Fields: Gracie 4
Flower: Kenneth 321

G

Gandhi: Indira 333
Gilmore: Scott 67, 100,
105, 106, 108, 110
Goodpaster: General 247,
251, 255, 259, 261, 263,
264, 266, 273

H

Harding: Gen Sir John 120,
121, 122
Hardinge: Kevin 295, 367,
368, 369
Healey: Lord Denis 143,
166, 171, 178, 180, 181,
182, 191, 193, 194, 195,
196, 202, 241, 242, 243,
247, 251, 253, 254, 258,
261
Hill Norton: Lord: Admiral
of the Fleet 299
Hitchen: Brian 226
Hunt: Gen Sir Peter 164,
173, 299

Hurd: Douglas 195

J

Jenkins: Clive 323
Jones: Professor Robert 369

K

Kent: The Duke of 327
Khashoggi: Adnan 363, 364,
365
Kielmansegg: General Graf
Johann von 229, 230, 231,
232, 234, 236, 245, 247,
255

L

Lea: Maj Gen Sir George 3,
169, 173, 202, 209, 213

M

Major: John 310
Mandela: Nelson 327
Manekshaw: General Sam
267, 268, 289, 290, 291
Montgomery: Field Marshel
Viscount 60
Montgomery: Major Brian
60, 61, 64, 65
Mountbatten: Lady Edwina
81, 82
Mountbatten: Lord Louis:
Admiral of the Fleet 170,
172, 173, 174, 178, 179,
180, 181, 202, 234, 236,
241, 248, 293, 302, 303

Mulley: Fred 166, 179, 180, 181, 182, 191, 195, 196

O

Olaf: King 270, 271, 272
Owen: David 325

P

Penny: Sir William 127
Pike: Gen Sir William 220
Pocock: Tom 1, 2, 3, 4, 29, 135, 144, 172, 274, 299
Profumo: John 278
Purdon: Maj Gen Corran 209

R

Rippon: Lord Geoffrey 260, 261, 262
Ritchie: Gen Sir Neil 112

S

Saint Bride: Lord 292
Scott: Lt Col Bruce 36, 38, 40, 41, 60, 62
Sheil-Small: Denis 67, 187, 188
Slessor: Sir John: Marshal of the Royal Air Force 298
Slim: Gen Sir William 59, 60, 61, 62, 63, 67, 103, 138, 241, 374
Smith: Ian 321, 322, 324, 325
Soames: Mrs Christopher 366

Sukarno: President 157, 160, 161, 162, 163, 166, 203, 216, 221

T

Templer: Field Marshal Sir Gerald 118, 179, 180, 206, 299
Thornycroft: Lord Peter 191, 192, 193, 199
Tonypandy: Viscount 310

W

Walker: Arthur Colyear (father) 8, 9;
Dorothea Catherine (mother) 11;
Nigel (son) 27;
Venetia (daughter) 27, 28, 31, 92, 229
Wallace: Alexander 14, 16
Walls: Lt Gen Peter 321, 322

Z

Zia-ul-Haq: Gen Mohammed 332, 333, 335, 336, 337, 338, 339, 348, 364